THE MANUFACTURING OF JOB DISPLACEMENT

The Manufacturing of Job Displacement

How Racial Capitalism Drives Immigrant and
Gender Inequality in the Labor Market

Laura López-Sanders

NEW YORK UNIVERSITY PRESS
New York

NEW YORK UNIVERSITY PRESS
New York
www.nyupress.org

Library of Congress Cataloging-in-Publication Data
Names: López-Sanders, Laura, author.
Title: The manufacturing of job displacement : how racial capitalism drives immigrant
and gender inequality in the labor market / Laura López-Sanders.
Description: New York : New York University Press, [2024] |
Includes bibliographical references and index.
Identifiers: LCCN 2023007542 | ISBN 9781479822973 (hardback ; alk. paper) |
ISBN 9781479822997 (paperback ; alk. paper) | ISBN 9781479823000 (ebook) |
ISBN 9781479823055 (ebook other)
Subjects: LCSH: Discrimination in employment—United States. | Labor market—United
States. | Racism—United States. | Capitalism—Moral and ethical aspects—United States.
Classification: LCC HD4903.5.U58 L667 2024 | DDC 331.13/30973—dc23/eng/20230223
LC record available at https://lccn.loc.gov/2023007542

This book is printed on acid-free paper, and its binding materials are chosen for strength
and durability. We strive to use environmentally responsible suppliers and materials to the
greatest extent possible in publishing our books.

Manufactured in the United States of America

10 9 8 7 6 5 4 3 2 1

Also available as an ebook

A mi Mamá, por enseñarme a valorar el aprendizaje

A mi Papá, por enseñarme a valorar la sencillez

A Bill, mi querido esposo, simplemente por todo

CONTENTS

Introduction

"Hi, you are here to build a Mexican enclave." Dave, the factory's general manager greeted me the first time we met. It was my first day working at HiCap, an employer of more than four hundred workers in the US South. I was walking with Carrie, the manager in charge of new hires, on a tour of the plant when she summoned Dave to come and meet me. Dave, white and fifty-something, was working with one of the plant engineers fixing a broken machine by the conveyor belt when Carrie called him. Dave approached us through the heavy forklift traffic. After the surprising greeting, he wiped his hands with a rag before cleaning two heavy drops of sweat traveling down his round face. Dave, I learned, was generally a soft-spoken man, but on the shop floor, he spoke loudly so others could hear him through the hearing protection. "Tell Marcus that I want him to bring your people, two at a time, until you have a solid Mexican enclave here. I want to weed out all of these people." Dave lifted his head and turned his gaze toward sections of the shop floor staffed with Black and white workers but not one Latino worker in sight.[1] "I want you to learn all the jobs on the line and build the enclave," he instructed me, as I remained quiet with my eyes wide open like a deer in headlights. I nodded affirmatively.

I was surprised to hear a manager use the word "enclave" in such a racialized form. While the term is controversial in the sociology of work and immigration, there is some consensus in defining an "ethnic enclave" as a structural form of immigrant integration in labor markets.[2] Dave's use of the term was not far from the scholarly definition.

"What I want are groups of Hispanic people working together as a team, under the supervision of a leader, someone who can be an interpreter or translator. We are going to bring in more of *your people*," Dave emphasized, "people who want these jobs. I am getting rid of people who don't *want to work hard* [my emphasis] and bring in people who do. Once the enclaves are set up, the idea is that one of you take the job of Kesha or Darius. One of these supervisors is going to have to go, and one of you will be taking their place."

When I started observing HiCap, a transnational business, I had already observed five other, similar companies at different stages of immigration-driven demographic change. I discovered that the representation of Latinos in light industrial manufacturing, relative to the integration of Black and white workers, varied in systematic ways. Some organizations had gone from having exclusively Black and white workers to having primarily Latino workers. Others had some sections of the plant, typically the worst jobs, staffed with immigrant workers, primarily unauthorized Latinos. Sections of the shop floor with all Latino and Spanish-speaking workers coexisted with those with a mix of Black and white women operators and with those with Black and Latino men. Still other shop floors were almost exclusively Latino. Workers and managers related a story of demographic change tied to the perception that immigrants were more productive than Black workers.

At HiCap, I observed the transformation of a Black and white to a Latina/o workforce as it happened on the ground from an "in-between" perspective. Hired as a bilingual supervisor, I observed the mandates of management and the responses of workers to these mandates. Unlike other organizations that sociologists have observed, in which the demographic transformation had already occurred or in which segregation rendered no new evidence, HiCap was starting a demographic shift that it coded "the project." The project aimed for a "Mexican enclave," as Dave noted, that could push existing workers aside and introduce their more vulnerable counterparts. The project unfolded over the course of seven months, using race, gender, and unauthorized immigration status to find workers who would transform the plant's ethnoracial composition from a primarily Black and white workforce to a primarily unauthorized immigrant workforce. The process became the focus of my research. I hoped to uncover the mechanisms that contributed to the racialization of the workforce by undocumented immigrant status, the relative valorization of workers, and the employer-driven shift of the color line in organizations in new immigrant destinations. *The Manufacturing of Job Displacement* introduces racial capitalism to the analysis of segmentation—or fissuring—in organizations, as it connects *the process* of capital accumulation to sorting mechanisms involving racial and legal categories of distinction and vulnerability.

My observations of a racialized displacement at HiCap—and at five other organizations—shed light on important yet unanswered sociological questions. Scholars have long known about displacement as it happens in neighborhoods, when one ethnoracial group moves into a neighborhood and another group moves out. In neighborhood gentrification, for example, a wealthier, often whiter, group moves into a neighborhood and displaces residents who can no longer afford living in the neighborhood, either because the cost of living increases or because real estate brokers entice them to sell their residences and move out. We know a fair amount about these neighborhood displacement processes. But scholars know much less about labor displacement, which is similar to neighborhood displacement in that some set of forces "push" out an established group. But how does this play out in practice? How do employers displace one group with another when federal law prohibits racial discrimination in hiring practices? How do employers deploy racial and gender bias when social norms call for more inclusive and equitable hiring practices?

This book answers these questions by pulling back the curtain on employer hiring practices. Behind that curtain, this book shows that a system of practices and behaviors creates racial inequality in the labor market. The practices result from the orchestrated actions of employers in determining who gets hired, remains employed, or gets driven from a job and displaced with the most vulnerable workers. I document the strategic maneuvers of managers to keep their own hands clean by compelling supervisors and employment agencies to systematically displace Black workers with unauthorized immigrants. My argument is that worker displacement does not occur solely because of unconscious hiring biases or social networks, as other studies maintain. Rather, using bilingual supervisors and profiting from the fragmented relationships between Black and Latino workers, employers intervene strategically. They use vulnerable and tractable unauthorized immigrant labor to impose and justify untenable standards that drive native-born workers out of their jobs and create vacancies filled by immigrant workers. In manufacturing displacement, employers deploy racialized ideologies to justify discriminatory practices on the basis that immigrant labor can save organizations, industries, cities, and even nations from ruin.

When I embarked on my research and became a part of this displacement "project," I did not expect discrimination to be so veiled and, at the same time, so rampant. I found that employers hide behind labor intermediaries to orchestrate systematic employment discrimination. What this means is that the more segments of society—especially segments with norm-defining abilities—pursue ideals of inclusion and integration, the more creative some owners and employers become in seeking to maintain racialized and gendered practices in their organizations. Despite civil rights legislation prohibiting discrimination against protected classes (race, gender, and nationality) in hiring, companies use these categories to hire new workers and get rid of workers they no longer want. Discrimination against the most vulnerable draws in many people, the victims, of course, but also those whose ambiguous social positions within the HiCap hierarchy put them in a position of having to serve two masters: on the one hand, the employer; and on the other, those with whom they share affinities of class, race, gender, or nationality.

Ethnic Supervisors in Displacement

Darius spit the apple-flavored chewing tobacco inside an empty Gatorade bottle. He had opened the Skoal container and started chewing at around 7 a.m. when he left the stoop of his small house, which sits on family land about twenty minutes away from Jessamine. He headed down a narrow two-lane highway to his supervisory job at HiCap. The parking lot was still dark when he pulled into his spot overlooking the factory. The thin layer of ice that had accumulated overnight on his black SUV in early January had not yet fully melted. He left the engine running to keep warm while he waited for the shift change at the factory. Listening to a Jay-Z tune, he relaxed in his car waiting for the day shift to start. As Darius later recounted, Thomas, his best friend and assistant supervisor, climbed into his SUV to join him.

Darius announced, "I promise I'll quit this year, I promise," trying to convince himself of something he knew well he would not do.

"The job?" asked Thomas.

"Nooooh! Noooo! Nooo! Smoking."

"Got me scared there for a minute," Thomas responded.

Yet as Darius said those words, his stomach twisted into knots. He told me that he had not talked to his friend about what was coming down at the plant, but keeping it a secret was killing him. Along with other supervisors, management had recruited Darius to carry out a new directive at the factory. Management had stopped hiring American workers; they wanted to get rid of workers at the plant who were "not working hard" so they could make room to hire new Hispanic immigrant workers.

For Darius, this meant that the Front End, the section he supervised, was probably going to be all Latino soon, just as third shift already was. Darius had not said anything about the changes coming to the plant to anyone, not even to Thomas, his closest friend. He was afraid that "Thomas would bring everyone down on him" if he told him what he knew. Besides, Darius only had a vague notion of the displacement project. What he knew was that management charged Marcus, a Black section manager, with leading the displacement and expected Darius and four other Black supervisors who worked for him—Raymond, Sammy, Connie, and Kesha—to cooperate. It was no wonder the chewing tobacco was burning a hole in his stomach.

As Darius and Thomas waited for the shift to start, Darius told Thomas that he had tried to quit chewing tobacco more than once, but the possibility of losing his job had him too stressed to quit nicotine cold turkey. They talked about the day that Dave announced at a cafeteria meeting in September 2005 that they were going to "get rid of people and bring in workers that want to work hard to replace them." Darius feared losing his job, but Thomas interpreted Dave's announcement as an idle threat: "They won't do nothing," he told Darius. Darius knew that the company was hiring bilingual supervisors to train Hispanic workers. He took another pinch of tobacco and put it in his mouth to help him think. He rubbed the flavored strings in his mouth with his fingers and spit into the Gatorade bottle. After a few minutes of chewing, Darius felt better, even about his job.

A week later, I was waiting outside the plant before the shift change. I parked next to Darius's SUV when I saw Marcus tap its hood, bringing Darius and Thomas back from their thoughts. Standing outside, Marcus pointed at his watch, signaling to Darius that it was time to get his gear on and get his people ready for the workday. Darius put away his Skoal container and tucked his Gatorade bottle, bottom filled with "tobacco juice," into a red backpack that also carried his keys and cell phone. He picked up a pair of yellow-tinted safety glasses, his favorites, and walked the distance between the parking lot and the plant with Thomas. Darius was still quiet. "I'm no talker," he said as we all walked down toward the factory entrance.

A wave of third-shift workers stormed out of the plant, their eyes wide open and their bodies still jittery from drinking the high-energy best sellers at the employees' cafeteria: Red Bull, Monster, and Rockstar. Some of the workers disappeared in their cars, ready to drive away for a good day's sleep, if they could find it. The vast majority of the workers leaving third shift were the Hispanic immigrants whom the plant hired only a few months before to replace native-born workers. Spanish filled the air as workers walked in pairs and small groups toward their cars. Darius greeted the remaining handful that spoke English but did not comment that the Black and white workers who had staffed the shift were now gone.

Darius had worked at HiCap for more than ten years and knew many of the line workers, supervisors, and managers on all three shifts. As management began hiring Hispanic workers on third shift and then on second shift, many of the workers Darius knew were no longer working at the plant. "I went to high school with some of these guys. I played ball with them. They're like family," he told me as the displacement was in full swing.

Getting to be a supervisor took Darius more than a decade, working every assembly-line job imaginable, "and putting up with all kinds of shit," he shared on repeated occasions. "I could spend another ten years trying to work my way up at a different factory, but no manager would make me a supervisor at my age and without a college degree." Besides, Darius had some unsuccessful attempts at switching jobs throughout the years and was convinced that recruiters were not going to look at his résumé. "When I applied for the job at HiCap, they were taking anybody who applied. . . . You know, they can fire me anytime, but I am not going down without a fight. There's no way I'm losing my job, . . . no way!" he said.

* * *

In 2006, as a graduate student in sociology, I packed everything I could fit into an old white sedan and drove from California to the US South to study immigrant incorporation and race relations. As part of this research, I learned about how Darius, Thomas, and many immigrants found themselves struggling with employment discrimination and exploitation. At that time, immigration analysts were writing about how Mexican immigrants, like myself, integrated in a place where few other Latinos settled. Initially, I wanted to shed light on the way in-between groups like Latino immigrants settled in a place that had a dichotomous Black-and-white color line. To my surprise, rather than studying incorporation in communities, I found myself in workplaces studying how employers manufacture a racialized displacement—using race to select and hire workers as substitutes for established workers. Racial categories—"Black," "white," "Hispanic," and so on—are bound up with meaning about the traits of individuals in those categories. Racialized displacement involves using beliefs about the fitness of individuals in racial categories for a particular job. In HiCap, management's beliefs about Latino workers as hardworking, obedient, and reliable compared to white and especially Black workers made Latinos ideal substitutes for the more established white and Black workers. Racial categories are also bound up with categories of nationality, legal status, and gender in ways that also made Latino workers seem like ideal replacements in the eyes of management.

As I talked to people and lived and worked with them, I discovered that immigrants and nonimmigrants struggled to keep their jobs when employers orchestrated, off the book, discriminatory hiring practices to substitute Black workers with more exploitable, Latino, unauthorized immigrant workers. This realization was puzzling because sociologists of organizations argue that large, visible employers take actions to adhere to principles of equality and inclusion and do what they can to protect their reputations.[3] I found that, in small cities where immigrants are beginning to settle, employers orchestrate racial and gender discrimination when they have access to a labor pool of vulnerable workers and when they can rely on labor market intermediaries to manufacture displacement. Labor queues, employers' ranking of workers, and job queues, workers' ranking of jobs, shift in response to organizational dynamics and "racialized shocks" in the new destinations where immigrants settle.

Changes in the racial and gender composition of an organization relate to the ways employers orchestrate displacement and the ways workers respond to changes in the organizational and political environment.

Sources of Ethnic Change in Organizations

A dynamic debate in the economics literature brings attention to a different face of immigration. Research on "the costs" of immigration essentially ignores race and focuses on the impact of immigration on the economic opportunities of native-born Americans.[4] For decades, economists have examined the common belief that immigrants take jobs away from low-skilled native-born Americans, lowering wages and contributing to inequality in US society. At the center of this debate is whether immigrants are *substitutes* or *complements* of native-born workers. One point of view, the immigrants as *substitutes* argument, affirms the public view that immigration has a negative impact on the employment opportunities of native-born Americans, particularly affecting low-skilled workers.[5] An opposing view, the *complement* side, contends that immigration does not negatively influence the life chances of native-born workers, as immigrants and natives rarely overlap in the same jobs.[6]

While some scholars maintain that immigrants value jobs differently than Americans do, others argue that since immigrants take the jobs that Americans do not want as they are presently constituted in areas with a supply of immigrant labor, employers hire them as *complements* to fill vacancies. This old debate, even to this date, gives the impression that immigrant incorporation into jobs happens organically—through market forces—and that job vacancies that immigrants occupy exist because native-born workers have moved out (on their own) from precarious jobs and into better ones. However, what do we know about job vacancies that result in the *displacement* of established workers in an organization or the act by which employers *substitute* native-born workers with more exploitable immigrants? Relatedly, what do we know about the way the racialization of employment affects the valorization of jobs? After all, organizations shift from having a particular ethnoracial composition (i.e., Black, white, or Latino) to having a different racial group performing those jobs, particularly if those jobs are "immigrantized" or "Browned."[7] The economic debate on immigration suggests that displacement is unlikely, and following this logic, the racial turnover in an organization is essentially *a myth.*

Sociologists have examined the issue of immigrant integration and ethnic succession in the labor market from the perspective of theories of labor market segmentation. Under the segmentation hypotheses, competition between immigrants and native-born workers leads to immigrants either *replacing* or *displacing* native-born workers from jobs.[8] One perspective argues that immigrants and native-born workers of the same skill levels are perfect substitutes for each other and that immigrants can displace the native-born in jobs.[9] This model paints a picture of the labor market in which immigration produces an upward shift in labor supply. Explaining how segmentation can drive changes in the demographics of the workforce, the segmentation/displacement hypothesis also predicts that with more immigration, wages decline and jobs become more immigrant dominated. The other side of the displacement/segmentation debate involves the view that immigrants are complements, not substitutes, of host-society workers. This view posits that immigrants and host-society workers do not compete for the same jobs, even when their skill levels are identical. For example, employers sort immigrants into jobs that are more precarious, that have poor mobility ladders, that have limited contractual arrangements, and that involve short-term relationships between the employer and worker.[10]

Empirically, however, there is evidence that employers sort documented and undocumented workers into different segments of the labor market. For example, immigrants generally work in jobs in the secondary segment of the labor market. These are jobs with lower wages and less stability.[11] Other researchers find that that labor market segmentation between immigrants and native-born workers changes over time. For example, under higher levels of migration, employers start considering immigrants and switch from hiring native-born workers to hiring migrants.[12] Barry Chiswick shows that some jobs are done primarily by undocumented workers in regions in the United States of high immigrant concentration.[13] In other regions, mainly native-born workers perform the jobs at the bottom of the labor market.[14] That is, employers may favor immigrants for service jobs in California, where immigrants are prevalent, but are less likely to switch to these workers in South Carolina, where they are less prevalent in the labor market.

What is clear in the research on segmentation and displacement is that the native-born and immigrants work in a segmented labor market, with migrants taking the lower-wage jobs. Furthermore, native-born workers are displaced when some employers switch from employing documented workers to employing undocumented immigrants.[15] Finally, in 1972, Edna Bonacich proposed a relevant variant of labor market segmentation—the "split labor market theory"—that supports the idea that immigrants take the lower-wage jobs while nonimmigrants protect the better jobs.[16] Similarly, most recent research points to the "fissuring" of workplaces as a form of labor market segmentation involving subcontractors and vulnerable immigrant workers.[17] Thus, labor market segmentation (or "fissured" workplaces) exists in the labor market, and employers use undocumented immigrants and subcontractors; but how this theory explains the process of change in jobs is unclear.

The vast majority of immigrants incorporate in secondary labor markets, so immigrants and native-born workers are unlikely to overlap in the same jobs. That is, immigrants are more likely to take undesirable jobs shunned by native-born Americans, jobs typically in the secondary labor market that are characterized as "3D": "dull," "dirty," and "dangerous."[18] One of the reasons immigrants take jobs at the bottom of the labor market is because they operate under a "dual frame of reference," earning disparate host-society wages to pay for community-of-origin needs and aspirations.[19] For immigrants from Central America and Mexico, the lifestyles they leave behind cost less than our lifestyles in the United States. In contrast, native-born workers compare their status to similar others in the US, not to similar others in a community and nation with lower wages and more modest lifestyles. Consequently, in contrast to their immigrant counterparts, native-born workers view jobs with low wages, poor working conditions, and no mobility ladders as undesirable.

The economic debate on the "costs of immigration" has explained how "succession" in labor markets works once the jobs have been degraded—become "bad jobs" that Americans no longer want.[20] A look at employment succession on the ground, however, shows that these arguments miss the *process* by which jobs become undesirable. This omission is noteworthy because the process is precisely that which distinguishes simple replacement from displacement.

Displacement, the form of replacement based on forced employee turnover, is difficult to document empirically because most researchers believe that they have seen replacement when, in reality, they may have witnessed the outcomes of a displacement process. Still, ethnographic studies on new immigrant destinations are beginning to document active displacement in different industries.[21] Vanesa Ribas has concluded that displacement and replacement are intertwined processes.[22] The employers in her study initially introduced Latino immigrant workers as replacements for African American and white workers in a meatpacking plant in North Carolina. Once the replacement workers were in place, social closure acted to apply pressure in the direction of further vacancies, and the ability of workers to bring in their coethnics sealed the deal. This research illustrates how employers are using immigrant workers as substitutes for, not as complements of, Black workers.

Unfortunately, public controversies about the impact of immigration—related to the claim that "immigrants take jobs from Americans"—shift the focus to immigrants and away from the system of stratification put in place by profit- and control-seeking employers, which produces their integration as replacements.

The Racialized Capitalism View of Ethnic Change in Organizations

I write this book to dispel the myth of displacement and move the analysis from "the cost" of immigration to theories of racial capitalism: the organization of the economy along racial lines to extract economic advantage from racial categorization.[23] I adopt an intersectional view of racial capitalism that, in addition to racial identities and racialization, includes multiple categories of vulnerability that employers deploy in racialized labor markets.

Understanding immigrant-driven demographic change in organizations involves looking at the ways labor markets operate in racialized organizations and how they become building blocks of racialized capitalism. Mechanisms such as segmentation in local labor markets call for an examination of dynamics inside organizations.[24] For example, employers might hire immigrants to occupy the same jobs as the native-born. However, because of differences in vulnerability, they assign immigrants to different tasks in an organization or to more exhausting work. Examining segmentation and the racialization of hiring practices within organizations tells us how employers valorize some workers on the basis of their identities and level of vulnerability.

The Manufacturing of Job Displacement draws from the growing literature on racialized organizations and racial capitalism.[25] Theories of racialized organizations see organizations not as race-neutral bureaucratic structures but as places in which race constitutes everyday life.[26] By examining the complicated nature of racialization in organizations through ethnographic methods, I expand conventional theories explaining shifts in the racial composition of workplaces on the basis of employer demand. We know that employer preferences exist and are expressed in subtle ways in the hiring process. Most research focuses, however, on the pre-hire phase of the employment cycle and therefore cannot reveal how worker vulnerability plays out or how the intersection of race, gender, and class affects the stratified work environments that immigrants join. One reason that this limitation exists is because our theories traditionally treat categorical groups as dichotomous and homogeneous. Yet a central characteristic of social relations in organizations is that power relations vary based on nuanced divisions. These assumptions make it difficult for researchers to detect the subtle but important issues of employee vulnerability that distinguish, for example, Blacks with a criminal record from those without and Latinos with legal documentation from those without.[27] This brings to the fore one of the benefits that participant observation delivers in the study of labor inequality related to immigration, namely, the ability to detect granularity in employment relations.

If ethnic displacement and replacement are going to be fully understood, there is a need to understand what happens in everyday life as white employers and their agents produce a system of racialized oppression that profits from the vulnerability of Black and unauthorized workers. While the theoretical difference between displacement and replacement lies in the genesis of the vacancies being filled, in practice displacement also activates agency in the form of resistance on the part of the group or groups being displaced.

For racial capitalism to explain the dynamics of displacement, we need to take into account how race articulates this process. For Cedric

Robinson, race is central to capitalism, as capitalism has its roots in a history of colonization, exploitation, and systematic oppression of people of color.[28] For example, the concept of racial capitalism establishes that throughout slavery, the value of Black people was in relation to the profits they brought to white employers. Similarly, class and gender are important to the degree that these categories of distinction contribute to the construction of labor markets in organizations that profit from people's differences. Categorical distinctions, however, tell us little about labor market inequality in static forms. Differences along intersecting categories are most valuable when workers and employers use difference to draw boundaries of inclusion or exclusion in workplaces. Robinson, for example, has theorized that racial capitalism illustrates a tendency toward fragmentation rather than homogenization. The case of zero-sum displacement in this book highlights how one of the consequences of racial capitalism is to divide workers along racial lines rather than unify them as workers.

This book asks, What are the vulnerabilities that shape racial capitalism in an immigrant worker displacement? What organizational processes and structures enable racial capitalism in organizations? How do Black, white, and Latino workers respond to racialized displacement? What are the consequences for the workers involved in racialized displacement? And how and why do employers get away with racialized displacement when large, visible organizations presumably take active steps to uphold principles of equality and inclusion? In answering these questions, *The Manufacturing of Job Displacement* applies a different lens to the myth of displacement.

The evidence portrayed in this book shows that the influence of ethnic labor intermediaries, while treated in some research on immigration, needs to take a more prominent role in the study of organizational racialization. Employers on their own cannot succeed in overturning the workforce using race, gender, and immigrant documentation status. To identify and recruit replacement workers, to hire them, to train them, and then to replace those who are already in their organization, they need a staff willing and able to follow directives and coordinate activities. Because employers are essentially circumventing the law by using race and gender in hiring—even when masking the categories of unauthorized immigrant status as "hard work" and gender in the sex-typed image of "heavy lifters"—they engage the cooperation of temporary employment agencies, bilingual supervisors, and existing native-born plant employees to orchestrate a displacement.

What role do intermediaries play in racialized organizational change? In *The Manufacturing of Job Displacement*, I highlight how the relationship between race, gender, and legality, underdeveloped in early organizational studies, played out at HiCap. The hiring practices witnessed in new immigrant destinations, however, necessitate revisiting traditional understandings of brokers in the demographic change that occurs in organizations. The participation of temp agencies in displacement, for example, is often mediated by the legal status of the workers, the gendered nature of immigrant work, and the settlement patterns of immigrants. The challenges that temp agencies face are reflected in comments I heard from the intermediaries hired to make recruitment seamless for HiCap management. "I am having a hard time finding people to fill all the positions on the different shifts," noted a bilingual recruiter in desperation. "You know that many of 'our' people want to work, but they don't have good papers" and "We can't find heavy lifters"—the code for men—"all we can find is women!" were the claims that recruiters commonly expressed when managers requested more male, Hispanic workers. The recruiters went to great lengths to find these workers, even looking for them in the streets.

One evening I was waiting for my paycheck in the lobby of the employment agency that supplied workers to HiCap and other organizations—I was an employee of Ready Hands temp agency, despite that the work I did was for HiCap. I was writing field notes outside the office of Peggy, the director of the employment agency, when she answered an incoming call. "No, Doreen, I am not just sitting here, . . . just waiting. . . . I'm desperate! I am so desperate to find Hispanics that—you are not going to believe what I did this afternoon. I ended up following a woman driving a van downtown because she looked Hispanic to see where she lived. Unfortunately, I lost her when she turned at a light. I don't care if this is risky. I need to find Hispanics!" The demand for Latino workers was not unique to HiCap or this agency. The agency that hired me for the job at Party Mix offered workers $50 to refer workers and $100 if the worker stayed more than ninety days on the job. White and Black workers I asked had not heard that the agency was offering money for referrals and hires. When I told Peggy that I was leaving to go back to school and write my thesis, she offered me a job scouting Latino workers. The opportunities were unparalleled for Latino labor intermediaries, in her view, and in the view of many Black and white southerners who felt that Latinos were leapfrogging them. Arlie Hochschild describes a similar resentment among white Louisiana workers, who objected to minorities "cutting in line."[29] My observations suggest some truth to this perception. These "opportunities," however, were limited from a social mobility perspective.

Bilingual intermediaries, my research shows, are central in racialized labor markets that rely on immigrant pools. Thus, the degree of an organization's engagement with labor market intermediaries patterns the management of human resources in organizations and the inequalities resulting from racialized practices. Labor intermediaries, while often missing from organizational charts, are ubiquitous in hiring processes. They enable employers to bend or, at times more accurately, break the law. That is, organizations rely on intermediaries in the form of headhunters, temporary employment agencies, and ethnic supervisors and mentors to produce, transmit, and act on stereotypes in the management of their human resources. In describing the influence of intermediaries in racialized hiring practices, I propose an analysis of the roles that brokerage and mediation play in racialized displacement.

Research on replacement or displacement has been conducted in cities with large and established populations of Latino immigrants and excludes regions in the US where immigrants are still relatively few but growing in number—regions conceptualized as new immigrant destinations.[30] Widespread industrial restructuring and the shift from capital-intensive production toward more labor-intensive modes of production, as well as right-to-work laws and the availability of low-cost labor, have increased the demand for low-skilled labor in many new destinations.[31] Immigration to new destinations has been driven, at least in part, by a combination of this restructuring and policy-related forces (e.g., enhanced border enforcement) that has made new destinations more attractive than some traditional destinations in the eyes of immigrants.[32]

In contrast to traditional immigrant destinations, where jobs have been segregated for many years, new immigrant destinations are a context where low-skilled African Americans and recently arrived immigrants can and often do overlap in the workplace.[33] Although signs of labor market segmentation are already appearing, the process of segmentation is far from complete, providing an ideal setting to study the mechanisms that drive it.[34]

The conclusions of the research that focuses on immigrant-native labor market competition in new destinations are mixed. Many studies show no evidence of competition and conclude that native-born workers eschew entry-level and low-skilled jobs such as those in meat and poultry processing and that Hispanic immigrant labor fills the resulting void in that labor market.[35] Martha Crowley, Daniel T. Lichter, and Richard N. Turner recently examined the economic impact of immigration on southern Blacks as a population and found no evidence of competition.[36] Because this conclusion is based on aggregated data, it does not rule out the possibility that low-skilled Black workers compete with low-skilled immigrants. Katharine M. Donato, Melissa Stainback, and Carl L. Bankston III, in an interview-based and telephone-survey study, found replacement occurring in the shipbuilding and oil industries in southern Louisiana, both industries with high turnover.[37]

Using observational data and interviews with African American workers, David Griffith's analyses of the blue-crab processing plants on the coast of North Carolina describe one of the few documented examples of competition between Black workers and immigrants.[38] Josh McDaniel and Vanessa Casanova show a unique case in the forestry industry in Alabama, where Hispanic immigrant labor was used almost exclusively to meet the growing labor needs of the operations, despite that they were located in areas characterized by high native-born unemployment.[39] Similar to Roger Waldinger and Michael I. Lichter's findings in Los Angeles and those of Mary Waters in New York, when new-destination studies find replacement or displacement, the central mechanisms driving the hiring processes are employer preferences and social networks.[40]

A common characteristic of existing research on replacement or displacement in new immigrant destinations is that most of these studies focus on meat- and poultry-processing plants.[41] Because these plants have exceptionally high annual employee turnover rates, they are perfect research sites for studying the hiring processes in this new context.[42] These turnover rates, however, lead to the same analytical issues that the network hiring studies have encountered, namely, that studying contexts with constant vacancies limits the ability to apply the findings to only those industries where naturally high turnover rates would aid employer efforts to use immigrant labor to replace or displace native-born workers.

I develop the concept of *racialized displacement* to explain intentional change in the worker demographics of an organization. The purposeful displacement of workers has flown under the radar of most research for multiple reasons. As mentioned earlier, some studies have taken place in organizations and industries typically suffering from high or extremely high employee turnover, so employers with an eye toward reconfiguring the demographics of their workforce had no need to create vacancies. These employers could focus solely on hiring to accomplish their goals. Racialized displacement also takes place in a relatively short time frame, so other studies have simply missed the window of opportunity to observe the mechanisms at work. Finally, employers, when they are hiring and firing based on protected categories (e.g., race, gender, country of origin), know that they are not acting in good faith as they embark on a project of racialized displacement. It is, therefore, quite likely that researchers looking in from the outside are completely misled by the purposeful obfuscation of the employers as this process unfolds. *The Manufacturing of Job Displacement* is able to detail the process because the displacement was observed over time and from a unique vantage point inside the organization that happened to coincide temporally with the occurrence of the displacement.

On Methods and Context

Although the methods for this research are detailed in the appendix, a brief description of my approach should provide context for the analysis in *The Manufacturing of Job Displacement*.

In 2005, I moved to South Carolina for thirteen months to conduct an ethnographic study on the incorporation of Latino immigrants in a new immigrant destination. Several years have passed since the initial work on this ethnography, yet the mechanisms I uncovered and describe in *The Manufacturing of Job Displacement* remain relevant today. Immigrants, exploited as much as ever, continue to take the blame for the interventions that employers use to manipulate the labor market. Furthermore, scholars continue to grapple with the intricacies of how labor market segmentation unfolds along the lines of class, race, gender, and immigrant documentation status. At the time of this research, South Carolina had one of the fastest-growing immigrant populations in the country, making it an ideal site for this study. The growth of the Latino population, primarily from Mexico and Central America, had been dramatic in relation to the growth of the Black and white populations. The Black and white populations grew by 24 and 26 percent, respectively, between 1990 and 2010, while the Latino population grew by 671 percent (from 30,551 to 235,682) during the same period.[43] The ethnoracial transformation in South Carolina was tied to processes of economic restructuring and globalization that mimicked processes observed in other regions.[44]

In the early 1990s, South Carolina attracted heavy manufacturing enterprises, such as BMW, which set up large operations in an effort to capitalize on low labor costs, right-to-work laws, and tax incentives. In addition to heavy manufacturing, a cadre of parallel light industrial manufacturing companies was also demanding low-skilled Latino immigrant workers. This reindustrialization, together with weak labor unions, resulted in an increasingly segmented labor market with skilled professionals at the top and flexible, low-skilled workers at the bottom. Initially, workers in low-skilled jobs were working-class white and Black individuals, but Latino immigrants, primarily men, became an attractive source of labor and a source of competition for African Americans and working-class white workers for jobs.[45]

Field Work and Research

First and foremost, this is an ethnography of work. More specifically, this is an ethnography of how employers, workers, and communities construct workplaces and labor markets in a structure where race, gender, and vulnerability intersect. It is not, however, an ethnography of a particular organization. I selected HiCap to study not that particular organization but rather the social processes that were emerging in a local labor market and that happened to be visible at that point in time at HiCap. The Institutional Review Board (IRB) that approved this research project was adamant that the identities of companies and participants remain anonymous. For this reason, the reader will find only a limited description of the actual site and site-specific activities in the descriptions. Pseudonyms are employed throughout the text.

Faye Crosby, Stephanie Bromley, and Leonard Saxe note that if people do not know they are being observed or measured, they are more likely to behave in accordance with their attitudes.[46] This is even more the case when studying a sensitive issue such as race and ethnic relations and discrimination in the workplace. To minimize the undue influence of social desirability, this study relies on participant observations to unobtrusively observe and document the processes and mechanisms involved in racial displacement in the labor market.[47] The study fits with other research that uses unobtrusive participant observation or naturalistic approaches to examine workplace dynamics, along with studies immersed in work contexts that document how attitudes and behaviors manifested themselves in specific situations and over a sustained period of time.[48]

In new immigrant destinations, immigrants integrate into one of two main segments of the labor market. The vast majority integrate into the lowest paid and least desirable jobs. Immigrant individuals in the lowest paid jobs tend to live in ethnic communities characterized by low-quality housing in areas with high crime risk. Because of the high concentration of immigrants in these neighborhoods, they are able to partake in the information and resources of their community. A second group typically consists of more established immigrants or those with higher human capital, who are more likely to work as brokers of immigrant services or labor. This segment of the immigrant population is also more likely to live outside the ethnic neighborhoods, in subdivisions side by side with native-born (primarily Black and white) neighbors. In an effort to capture this heterogeneity in my research, I designed this ethnography in two phases. The first phase saw me living in Bristol Apartments, where I met the immigrant participants with whom I labored for the first six months, when I did everything I could to fit in as a newly arrived immigrant from Mexico by way of California.

After six months in the lowest segment of the immigrant labor market, I moved to Jessamine Homes, a higher-income working-class subdivision that was a world apart from Bristol Apartments, even though it was less than a mile away. Here, I lived with a white family on one side of my rental and a Black family on the other side. There were two other Latino supervisors living on my cul-de-sac. As I moved to Jessamine Homes, I also obtained a position at HiCap as a bilingual supervisor. This completed my transition into the second phase of my ethnography, which led to the data that inform *The Manufacturing of Job Displacement*.

A key strength of this approach is that it afforded me intimate access to both the high and low class structures that are central to the analysis of racialized displacement. The benefits of sampling in both workplace segments were not limited to observations of the occupational heterogeneity in the Latino immigrant population but included the enhanced access that allowed me to interview people with varied race, occupational, and gender characteristics, whom I had observed for an extended period. In ethnographic work, this access promotes cognitive empathy while simultaneously providing an opportunity to validate observations made while in the field.[49]

The appendix on methods covers my positionality and other aspects related to my work roles during this research. As you read the following chapters, consider that ethnographers are the instruments of data collection. The data they collect reflect their unique perspective. I observed the racialization of organizations from multiple vantage points. I bring to my analysis my experience as an immigrant (Mexican-born) woman, as a member of the precariat working low-wage jobs, as a bilingual supervisor, as the daughter of a once undocumented father, as someone who was detained and deported by immigration authorities, and as a new American living and working with immigrants and US-born individuals. For more than twenty years, I have studied the immigrant experience in schools, workplaces, neighborhoods, community health clinics, and churches.

The Firm: HiCap

HiCap was a midsize firm (with more than four hundred workers) located in South Carolina that used a modern assembly line to manufacture complex commercial equipment.[50] Prior to the displacement, the demographic composition on first shift was primarily white and Black, with Black men vastly outnumbering white men. As a result, work teams with men were primarily African American, whereas work teams with women typically had a mix of Black and white employees. At the supervisory level, the vast majority of the production supervisors on first shift were Black, with only three Hispanic bilingual supervisors at the start of the study.

Operators typically worked an eight-hour shift. Managers assigned them to jobs that required constant concentration whenever the assembly line was in motion. Almost all the jobs on the assembly line were timed. With the exception of a couple of jobs that required lifting a baseplate assembly heavier than fifty pounds, the jobs were not gendered, and most jobs could have been performed equally well by men and women alike. The company advertised the jobs as "unskilled," as the tasks often seemed trivial to those who were not performing them. However, workers who arrived with little familiarity with assembly-line operations initially found these jobs to be difficult. Workers were required to complete a job cycle (e.g., securing an inductor assembly to a baseplate and running several wires through a grommet) in eight seconds. Most jobs required the use of specialized tools (e.g., screw guns and alignment fixtures). Some jobs involved the use of heavy equipment and required workers to be responsible for their own safety and the safety of their coworkers. Within a week or two on a job, an operator would start performing many of the simple tasks such as placing a grommet or assembling inductors, but many of the other tasks required more experience and persistence.

The recruiting and hiring of workers for the assembly line was directed by the plant's general manager, Dave, the white man I introduced earlier in the introduction. The implementation of his decisions, however, was split between a temporary employment agency, Ready Hands, and the plant's Human Resources (HR) office. Ms. Roberts, in HR, handled all personnel matters related to permanent plant employees, while the agency handled personnel decisions related to temporary workers. During my tenure with HiCap, the company hired all new operators for the assembly line through Ready Hands.

HiCap had the policy of starting all new production workers at the same pay rate with direct hires, converted from "temp" to permanent status, starting at $13.50 per hour. Workers hired as temps through the agency started at $7.50 per hour and moved to $8.00 per hour after thirty days, with some earning $8.50 per hour after being with the agency for an extended time. To evaluate the attractiveness of these pay rates, it is useful to compare them to the distribution of pay for low-skilled workers in South Carolina's manufacturing sector at the time. The temp rate of $8.00 per hour represented the twelfth percentile for white workers in the low-skilled manufacturing sector, the twenty-fourth percentile for African American workers in that sector, and the forty-first percentile for Hispanics working in the sector. The relatively low figure for whites shows that they had many other manufacturing opportunities that were more lucrative and might explain why almost none of the temporary employees hired while I was at HiCap were white. The temp wage of $8.00 per hour falling in the twenty-fourth percentile for African American workers, however, provides evidence of its attractiveness to that group, and the fact that it fell in the forty-first percentile for Hispanic workers would have made it even more attractive to them.[51] By comparison, the starting wage for direct hires of $13.50 per hour (the lowest that any of the permanent HiCap plant employees would have been making during my study) would have been quite attractive to the white employees, for whom it would have fallen in the forty-fifth percentile of all manufacturing jobs for which they would have been qualified. And that attractiveness is only amplified for the low-skilled African American workers, for whom that wage would have put them in the sixty-third percentile. With so few opportunities in the region paying more, it would be an understatement to say that any forces that motivated plant employees to abandon these positions would have had to be strong.

Contrary to the data for the manufacturing sector as a whole, HiCap had no wage differentials based on race. The primary wage disparities in this workforce were related to the distinction between permanent and temporary employees. An argument can be made that a movement to hiring temporary workers is a movement toward hiring cheaper labor. However, immigrant workers hired as temps generally came into the factory without HiCap-specific knowledge or the English fluency required to perform independently many jobs on the manufacturing line. This increased costs due to the hiring of bilingual supervisors and disruptions in production resulting from frequent errors. HiCap, it should be noted, also paid considerably more than $8.00 per hour to the temp agency for each worker, driving the price of these workers toward the level of a direct hire at the plant.

Wages and economic benefits are not the whole story in determining whether workers eschew a job, creating vacancies for others with different expectations to fulfill.[52] Indeed, job satisfaction is related to the "objective" characteristics (e.g., wages and other economic benefits) of a job, but it is also related to workers' subjective perceptions and values, such as control over work, job security, and opportunities for advancement.[53] The bulk of the literature on replacement and displacement highlights working conditions in meatpacking and related industries that would drive away most native-born workers. Ethnographies on meat-processing plants demonstrate how workers have little or no autonomy, work in cold and damp environments, have no breaks, and are unable to develop relationships due to noisy work environments.[54] Given the unpleasant and often dangerous working conditions documented in these studies, the constant churning and employee turnover that characterize these workplaces support the conclusion that only the most desperate workers will stay. The question that emerges is how the demographics of the labor force shift when working conditions such as those defining meatpacking plants are not the starting point.

At the start of this study, HiCap did not exhibit the characteristics described in most prevailing studies on replacement. In fact, a significant number of the native-born line workers had been at the plant for several years, showing at least some attachment to their jobs. When I started working at the Front End, the section I observed from start to finish, over 60 percent of the workers were permanent factory employees, many of whom had worked at the plant since it had opened several years prior. Many of these longtime workers were also relatives or close friends of the newer workers in the section. This type of social structure led to a working environment that combined work with friendship, music, prayer, and game playing.

Explaining Displacement and How It Is Manufactured

The Manufacturing of Job Displacement examines how employers get away with displacing workers under a system of racial capitalism, a system in which employers promote and retain workers on the basis of their vulnerability. The book has three primary goals. First, it makes the case that to understand the difference between categorical displacement and replacement, we need to examine how intermediaries enable the racialization of discriminatory hiring practices and how employers use veiled discrimination to create vacancies and displace nonimmigrant workers. Second, the book shows how racial capitalism explains the practices of employers, the commoditization of unauthorized immigrants (i.e., replacing their personhood with an identity of being a labor object to be used and discarded at the employer's convenience), and the ability of employers to distort the perceptions held by legally authorized workers who face racialized displacement. One of the book's significant contributions is that it challenges simple narratives of ethnic succession, instead shifting attention to organizational racialization. Additionally, it shows that the ongoing debate about the forces at play when unauthorized immigrants "take" Americans' jobs is not only more complicated than popular discourse allows but mistaken. Third, the book argues that the intersection of race, gender, and documentation status is central to understanding how individuals respond when working conditions turn dire and how resistance shapes "ideal worker" schemas and accessibility to jobs.

Organization of the Book

Chapters 1–4 of *The Manufacturing of Job Displacement* focus on the *process* of orchestrated displacement in racialized organizations operating under racial capitalism. I show how displacement that relies on subcontractors and ethnic intermediaries influences the racialization of organizations and labor markets and fissures workplaces. The chapters illustrate the mechanisms that transformed HiCap, the main case study used for this research, from a biracial (Black-white) to a triracial (Black-white-Latino) composition over the course of only a few months. Chapters 5 and 6 focus on *the context of displacement* that creates the conditions for fluctuations in racialization.

Chapter 1 explains how HiCap wanted to hire undocumented Latino workers and get rid of Black workers. Employers preferred Latino immigrants because they viewed them as vulnerable, easy to exploit, and lacking rights and legal recourse and because they perceived them as more productive despite lacking evidence of their supposed superiority. Systemic constraints, however, prevent employers from liberally acting on their racialized preferences. It is illegal for employers to use race, nationality, or gender in hiring. Additionally, large, visible organizations the size of HiCap tend to uphold, at least ceremonially, values of equality and inclusion, and they calculate the risk of litigation. Thus, if companies want to hire unauthorized workers, how do they go about it? The chapter shows that employers hired Latinos using ethnicity as a proxy for documentation status. Additionally, employers carry out racialized displacement because they have access to vulnerable workers who can secure "good papers" in the black market. Hiring unauthorized Latino immigrants with good papers, a category that stratifies racialized labor markets, enables employers to commoditize unauthorized immigrants, displace low-paid Black and white workers, and lure unauthorized workers into exploitative jobs.

Chapter 2 opens with HiCap's need for a pool of readily available workers to replace the first groups of Black and white workers who left the plant when the company hired Latino immigrants as displacements. How did the company hire about three hundred Latino workers when law and social convention restricted them from openly engaging in racialized hiring practices? It enlisted subcontractors and labor intermediaries. The chapter focuses on the racialized employment infrastructure that HiCap relied on for labor displacement. A central mechanism in displacement and the racialization of organizations involves subcontractors such as temporary employment agencies and labor intermediaries—particularly bilingual recruiters and supervisors ("brokers"). HiCap contracted with Ready Hands, a temporary employment agency, to supply immigrant workers, while bilingual supervisors, also employed by Ready Hands, managed shop-floor training and social relationships. This coordinated system stratifies labor markets under racial capitalism by isolating workers from employers and preventing them from establishing class relations with others. Displacement blocks solidarity along racial and gender lines by tactically promoting racism and schemas that fragment Black and Latino solidarity.

Chapter 3 shows how once HiCap had hired workers with good papers and created an intermediary- and subcontractor-driven infrastructure to train and hire additional immigrant Latinos, it carried through its racialized displacement through forced vacancy creation—when employers "push out" existing employees to create jobs for the vulnerable workers they want to hire. In essence, once Latino immigrants were at the door, the company needed openings that immigrant workers could fill. It was illegal, however, to fire workers merely because they belonged to a protected class, and employers wanted to protect their reputation. How did HiCap create vacancies for the immigrant workers the company was hiring? First, HiCap fired people it could easily terminate, mostly workers who were employed by the subcontractor (Ready Hands) and classified as temporary. Then, the company deployed different strategies to push out workers who were permanent employees of HiCap and had long-standing relations with fellow workers and supervisors. To get buy-in from supervisors, who would carry out the displacement, and sustain a narrative that the displacement was justified, employers promoted an ideology of "hard work."

Chapter 4 engages a different puzzle in HiCap's displacement project. Managers wanted to replace the current workforce with Latino men, but they were only partly successful; the workforce at the Front End, the main section at the plant, changed to roughly 50 percent Latino, men and women. HiCap had hoped to have in place a mostly male Latino workforce. In a nonunion plant located in the state with the lowest union density in the country and with the cooperation of intermediaries, it seems likely that an employer would be sufficiently powerful to fully implement any desired changes in a workforce. So why not here? Part of the answer is the way workers "did gender" when confronted with racialization and the threat of losing their jobs. The chapter shows how men and women with limited options but a willingness to resist displacement used vulnerability affinity (sometimes including Black men with a criminal record aligning with unauthorized Latino women operators). While workers "do gender," they also "do race" to protect their jobs. This chapter presents another situation in which workers resisted organizational threats and fought back by deploying their agency against employers. Although employers achieved their goals, the displacement at HiCap did not go in the direction that employers initially envisioned. This chapter explains what can work for employers and how unexpected consequences can result when workers resist displacement. Additionally, the chapter shows how displacement locks the most vulnerable workers in exploitative and degraded jobs. In the case of HiCap, the vulnerable workers who staffed the organization under an exploitative regime were unauthorized Latino women, Black men with a criminal record, older

Americans (Black and white) depending on employer-sponsored health insurance, and employees (Black and white, men and women) on the threshold of retirement. With regard to the binary of "good papers / bad papers" that marks immigrant vulnerability, the displacement at HiCap consolidated on documentation status as the company pushed out documented workers who resisted.

Chapter 5 moves away from the HiCap case to focus on the broader forces that can alter racialized displacement. The chapter examines how anti-immigrant legislation and social movements (i.e., the immigrant marches and countermarches taking place in the spring of 2006) marked a turning point in immigrant labor market disadvantage and the unrestrained, and racialized, demand for immigrant workers that fueled racialized displacement processes. Additionally, the chapter examines the effects of surveillance in the labor process (i.e., E-Verify) in the context of chaos and uncertainty related to immigration reform. In discussing the policies targeting employers of immigrant workers, the chapter begins to foreshadow the shifting and contingent nature of racialized displacement under racial capitalism.

Chapter 6 returns to the central question of the book and shows a different form of resistance to displacement. At Jessamine, the community where I conducted research, the economy faced disruption, while immigrants experienced a crackdown on "illegal" immigration in the form of E-Verify mandates and other employment-based policies.[55] The result was a shift in the immigrant experience from welcome to rejection. The chapter discusses the *racialized shocks*, which are defined as events or policies such marches, factory raids, employment enforcement, and documentation scrutiny, that drive undocumented workers away from new immigrant destinations and influence immigrant perceptions that Americans no longer want them. The visibility of Latina/o immigrants in workplaces and neighborhoods decreased dramatically as they found their livelihoods hanging from a very thin thread. The chapter makes the case that the effects of racialized shocks drove the unauthorized away from some new immigrant destinations and, in many cases, back to their home nations. This chapter cements how racialized displacement under racial capitalism is contingent on broader societal and economic forces and shifts in response to social action and nativist behaviors.

The book introduces a process that more adequately explains displacement in locales, such as new immigrant destinations, where African Americans and immigrants compete for the same jobs. In contrast to other studies that have inferred, after the fact, the existence of replacement processes, this book provides a clear view into the inner workings of a racialized displacement process, documented as it was occurring. One of the key unknowns when looking at organizations after they have categorically segregated (be it by race, ethnicity, or gender) is whether the redefinition and revaluation of the jobs caused the segregation or was caused by the segregation. In that light, a key contribution of the approach used in this study is that it provides a window through which one can view the dynamics of a process that is typically unobservable.

The Manufacturing of Job Displacement reassesses theories of labor market segmentation, queuing, and split labor markets to show the intricate relationship between capitalism and racialization, and it sustains that racial capitalism allows for a stronger analytical examination of labor market inequality. The book tells a story of how employers, workers, government, and communities construct workplaces and the labor market in a structure in which categories of marginalization and vulnerability intersect to make precarious labor conditions. Along these lines, it explains how employers manipulate the market using race, gender, class, and legal status, shifting the deracialized debate on the cost of immigration to include the intentional analysis of racialization in the hiring of immigrant workers. The book shows that to understand labor market inequality in the twenty-first century, there needs to be a thorough analysis of the historically prevailing intersecting categories of difference and vulnerability and the changing and contingent mechanisms of *racialized displacement*.

1

Racialized Hiring

Getting Hired

Would I get in? What was the HR manager going to ask me, a Mexican woman recruited to supervise Latino workers? I dictated field notes in my recorder sitting in the parking lot outside HiCap, a large manufacturer of air conditioners in South Carolina. At the time, I didn't know that the company was about to displace its current workforce, shift the color line of the factory from Black and white to Latino. Working as an operator, I had studied other companies whose employees were already mostly Latino, but that day in October, I was waiting to be hired as a supervisor in a company that I would soon discover was about to embark on a racialized worker displacement. I was waiting for the company's human resources manager to interview me. An employment agency sent me to HiCap, which was hiring bilingual supervisors for what I was told was a "new project" involving Latinos. I briefly fixed my eyes on the large glass doors at the company's entrance. Then I wondered, Why does the company want Latinos when they could more easily hire Black and white workers in South Carolina? Why are they hiring bilingual Latino supervisors?

It was pouring rain in South Carolina on this fall morning. My stomach was in disarray. I'm the nervous sort, and I could feel my heart pounding fiercely and my legs shaking. In five other jobs I performed for this research, an employment agency or a subcontractor hired me directly, without the need to interview with company human resources personnel. In part, this was because all these jobs were the typical jobs that exploited Latino immigrants find (e.g., janitor, factory operator, warehouse employee), those at the bottom of the "bad job" spectrum.[1] Thus, when I interviewed for the bilingual supervisor job at HiCap, I learned that the hiring of Latino bilingual supervisors was as complicated as hiring Latino operators. Complications stemmed, however, from issues related to documentation status and the company's claim to be colorblind.

At the time, I did not know much about this process. I was there to see how companies hired ethnic intermediaries. I closed my umbrella in front of the two large glass doors at the company entrance. I told the security guard that I was there to interview with Ms. Roberts.

"Are you with the staffing agency?" he asked.

"I am."

"Sign your name and go straight down the hall."

I knocked at the door of the small room the guard pointed me toward. Barbara and Yvette, two white women, greeted me. They were sitting in front of small desks looking at computer screens. "Carla asked me to come and interview with Ms. Roberts," I noted. They looked at each other. I repeated my name twice, and Yvette, the shorter of the two women, checked my name to see if Ms. Roberts was expecting me. "Just give me a few minutes. I'm going to check. You can wait outside." The waiting room was three chairs lined against the wall in a room that looked dirty and unkempt, as though no one had cleaned it in years. The chairs and floors were stained and dark with dust and spills. Five minutes later, Yvette came out. "Ms. Roberts is expecting you." Four doors down the hall, Ms. Roberts greeted me at HiCap's human resources office. She was a tall, well-dressed Black woman with an elegant demeanor. "Please take a seat. Please feel free to hang your coat and umbrella there," she offered as she scanned my résumé. Before I could say anything more than "thank you," she asked, "You say you have production experience, can you tell me about it?"

"I worked in textiles for a little while, at Carolina Mills, as a patroller."

"This position requires that you train people, have you ever done that?"

"I worked for Hyatt hotels as a training manager in Mexico and trained every new employee I hired," I answered.

"Your position requires that you make sure that everything works well in your area. There are going to be times that you are going to hear things that you don't want to hear. . . . Sometimes things don't work well, and there are tensions in the plant. . . . When this happens, you talk to your manager who deals with this. Are you okay with that?

"Yes, I am okay with that," I responded, but I was so nervous that I did not ask her to elaborate.

"In this job, you will be working with Spanish people. . . . Do you know that? I mean, do you have experience managing Spanish people? You'll be a sort of interpreter."

"Yes, Carla from the staffing agency mentioned that. And, yes, I can be an interpreter. I mean, I speak English and Spanish." I was not sure what to say or what she meant by managing Spanish people.

"Have you had experience with scheduling?"

"I have managed schedules working as a coordinator in education. I am a student working on my thesis, and I have to schedule my classes and work all the time," I said foolishly, as I did not know she was asking about "production schedules," which involve a different set of skills and tasks than organizing one's calendar. Supervisors use production schedules to assign workers to tasks, make sure that the different models that clients order correspond with the models produced on the floor shop.

Ms. Roberts looked at my résumé again before closing, "You people are always more qualified that we usually see here, but if you are here, I don't see why we can't hire you. You just can't wear those heels here." I made the mistake of wearing boots with heels. "They're dangerous. You could get one of those heels stuck in the conveyor belt. I've seen that happen, and I don't want you to get in an accident. Get yourself some work boots, the kind with steel toes, before you start."

Just like that, I was hired. Other bilingual supervisors went through more involved interviews. They interviewed with Ms. Roberts, an engineer, and two managers, but at the start of the displacement, few people were prepared for what management had in mind. What seemed clear from the beginning was that hiring bilingual supervisors was connected with racialization. Ms. Roberts noted that I was going to be supervising "Spanish" people, the term many southerners used in reference to Latinos.

After the interview, Ms. Roberts took me in tow. "Follow me. I am going to show you the plant." We stayed on the edge of the plant walking within a three-to-four-foot-wide walkway flanked by two yellow lines on the cement floor. The shop floor was chaotic and overwhelming. Assembly parts traveled the floor with forklifts honking at every opening and intersection and hovering with parts over the manufacturing floor. Operators brandished automated riveting guns, attaching wires to assemblies filing past them on a conveyor line. Many talked affably. "Come, let me show you the Front End," Ms. Roberts said as we went into a large department at the head of the plant's serpentine conveyor belt. She waved to a tall Black man standing near a desk and talking on a radio pinned to the edge of the left shoulder of his T-shirt. "That's Darius. You might be working here, with him," she noted as we paused at the Front End. I looked around and saw white and Black workers, mostly women and mostly Black.

As I observed the plant, the absence of "Spanish" workers on-site puzzled me. After the Front End, we went section by section, and I counted only white and Black employees, not one Latino, throughout the different sections of a shift with more than two hundred workers. The overwhelming majority were women, with roughly even numbers of Black and white operators. The vast number of the men in operator positions were Black. Supervisors were primarily Black men and women, and management was roughly 80 percent white. Supervisors were generally one step removed from the operator position and oversaw the work of operators on the assembly line. In contrast, managers directed the work of supervisors and had authority over both supervisors and workers. We kept walking toward the back of the production area, with Ms. Roberts naming people in management in each section. We passed several more departments, including offices and two large cafeterias, and still no Latinos in sight.

After what seemed like a mile, we slowed down near a production area isolated by stacks of boxes and shipping supplies. We worked our way through the walls of foam and cardboard and reached the stairs of a metallic platform. Stopping at the top of the platform and looking several feet down, we heard, "Poool-it! Poool-it!" The sound was coming from a group of Hispanic workers yelling in accented English below the platform and behind the walls of cardboard boxes. There they were. Hidden in the back of the factory, completely out of sight in the Back End, was a section that employed the only group of Hispanic workers on first shift. The young men and women focused on their work, moving quickly and quietly. The only words we could hear were "Poool-it! Poool-it!!" They were alerting the two white men on the other side of the conveyor to pull units from the production line when they were ready for shipment or quality control.

The Back End was a small section in an isolated area staffed with about sixteen temporary operators. It performed a set of relatively simple industrial processes that new employees could learn in a matter of hours. "The project" started on first shift in the Back End. This section had changed from having a primarily native-born to a primarily immigrant workforce. Roberto, the bilingual supervisor assigned to the section, trained and supervised the Hispanic immigrant workers. In Roberto's words, "replacing native-born workers with Hispanic immigrants happened as fast as the temporary agency could terminate native-born temps and hire the new workers." Consequently, the composition of the labor force in the Back End was rapidly transformed—overnight—as the company pushed Black people to quit and hired a steady stream of Latino workers. The Back End went from 80 percent Black and 20 percent white to 90 percent Latino and 10 percent white. Roberto told me that it was easy for him to replace the Black workers in his area because he had a small workforce, and the original workers were not permanent factory employees.

Racializing Illegality in Hiring

A central aspect of displacement involves the targeted selection of workers for job placement as vacancies opened for various reasons. HiCap employers wanted to hire undocumented workers because they viewed them as vulnerable and easy to exploit, workers with limited rights and legal recourse. As a result, to secure unauthorized workers, managers directed their labor intermediaries to hire Hispanic immigrants using race as a proxy for unauthorized documentation status. Sociologists have found that the use of the Latino ethnicity as a proxy for "illegal" documentation status is an issue that is central to racialization processes in the immigration system.[2] In most contexts in the United States, "illegality" is not an objective, race-neutral term. "Illegality," according to the sociologist Cecilia Menjívar, "has become synonymous with 'Mexicanness' and with being Latina/o. Like race, which is a fundamental organizing principle of social relationships, 'illegality,' has become an axis of stratification with effects similar to those of other racial hierarchies."[3] Speaking Spanish cements the racialization of "illegality" for Latinos. As I argue in chapter 2, enlisting bilingual intermediaries to hire and integrate Spanish-speaking unauthorized immigrants in the labor market serves as a mechanism of racialization and stratification in hiring. Thus, when employers use Latina/o (or Mexican) as a category for hiring, they are racializing a documentation status as "illegal." When they systematically hire Spanish-speaking Latino immigrants to displace Black individuals, as in the case of HiCap, they are using race, language, and nationality in discriminatory practices.

Targeted selection using protected categories such as race, gender, language, and nationality, however, is illegal and an institutionally sanctioned practice. First, the Civil Rights Act of 1964 prohibits the use of these categories in hiring and reinforces the law through Equal Employment Opportunity Commission (EEOC) compliance directives. Yet, even if we were to leave employers' use of "Latino" as a proxy for immigration status to the side and consider immigration status at face value rather than in its racialized form, employers still have to grapple with mechanisms (i.e., E-Verify) that make hiring unauthorized workers difficult. Many native-born residents resented employers who hired immigrants. Some white residents went so far as to march in the streets of Jessamine to show their discontent.[4] Thus, using race and immigration status in hiring carries risks to employers. Second, research suggests that HiCap, a large, visible employer with more than four hundred employees, will take active steps to demonstrate legal compliance and equality of opportunity. Carly Knight, Frank Dobbin, and Alexandra Kalev found in their study of litigation and diversity that large firms are more responsive to lawsuits than smaller firms are and that large firms can become more diverse at the managerial level as a result of litigation.[5] Furthermore, employers are likely to protect their reputations and avoid the high costs of appearing in court.[6] We would expect a large firm like HiCap, primarily staffed with white managers and directors in its headquarters and throughout the organization, to protect its reputation through proactively avoiding litigation over racial and gender discrimination.

In essence, employers face the dilemma of retaining control—such as hiring the workers they want—yet maintaining legal compliance. How, then, did HiCap, a large, visible company, hire the workers it wanted? HiCap maneuvered to hire Latinos with good papers to signal compliance with both immigration and EEOC laws.

Hiring Workers with Good Papers

Having good papers, in its simplest form, means meeting basic bureaucratic requirements to work. In the United States, the Social Security Administration confers the right to work through issuing a Social Security card. As anyone who has applied for jobs knows, Social Security cards are nothing more than a piece of cardstock with a nine-digit number printed in fragile ink. There is no picture legitimizing the identity of the cardholder. Yet, the card has incredible power. It opens the door to jobs. It ties government employment law to private employment practices. And it separates the documented from the undocumented in the scramble for formal employment. Good papers can consist of a Social Security number and a driver's license, a "green card," or some other form of identification issued by federal or state government. The documented have good papers.

HiCap was similar to other companies. While managers at HiCap preferred unauthorized immigrant workers—a preference that managers and other representatives stated many times while I worked there—the company hired workers who had "good" papers and fired those with "bad" ones. The challenge was for unauthorized immigrants to find good papers. Having good papers, however, is not solely a bureaucratic status. It is also an avenue for immigrants into exploitative jobs because, for employers, hiring workers with good papers is how they begin the process of circumventing the law and carry out racialization projects such as the manufacture of displacement.

In an environment of restrictive labor policy toward immigrants, these workers find themselves with limited recourse to meet the bureaucratic requirements for a job. Undocumented immigrants "borrow," "lease," or "purchase" Social Security numbers from friends, kin, or black-market entrepreneurs. Some immigrants in the borrowing and leasing categories access valid Social Security numbers from young family members who are not yet eligible for employment or outside formal employment. Others borrow or lease good papers from older immigrants who are either retired or about to retire. Those who purchase are further away from good papers.

The purchase of a Social Security number in the black market highlights how immigrants take risks when they aim for better jobs. Unauthorized immigrant workers encounter shady individuals looking to benefit from immigrants' barriers to employment. Lucy, whom we will meet again later, and her husband, an immigrant couple, told me that a drunken man, who appeared to be native-born, approached them in a gas station and in broken Spanish offered them his Social Security number for $100. This number was associated with a criminal record and became an invalid document for employment. While this is not how Social Security numbers are typically acquired, the ubiquity of identifiable immigrants and their propinquity to people who lightly value the cards means that these kinds of exchanges can happen. It also means that the situation of unauthorized immigrants is so precarious that they spend their hard-earned dollars on documents that often have no value to get the jobs ranked high in their job queues.

Although employers use employment agencies to hire workers with good papers when creating and filling displacement vacancies, immigrants seeking long-term employment assume the risk of discovering that their papers are bad. For example, Gabe, a Mexican immigrant whom HiCap hired to replace one of the white men at the Loading Corner, used a purchased Social Security number to work at HiCap. Two weeks after he started, and while he was still in training, the temp agency called him to tell him that his "papers came with a problem, they are not good papers," and "terminated" his contract. Typically, the agency terminated workers with bad papers with a phone call in the evening so that workers did not report to work the next day. While the agency paid Gabe for all the hours he worked at the company, Gabe lost the $20 the agency discounted from his wages for the verification of documentation and $100 for the bad papers he purchased. Similarly, the temp agency hired Brenda, a Mexican immigrant who lived in my building. The papers, that is, the Social Security number she purchased, came with a criminal record. While she wanted to continue working at the company, the company told her that with new, good papers, they could hire her for night shift, where nobody knew her. She refused because she had two small children at home whom she could not leave on their own at night. Undocumented immigrants often must kiss many frogs before they find the prince of good papers. More broadly, the good papers strategy used in displacement results in a system in which employers maintain compliance with the law while feeding gray economies and placing immigrants at risk when participating in the black market for papers. The search for good papers is a revolving door in which workers come in and out of the job until the company finds the workers who have valid permits for work—whether they are theirs or not.

Having false papers carries material and cultural costs for immigrants. The overwhelming majority of immigrant workers at HiCap acquired their papers from immigrant entrepreneurs who also printed false IDs. Even if workers have a good Social Security number from kinship ties, they still need a corresponding ID that has the name belonging to the Social Security number. Once undocumented immigrants obtain their employment ID, they get a new name and relinquish their identity. Detached from their name, they cease to be Ramona Gonzalez, Adriana Perez, or Jorge Valdez to become María Gonzalez, Ashley Petersen, or Richard Smith. The necessary switching of identities that labor restrictions impose on immigrants means they can be younger or older than they really are. They often acquire a criminal background or are liable for child support even if they never committed a crime or had children.

Borrowing papers is a scenario with lower risks for immigrants and employers. Purchasing good papers to get a job has the highest level of risk. When getting a job involves purchasing a Social Security number on the black market rather than borrowing or leasing it from trusted others, immigrants partly rely on luck and partly on the ability to pay higher fees. "You have to get lucky to get good papers. It's pure luck. . . . You'll probably know within two weeks [if you have good papers] because they check," Richard told me as we were eating hamburgers and fries at the cafeteria at HiCap. "Carla told us," he added, "I'm gonna let you work for two weeks, and by then I'll find out if your papers come back with a record. If after two weeks I find that they are no good, then you are going to have to leave. I'll go to the plant and drag you out by your hair."

Richard's comment illustrates that while employers give the appearance of following the law, they are not immune to the allure of false documents. They hide behind the temporary agency, which is in charge of the dirty work. The agency scrutinizes and fires immigrants. The two-week period the agency gives workers to see if their papers are good is the time the government agencies take to check for a mismatch between a worker's Social Security number and their identity. Thus, both employers and the state give workers hope and then kill that hope. Even when workers know the risk, work is so essential to their livelihood that they hold to the illusion that their papers might be good and that they might stay employed.

Juan: The Unbearable Burden of Bad Papers

Juan had not missed a day of work. Suddenly, however, he missed three days in a row without notice. I found myself going through the mental checklist of reasons that might explain his disappearance. Juan had been at the plant for two months and had survived the time it typically took the temp agency to check workers' papers for a criminal record. Supervisors praised him as a model worker as he had adapted to factory work with ease and had surpassed many plant employees in skill. When the factory had short production schedules, he volunteered for other shifts. He had sent no signals that he was ready to leave the job. He had good relationships with supervisors, and no-call, no-show behavior was uncharacteristic of his work ethic. "I need to work a lot because I need to make money. I am here to help my brother go to the university. I came here so that he can do that, so please give me as many work hours as there are. I don't mind hard work."

I even started wondering if there had been some US Immigration and Customs Enforcement (ICE) actions in the area, but I was certain that I would have heard about it. Unfortunately, for Juan and other workers in his situation, getting a job in the formal economy is only the first hurdle on the path to long-term employment. In many cases, workers left jobs despite their willingness to go above and beyond for their employers and the clear preferences of employers for workers with this attribute. Having documents that failed the criminal background check was one important and common barrier to their employment.

Similarly, but pointing to delays in the ability to meet good paper requirements, Juan shared, "I bought my Social Security number. When the staffing agency hired me, they knew my papers were not mine. They had to know. I don't know why it took them so long to find a problem, but I guess they did, and now they're telling me I can't return to work. Carla asked me to go pick up my check from Ready Hands, and when I arrived, she asked that I turn in my ID."

Juan and other workers in fragile employment situations interpret an organizational lag in the verification of employment eligibility as a "pass to work." In their hope for employment stability, as soon as the two weeks for the typical background check pass, workers are likely to grow confident that they have made it past the potential barriers to their employment. At that point, immigrants frequently begin to develop an attachment to the job. Consequently, if employers dismiss them from employment after the expected verification period passes, bewilderment and frustration ensue.

This frustration manifested itself in immigrants feeling unfairly treated. For example, a few days after Juan was a no-call, no-show, I spotted him sitting on the hood of my car in the HiCap parking lot waiting to talk to me. When the shift was over and he saw me walking to the car, he jumped off the hood and approached me. "I've been waiting to talk to you. I need your help to return to my job. They fired me because of my papers," he said clinching his teeth. He added, "I told Carla, 'Let's be honest. I am not the first or the last Mexican in this situation. You know quite well that the Social Security numbers that we use are no good, well, at least that they belong to other people. Here we are all 'illegals.' I am really upset because they let me work, and it was a mistake they made. They made the same mistake with two other people, too. . . . You know, we come here to work, nothing else, just to work."

Displacement processes that rely on undocumented immigrants navigating black markets to get a job racialize Latinas/os and carry consequences in their hiring into better jobs—jobs outside the informal or ethnic economy. The bad papers that immigrants purchase to get hired into better jobs are bad not only because they situate undocumented immigrants at risk of deportation but also, as the sociologist Douglas Massey has noted, because the criminal justice system affects Latinos/as in ways that are similar to how it marks Black individuals.[7] For example, workers like Juan who paid $200 for a Social Security number to work and earn a living, often acquired a criminal label by proxy. In Juan's case, the employment agency checked the validity of Juan's papers and found that his papers "came with issues." The employment agency then called him at home to tell him that his contract had ended and that he should not return to work. Juan was so frustrated that he went to the office and asked Carla, the agency's bilingual recruiter, why he could not return to work.

"There is an order of arrest under your name," Carla told him.

"Is the order of arrest under my real name?" he followed.

"The order of arrest is under the name of the person whose Social you have," Carla explained.

This kind of exchange is frustrating and humiliating. I personally had an analogous encounter with a recruiter while conducting this research, and I was heartbroken for several days—and I am a US citizen. At Carolina Mills, Avery, the labor intermediary, was a white woman who scrutinized every Latino person she hired. Consider, for example, how she questioned my legitimacy to work. Before I was hired, I had to complete several training sessions. At the end of the training, I was studying the Environmental Protection Agency (EPA) standards when I was called to the human resources office to meet with Avery. I assumed that she was going to offer me the job. All week, she had been calling white workers who started training with me to hire them. That same day, she hired a white man and a white woman. I thought I was next. I had passed all the safety requirements and written tests, and the manager saw me perform the technical rounds with proficiency. But the agency was not calling me to offer me a job but to question the legitimacy of my citizenship and associated right to work.

"There are some problems with your ID," Avery noted when she saw me come into the company's administrative department. She said it loudly in the open-floor office, and I felt the eyes of the office personnel placed on me.

"Why?" I asked.

"Your Social Security number came as not recognized in the system," she answered dramatically, placing a pink fingernail on a box in a form she waved in front of me

"My name looks right," I affirmed. "What's really the problem?" I asked.

"That you said you are Sanders, and you're not."

"Yes, I am," I said in what felt like a cry from my lungs assuring that I did belong there. I felt compelled to explain, like when a person explains to her friends when the server tells her in front of them that her credit card was rejected. "My husband is a US citizen," I said, with anxiety creeping into my voice.

"That's fine, honey, but are you?" she answered condescendingly, in a police-like tone, looking at me with suspicion.

"As soon as I get home from work, I will send you an email with my proof of citizenship."

I answered upset, humiliated, and confused. The embarrassment I felt was coming from having seen white workers get hired without scrutiny or questioning. It also reminded me that even when immigrants gain access to citizenship, as in my case, they are forever suspect. They have to prove their legitimacy to work and claim rights when others do not. Before leaving the office, I tried to smile with the office assistants sitting behind Avery, but they lowered their eyes before I had a chance to make eye contact. I felt that they were thinking that I was undocumented and that I was probably not going to return the following day. My papers were legitimate, but that did not prevent the emotional abuse that gate-keepers inflict on workers when employers segment the market with stereotypes of good and bad papers.

In Juan's case, his supplier assured him that he was getting good pa-pers and that he could apply for any job. Juan believed him because he paid top dollar for the Social Security number ($200) and, importantly, because he, like many immigrants, trusted the rationality of US employ-ment relations. That is, employers want workers who will work hard, and Juan was there to respond to that call. Consequently, Juan doubted Carla, the intermediary, for making hiring unfair. "I don't believe it," he told me in reference to the encounter with Carla. "Tomorrow I am going to go to the police to find out if it is true that there's an order of arrest under my name."

Immigrants make every effort to preserve their dignity in labor mark-ers that exploit their vulnerability. They aspire to save face and divest themselves from the mark of a criminal record they gain by proxy. Un-like the way the criminal justice system racializes Black people with a criminal record and excludes them from most jobs, undocumented im-migrants like Juan consider the mark of a criminal record as a tempo-rary barrier to employment, a bureaucratic transaction gone wrong, an anomaly to correct. "I don't think it's fair that I lose my job. We could have reached an agreement. I really need the job. I came here to work," Juan told me. However, even if undocumented immigrants can dissoci-ate themselves from the mark of a criminal record by not using the bad papers, they close a door on trusted hiring agents once they activate that label. Juan and others had to wait about a year before they applied again for a job at HiCap. A year was an arbitrary limit that the hiring agency imposed to avoid the risk of being caught.

The difficulty for many workers in accepting employment loss because of deeds they have not committed lies, in part, in the feeling that employers, for some reason, single them out. On one level, undocumented workers are aware that the restrictions on employment apply to a large number of immigrants and that their documents can come with baggage, but on another level, they question the fairness of the system, and my interviews show that workers begin to associate hiring practices that deny them employment with racial discrimination at large.

Besides Juan, many other Latino men left HiCap because of criminal records attached to "their" Social Security numbers. At the peak of the displacement, the last week of March, Manuel arrived to work without his brother Jose and his uncle Genaro. As he was getting into gear to start the shift, Darius caught his attention. "Manuel, where're your homies, Jose and Genaro?" Manuel usually arrived every day with these men. "They're not coming. Carla called them and told them, no more work," he answered, and Darius waited for me to interpret. "Man! I needed them here today. Leah and Therese called in sick, and I was really counting on them to cover for the ladies." During lunch, Manuel told me, "Their papers came back with a record." He continued,

When you buy the papers, you don't know if they have a criminal record. . . . You have to run the risk. Everything happens in the moment. You pay for them, and they give them to you. . . . There are no guarantees, and what happens after that isn't their problem. They [his brother and uncle] are thinking about buying other papers, but they are going to have to apply somewhere else because people here already know them by their old names. Carla told them that if they get good papers, maybe she can place them in a job here on second or third shift, where people don't know them. . . . But this time they have to be good papers. Otherwise she said she'll never hire them again.

As Carla illustrated, some agencies make accommodations to keep workers employed. In formal employment, however, bureaucratic rules and social relations on the shop floor limit the power of agencies and immigrant networks. Under the racialized displacement at HiCap, employers maintained a law-abiding stance and created the narrative that they were not giving preference to Hispanic immigrants. Thus, despite that people involved in the hiring of unauthorized immigrants wanted to keep the good employees employed, quite frequently things simply did not work out.

Hiring with bad papers is not race or immigration status neutral, as it generally affects Latina/o immigrants. Similarly, hiring with bad papers is not gender neutral, as it generally affects unauthorized Latino immigrant men. Instances of legal questions that applied exclusively to immigrant men and contributed to pushing them out of jobs in the formal economy—the "better jobs" for immigrants—also related to buying papers from people with child support obligations. Andres, a young and enthusiastic man from southern Mexico working at the Front End at HiCap, stopped me one afternoon as we were returning from the morning break. "Laura, can I ask you a question about my paycheck?" I nodded and said, "Sure, what's the problem?" Andres reached into his back pocket and pulled out a wrinkled stub, detailing the previous week's pay. "Well, it's my pay. I know we have to pay some taxes, but I worked overtime last week, and my check was way smaller than the weeks before." Then he pointed to the section on deductions and said, "What is a 'garnishment,' and why is it so much money?" I had never seen this on a pay stub, but as I looked up, I realized that we were only a few steps from the Ready Hands office. We stepped in, and I asked Barbara to explain it to me. "Oh, honey," Barbara struggled to contain her laughter. "I hate to say it, but Andres, here, is behind on his child support! The court has garnished his wages, and I bet he didn't even know he had kids. They must have just discovered that he's working here. That's gonna be an automatic deduction on all his future checks." Andres was listening but could not understand Barbara. "What did she say? Why is she laughing?" I walked away with Andres and explained to him that the real owner of the "Social" that he was using was behind on his child support and that the courts would take a pretty big chunk of whatever he made using that ID. He stopped walking as the news hit him. "Motherfucker! Oh . . . sorry . . . but what can I do, Laura?" I told him that I did not know but that Barbara said that the deductions would be automatic. After work, Andres went to Ready Hands to talk to Carla. He called me later that evening. Carla told him that there was nothing he could do but get better papers and that, since he had been working extra hours on the off-shifts, everyone at the plant already knew him as Andres, so there was no way for her to rehire him at HiCap with a different name. Andres thanked me for training him at HiCap and said that he hated to quit, but there was not even enough left from the checks to pay for his food, so he had to get new papers and find a different job. Child support issues with papers were not nearly as common as failures due to criminal records, but when they occurred, they "pushed" workers out of jobs in the formal economy. Additionally, this situation concretely created yet another impediment to finding Latino men for HiCap and slowing down the company's desire to have Mexican enclaves staffed with "heavy lifters," the term employers used to degender and deracialize their hiring. Plant supervisors used the expression to categorize men in general, but they started using it in reference to Latino men almost exclusively after the first Latinos arrived at the first shift.

As noted earlier, for the unauthorized, working involves staying on the right side of a fine line separating "good" and "bad" papers. The line shifts somewhat depending on the agency involved. Yet the main characteristic of good papers, those accepted for employment, is that the papers have no association with a criminal record (resulting from the deeds of the original holder of the taxpayer ID) and do not result in a no-match letter from the IRS (resulting from the name not matching the taxpayer ID provided). My observations and interviews with Hispanic immigrants revealed a gender distinction in access to good papers, with women having fewer issues with their papers than men did. Although a detailed analysis of false papers is beyond the scope of this book, it is likely that the higher frequency of problematic papers experienced by immigrant men relates to an elevated rate of criminal history for males in the pool of native-born individuals willing to sell Social Security credentials. All unauthorized immigrant workers coped with the economic and psychological stress of uncertain papers, but this issue more severely affected men, at least in employment; and the gender distinction had profound implications for the displacement process at HiCap.

Astrid, Whose Friends Call Her Lourdes: Good Papers and Women

On a day in May, I was preparing for work at a janitorial job I had every other night when I worked at HiCap. I received a call from Astrid, a Mexican woman from Campeche. Mariela, introduced me to Astrid, and Carla suggested she ask me to give her a ride to work since we all lived in the same neighborhood near Pioneer Road. For almost two weeks, I picked up Astrid every morning on my way to work at HiCap outside Mariela's trailer. This day, I wrote in field notes, I received a call at 10:20 p.m. from Astrid.

"Laura [sobbing], I am calling to tell you that I am not going to work tomorrow."

"What happened? Are you okay?" I asked, worried how she was doing.

"They called me from Ready Hands. Carla left a message with my husband saying that I shouldn't go back to work tomorrow. I think is because of the Social. It didn't clear. It's the only thing I can think of. What else?"

The interaction with Carla further illustrates the uncertainty that workers faced constructing identities through papers. Moreover, immigrant women in precarious jobs had a hard time navigating this insecurity. Carla, the Ready Hands recruiter, told Astrid that the Social Security number she provided had the wrong date. Astrid called Doña Jacinta, a woman who sold Social Security numbers to immigrants hoping to be hired. She issued a "corrected number," according to Astrid. Carla checked the number. It cleared, but the new number was for the constructed identity of Tracy rather than Astrid or Lourdes.

"She didn't tell me, and I didn't know," Astrid told me. "In my other job, I used my real name, Lourdes, but I stopped using my real name in case I could regularize my papers someday. I don't want to have problems," she added, with the hope that many unauthorized immigrants harbor of one day regularizing their status. In the end, Doña Jacinta omitted telling Astrid that the name with the correct number was not Astrid but Tracy, and Astrid lost the job. "I cried when my husband told me that I lost the job. I was already getting used to the work," she said.

The day after I heard from Astrid, the ride to work was cheerless without Astrid in the car. I told Mariela that I had heard that getting a "good Social" was all about luck. She snapped in disbelief. "No, that's not true at all! It has to do with who you buy papers from. Often, people buy the cheapest papers they can find, and then they get all embarrassed when the papers don't clear. All for not having paid a little more." I said it made sense. "There are people who make a business out of this," she said. "It's a big money-making business. Most people don't check the papers for criminal record before they use them. I had mine checked in an office. . . . I paid $15 to find out if the papers had a criminal re-cord, . . . but most people don't do that." She paused and lowered her head, playing with the zipper on her purse and lost in thought for a few minutes before she spoke. "It's crazy, the things we do. . . . We become illegal in this county just to have a little bit more," Mariela said alluding to leaving Mexico because her partner abandoned her with two young children, unable to make ends meet selling newspapers in Mexico.

In contrast to the more rational analysis of women like Mariela, men adopted a laissez-faire stance on papers. This can be because immigrant men's labor pool is wider. If jobs in the formal economy do not work out for men, they have alternatives in the informal economy via more estab-lished networks—men typically preceded women as economic migrants in destinations like those in this research. Richard's conclusion was that it was all "a matter of luck"—"Si Dios quiere" (God willing), a faith-based colloquialism portraying the common approach that men took to issues over which they felt they had little control. Mariela's pointed rejection of Richard's explanation and her commentary on the acquisition of papers, however, provide an additional explanation for why women have relatively fewer issues with their papers than their male counterparts do. It is hard to judge motivation or rationality because men and women have different labor market constraints and opportunities, and they shift.

* * *

"Do you know the rumor around the factory? There is a rumor. . . . They're saying that all the Front End is going to be Mexican. Is it true?" Thomas asked me as we waited for the shift to turn over.

"The Front End . . . is going to be all messy?" I wanted him to clarify, as his question surprised me.

"No, not Messy, Mexican!" he clarified.

"Where did you hear that?" I asked.

"That's what I heard," Thomas said, not wanting to say who was spreading the information.

"Yeah, that's what I heard too. Like what they did in the back, in finishing, in polishing, in other areas," Darius intervened with his serious voice. "They are saying that they are going to bring all Mexican people like you and other bilingual supervisors."

"What are you going to do if they do make the area all Mexican?" I asked.

"Nothing, there's nothing we can do. Because here we do what they ask us to do. . . . Like when there is foam on the baseboards and we write it down without fixing it, then they call us and ask why we didn't fix it, and we say because we were told to write it down. If they don't like it, they'll move us somewhere else, but we'll stay here [in the plant]."

Although the sense of despair in Thomas's and Darius's responses undercut the men's active resistance and agency to derail displacement, my data show that these responses emerged from a sense of helplessness that Black men faced because of a lack of employment alternatives outside of HiCap, related to men at the plant having criminal records. While the social and cultural distance from "Mexican" workers that Black male employees experienced may have seemed unbridgeable, their shared precarity linked them in an ecology of exploitation. That environment explains much of how Darius, Thomas, and other Black supervisors wielded authority, much to the advantage of HiCap's management.

Native-born men working in places like HiCap, especially Black men, roughly a third of whom, nationwide, have felony records, found that their previous run-ins with the law severely limited their current options.[8] One afternoon when displacement was in full force and many conversations at the plant involved applying for other jobs, Darius called me over to the supervisor desk. He pulled a folded newspaper page from the back pocket of his jeans. "I found this ad in the newspaper, and I thought, 'This is the job for Laura.' They are hiring. . . . They're even closer to home for you. I was going to apply myself, but I thought, . . . 'No, this is for Laura,'" Darius told me after he showed me an ad for a job at a prestigious manufacturing facility that was hiring production supervisors. Darius often showed kindness and generosity toward me. This thoughtful gesture was one of the many instances in which he treated me with kindness even at a time when the social relations on the shop floor were fraught with interracial tension. The gesture additionally demonstrates a measure of goodwill that exists on the shop floor and a sign of a missed opportunity for cross-racial solidarity. I read the ad, and Darius suggested that I apply, highlighting all the advantages of the job. After he was done talking wonders about it, I asked if he was going to be applying. I reminded Darius that I was leaving the plant to write my thesis and finish my graduate program.

"You aren't going to apply?" He lowered his head and immediately looked back up. To this, I responded, "No, but you should apply. This job is perfect for you, not for me."

Darius's response initially puzzled me. For months, I had wondered why a man like Darius, someone with the manufacturing skills that many engineers and managers envied, fought so hard for the job at HiCap. Looking at Darius's experience in manufacturing, I assumed he could get a job elsewhere without having to deal with the biases that permeated hiring practices at HiCap. Furthermore, I knew that Darius's educational qualifications surpassed those of many of the workers moving into better jobs. He told me that he had earned an undergraduate fellowship to pay for his studies at a top university in the South.

Darius's reluctance to apply for better jobs did not make any sense until he told me that, after two years studying prelaw, he dropped out of his university program and moved from the South for a while because, in his words, "he got in trouble." Darius's dreams came to a halt when he "was hanging out with the wrong crowd and ended up getting arrested." He lived in the North for a few years and returned to the South about the same time that the factory opened. Like many at the plant, he "got the job because they were hiring everyone that applied." Darius further explained the reason why he put up with discrimination and abuses at HiCap and took no action in applying for jobs. They won't take me. . . . You see," he paused briefly; continuing, he confessed,

> I have a criminal record. . . . They don't take people with criminal re-
> cords. . . . I've tried Michelin, BMW, GE, . . . but, no, they don't take
> people like me. There just ain't no second chances for people like me.
> The only way to clear my record is to get a pardon from the governor.

I've written, . . . but he never even answers my letters. I've been thinking about writing to Oprah. I want someone to listen to my story and see if I can do something. I only got this job because, back then, they were taking everybody who applied.

In his case, a criminal record locked Darius in a bad job, creating the perception that his options outside HiCap were limited.

Darius was not alone in his predicament. In fact, the company hired many of the permanent plant employees before it routinely checked criminal backgrounds. The men at the Motors Table told me that they would not have passed the screening to which the company subjected its current temporary workers. Knowing that this was the case, if not for themselves, then at least for some of their closest coworkers, the native-born men responded to displacement pressures with concerted and strategic efforts to have the process result in as little impact to them as possible.

Darius's case resonates with an influential literature on the way a criminal record creates barriers for Black and Brown men to find work. The sociologist Devah Pager has made a strong case for the way "the mark" of a criminal record negatively influences the employment opportunities of Black and Brown men when compared to their white counterparts.[9] The case of HiCap adds to this research in that the mark of a criminal record influences the responses of Black men in situations of displacement and demographic turnover in organizations. In my research, a criminal record frequently locked Black men into bad jobs. Men like Darius did not apply to other jobs because they knew that they stood no chance of being hired. In light of these barriers, Darius and some of his friends fought to maintain their jobs and a sense of control through a combination of fealty and bottom-up acts of resistance. It was as though they were playing out Hirschman's schema.[10] Blocked from exiting HiCap, Darius and others combined loyalty and voice in changing amounts. In contrast, when temp agencies terminated immigrant workers for bad papers, the agencies merely fulfilled many immigrants' expectations that they were part of a disposable workforce. Neither resistance (voice) nor fealty (loyalty) was an option. Furthermore, since the immigrant men ranked at the top of the low-wage labor queue, their employment situation was less precarious than the situation of the native-born men with a criminal record. In essence, the mark of a criminal record permanently locked native-born men in bad jobs, while the proxy mark of bad papers was a temporary setback for immigrant workers.

Employers and staffing agencies understand that documentation status is a challenge for immigrants. Good papers give immigrants unencumbered entry into positions as supervisors, interpreters, recruiters, or shop operators. Bad papers, on the other hand, restrict the freedom that immigrant workers have in being hired and promoted in the organization.

However, the importance of papers goes beyond the binary of "good" and "bad." Having good papers intersects with the racialization of labor power. To illustrate, HiCap followed an invisible organizational hierarchy in which bilingualism increased the desirability of a worker but decreased their exploitability. In this "labor queue of exploitability," monolingual individuals are more valuable to employers as they tend to be more vulnerable than their bilingual counterparts. This means that on the shop floor, I encountered only a handful of immigrants who worked with legitimate documents. When examining their employment trajectories vis-à-vis their undocumented counterparts, I found that companies placed documented immigrants in skilled positions or excluded them from formal jobs in their organizations.

In low-wage jobs like those at HiCap, employers exclude legally authorized workers. At HiCap, Javier, David, Arnulfo, and Che were four employees who, to the best of my knowledge, constituted the total number of documented immigrant operators at HiCap. Each arrived and departed the plant during the period of this study. I focus on Javier's case to highlight how having good papers at the plant made some immigrant workers targets of displacement yet more likely to escape the exploitation inherent with holding a job at this company.

Javier: How Authorized Immigrants Get Displaced

Javier, a thirty-year-old Peruvian, arrived in Florida after his parents legalized his status. He was proud to be a US citizen and told everyone willing to listen how his parents worked in the United States for thirty years and earned their right to legalize their four adult children. When Javier joined his parents in Florida, he found work as a maintenance technician in two Miami hotels, making $10 and $12 an hour. He had a high school education from Peru and training in car mechanics. Florida was not a good place for him to work. It was "good money but with a bad schedule." He started on his first job at 7 a.m. and returned home at midnight from his second job. Miami was also too expensive, and the only way he could pay his high rent and other bills was working at the two hotels.

Like all the migrant workers in this research, Javier moved to South Carolina seeking a more affordable cost of living and a new life. "With the amount I paid for rent in Florida, I could rent a mansion in South Carolina," he joked. Javier liked working hard. When he arrived in South Carolina, he found work as a painter. But he wanted a job that had more stability, and his fiancée, Sylvia, connected him to the job at HiCap, where she had worked for more than a year. When Javier started at the plant, he was curious about the company's plan to hire only Hispanics. "I've heard that this whole area is going to be all Hispanic. The recruiters at the agency told me that they were going to replace all the people in this area with Hispanics. They told me that the company wants to get rid of people that have been working at the plant for a long time and replace them with Hispanics." Since the day I met him, Javier paid close attention to Latino turnover at the plant.

Although Javier expressed a lot of enthusiasm about working at HiCap, managers were less receptive to him than they were to other Hispanic workers. Kesha and Marcus initially thought that Javier had "the right attitude for the job," but he soon gained a reputation for "not cutting it," as he complained about every job that supervisors asked him to perform—not surprisingly, as these jobs were tedious. His first job at the Front End was sorting screws and cleaning baseboards before assembly. Three days into this job, he requested a meeting with Marcus, the section manager. Most workers try to avoid, rather than seek out, meetings with managers. Javier was not like other workers. After his meeting with Marcus, Javier said, "This job is too boring. You're not going to keep anyone here. I'd like to move to another job." Javier expressed himself with the confidence and sense of empowerment that good papers acquired via naturalization give to some immigrant workers.

Being short of "heavy lifters" and interpreting Javier's request as wanting a more challenging job, Marcus moved Javier to the Transfer Corner, a job that involved heavy and constant lifting and twisting. After a day at the Transfer Corner, Javier complained about his back hurting and requested a transfer to a different job. Marcus ignored his plea. In response, Javier brought a back support with suspenders that he strapped on top of his shirt.

"Why are you wearing that?" asked Marcus when he saw Javier wearing the back support.

"My back hurts, and I want them to know that," Javier responded.

"You can't wear that! PPE [personal protective equipment] has to be OSHA [Occupational Safety and Health Administration] approved," Marcus said and shook his head.

"I'll wear this until I get moved to a different job," Javier responded defiantly. "Tell him that I want to be working in the department in the back, the one where they work with the copper lines." This was also the department where his fiancée, Sylvia, worked. "They work well there. People get along, and they work more hours. They are all Hispanics. Tell him that I want to move there."

"No. I don't do trades like that," Marcus said, closing the conversation as he walked away.

Marcus kept Javier at the Transfer Corner until Kesha protested. Javier was creating gaps on the line because he was not moving fast enough for the job. "He's not cutting it," Kesha told Marcus in her request to transfer him. "I hope he quits. You know what I am saying?" she added. Later that day, Marcus came to the area and told the supervisors that he needed someone to go to the back to clean units with alcohol, permanently. Kesha suggested to "send one of the slow ones. I am thinking either Javier or David"—the two officially documented Hispanic line workers at the Front End at the time. "Send Javier," instructed Marcus. Later in the day, Javier said that Dorothy, his new supervisor, needed another person in the area. Kesha sent David.

The job cleaning with alcohol was a virtual black hole for workers. Without rotations, most workers lasted less than a day on this job. Unfortunately, employers needed someone to clean with alcohol, and the managers saw the job as a solution to most personnel issues. If they moved an "issue"—workers whom management perceived as troublemakers—to alcohol and the employee quit, then that was a win. If they moved an issue to alcohol and the employee stayed, then the worker performed the undesirable job without creating turnover, and that was a win. To everyone's surprise, Javier refused to quit. He was determined to stay at the plant. Javier was saving for a house down payment, and he wanted to stay at the plant at least until he made enough money for the purchase. Additionally, the HiCap job afforded him the opportunity to work with his fiancée. Sylvia had fewer options than Javier had due to her lack of proper work documents, a situation that essentially trapped her in the HiCap job.

Three months after Javier had started at the plant, Dave, the plant general manager, called me to translate a meeting at Javier's workstation. When I arrived, Javier said without preamble, "I have been working here for several months. I've been asking to be moved to another job, and nobody does anything. I know what they are doing here. What are they thinking? Are they thinking that because I am Hispanic, they can do anything they want with me? I am not illegal, like the others. . . . Tell him that I know what my rights are and that they need to give us safety equipment."

I started translating for Dave. He listened attentively before responding. "Tell him I am going to change things. I'll send a mask and ventilate the area," Dave promised. He instructed me to talk to Marcus about sending a fan and giving Javier a paper mask. That evening, before the end of the shift, a small fan and a paper mask arrived at Javier's workstation, but those did little to solve "the problem of Javier."

About a week later, Dave came to the Front End and asked if I could step away from the line for a few minutes. He was furious. He needed me to interpret a meeting with Javier. "We are having issues with the operator working on the catwalk. He is wearing a face mask that he brought from home, and operators are not allowed to bring their own safety equipment to work." I told him that Javier was probably wearing the mask because the alcohol makes the operators nauseous and sick. Dave dismissed the comment. "I don't think it's the job. Marcus already told this guy that the PPE that operators wear around the plant has to be approved by OSHA. If he wants to wear a mask, it has to be OSHA approved. We don't have masks like the one he is wearing. . . . OSHA would have to approve it." We walked over to Javier's workstation. Dave stood next to me facing Javier. "Tell him that he can't wear that mask because it isn't OSHA approved." Javier nodded behind his heavy-duty respirator.

He cleaned a couple of more units and then stopped. Turning his face and torso toward Dave, he extended his arm with the alcohol-soaked rag and placed it under Dave's nose. Dave reacted, stepping back. The fumes of the alcohol hit his eyes and nose, and the drops of alcohol fell on his brown work boots. Javier smiled while breathing heavily through the mask, revealing his dark eyes behind a pair of thick glasses. "See . . . that's why I need this mask. Tell him that I am wearing it because the alcohol gets in my nose and throat. Without the mask, my nose bleeds." The move infuriated Dave even more. "He cannot bring his own safety equipment. Is this clear?" he responded to me, avoiding a direct confrontation with Javier. Dave turned around and returned to his office. "Who is that guy?" Javier asked as we lingered with the unresolved issue. "He is the plant manager," I said. "I have to take care of my health. I cannot believe that they care more about the need to inspect the mask than the safety of the workers. You'll see how they worry when they have to face a lawsuit," he said, repeating a threat that I had heard him make on several occasions.

Two days after the incident with the mask, Dorothy, the Black manager in Javier's section, asked that I meet her at Javier's workstation. She was standing near the entrance to the ramp where Javier cleaned the units. She pointed to Javier and said, disturbed, "He is not wearing his safety glasses." I told her that earlier that day, during break, Javier asked that I accompany him to the security office to borrow some safety glasses. The security guard said that he "didn't have any" and sent us to human resources. The office was empty, and the break was about to be over. A couple of days before this incident, Javier had forgotten to wear his glasses, and nobody said anything about it. With this precedent, he decided to go back to the assembly line and avoid getting in trouble for leaving his workstation unattended. Dorothy heard the explanation patiently. "I understand. It's not me. Dave just came in to tell me that Javier is not wearing safety glasses. I hadn't noticed because he is wearing prescription glasses, but Dave wants me to give him a write-up." Javier asked if he could go pick up the safety glasses from his car. "I am not sure the security guard would let you go out and come back in," Dorothy said in a sympathetic voice. "Here! These are the keys to my car—can you go and get the safety glasses for me?" Javier said, handing out the keys to his car. Instead of going to his car, Dorothy found him another pair of safety glasses. Dorothy said in frustration "I don't know why all of the sudden 'they' are looking at him. The guy was wearing the mask for several weeks, and they just now decide that he can't wear it. What's wrong with him wearing it? Now they want me to give him a write-up for this business with the glasses. What's going on? I think they're trying to get rid of him." And they were. Typically, a temporary employee who was problematic would be the subject of a phone call to the staffing agency, and that employee would simply not return the following day. But because of Javier's repeated threats of legal action and because HiCap was concerned about legal issues and legal responsibility, the company made sure that either Javier quit on his own or it had a solid case for termination.

As I walked with Javier back to the Front End, he told me, "What a week! I don't know what's next." He had lasted longer than any worker at the alcohol cleaning station despite efforts to get rid of him, and longer than any other documented worker, and he was not going to give up easily. He requested a meeting with Carla, and one day, during an impromptu visit, he approached her.

"The alcohol eats your liver and causes cirrhosis. You know that, don't you?" Javier asked Carla, the agency's bilingual recruiter, just outside HiCap's human resources office. He raised his hand and waved his index finger in front of Carla's face. "If I go to a doctor and they tell me that I am sick because I am working with highly concentrated alcohol in my job, the job that they have me doing at the plant, I am going to sue the company!" Javier's fiancée, Sylvia, was standing next to him with her hand lightly pressed on Javier's arm. The pressure sent signals to moderate Javier's frustration and prevent the storm that was about to fall on Carla.

"What are they thinking? What are *these* people thinking! Are they thinking that I am illegal, or *what*?! Just because the illegals don't complain and say nothing when they abuse them, they think that I am not going to complain. They think that I am going to say nothing? I am a US citizen! I can sue them!" The volume of his voice had increased, and now the security guard standing a few feet away from the office could hear him. The guard lifted his head and instinctively placed his hand on the gun holstered on his belt. With a facial gesture, he was silently asking Carla if he should intervene. Carla signaled with a reassuring nod of her head and a slow blink of her eyes that she had things under control. Javier followed Carla's eyes, still fixed on the guard, and took a deep breath, trying to calm himself down. Carla returned to Javier and said calmly, "I told you when you started, factory work is not easy. This is not a job for everyone. The company wants people that can work hard and do the hard jobs. If you don't like it, you don't have to do this job. You can leave anytime, and I'll bring someone else to do your job. I have piles of applications on my desk. There are so many people who would gladly take your job and start tomorrow. Go ahead and sue, but think about it before you do it. The agency has strict policies about papers, and we only hire people with papers. So . . . you'll be wasting your time." Carla's response was both firm and scripted. This was not the first time I had heard Carla saying similar things.

"I am not dumb! You and I know quite well that the people working here are working with false papers, papers that are not theirs. . . . But that's not what bothers me. . . . What bothers me is that they are treating all of us, even citizens, like me . . . they are treating us like il-legals. Why do I have to do a job that makes me sick, ah? Why?" Sylvia pressed on Javier's arm, leaving a print on his skin, begging Javier to calm down. Carla looked at him attentively with her deep blue eyes wide open. Other workers had confronted her in the past, but only a handful had the potential to act on their grievances. She could do little. Like the bilingual supervisors at the plant, she brokered between workers and employers, and her main objective was to keep both groups engaged in a well-functioning relationship. She knew he was right. She knew that Javier and Sylvia and everyone, at least the Hispanics, at the plant knew too. She told me in an interview several months after the exchange that acknowledging Javier's complaint would have meant closing doors to employing many immigrants whom she truly wanted to help. Wanting to end the conversation and hurrying out of the plant, she responded calmly, "Why don't you come to the agency and talk to Margie, the man-ager, about this? Maybe she can talk to your manager so they can assign you to another job." Her closing comment elicited a skeptical smile from Javier. "Yeah, maybe I'll do that. Thanks, Carla," he said, unconvincingly. Besides venting his frustration, not much came out of the exchange. The agency had a cover story.

After Carla left, Sylvia tried to calm Javier down with a soothing tone. She reminded him that proceeding with his threat to sue the company could have personal ramifications for them: "Javier, . . . you have to understand. It's not in the company's best interest to do anything against the illegals because it would mean recognizing that they are hiring people without papers, and immigration would come here and close the plant, . . . because, yes, they do have people that are working against the law, but it's not because they want to break the law. It's because they had no other option. They have no other option! No options! Do you understand? I wish you knew what this means. Think how lucky you are to have papers, how lucky you are that you don't have to come to work and be worried about immigration. You can stand here and speak your mind, . . . tell them that you are going to sue them. You can go to another company and find another job, but we can't. If we don't complain, like you say, it's not because we don't want to. It's because we can't." She stopped as her voice was starting to break. Javier tried to pull Sylvia toward him. Gently, she pushed him away. She looked at him straight in the eyes and said softly, "I don't know what you're doing. You want me to lose my job? You want me to go back to cleaning houses? Things are going well for me here. I am close to becoming permanent. You know damned well these jobs are not easy to find. Don't do this, Javier." Javier did not say a word. He found her hands and pressed them tightly. Still holding his fiancée's hand, he looked at me with a mix of impotence and compassion and thanked me for accompanying them to talk to Carla. They left, and he nodded to the security guard on his way out.

While Javier's documentation status facilitated his ability to express grievances, his interconnectedness with others with undocumented status neutralized much of the power typically conveyed by his status. In this case, that Sylvia, Javier's fiancée, was herself undocumented effectively constrained his options.

"Tell them to make him a floater," Marcus directed me to notify the agency to change Javier's status. Two days after the exchange with Carla, Marcus could not have imposed a stronger sanction on Javier. Floaters only worked a few hours a day, and some days they did not work at all. A reduction in work hours translates into lower pay or no pay at all, and this ultimately proved incompatible with Javier's reason for working full-time. For most immigrant workers in my research, being made a floater was little different from being fired. Javier quit after a week working as a floater. In retrospect, Javier was one of many documented workers constrained by limited English proficiency who found themselves in jobs where they were subject to the same treatment as Black workers, the workers whom employers perceived as "having an attitude" and the workers they ultimately target for displacement.

"Stateless."

"*Sans papiers.*"

"Irregular."

"Unauthorized."

"Undocumented."

"Illegal."

Bureaucratic requirements "mark" immigrants in the employment context. They label immigrants with the "illegal" credential. They are an aspect of what sociologists call "symbolic violence," creating boundaries that ease the process of controlling "others."[11] But these labels extend beyond unauthorized immigrants and similarly mark Black and Brown Americans with a criminal record. The damaging labels that restrict and animate prejudice against immigrants are several, fluid, and vary across nations and historical periods. Nevertheless, these labels not only reify people and present material barriers for immigrants, like the Latino workers whom HiCap recruited, who have to maneuver for access to jobs and a dignified living, but also underlie the new identities that many immigrants must adopt. Working without legal status or, as my interlocutors called this state of liminality, working without "good papers," immigrants live lives in which risk assessment guides everyday decisions. At the forefront of their decisions are plans to avoid deportation while still earning a decent living to feed their families, pay their rent, support their children's schools, and pay for private health-care services, minus the fear of deportation and the burden of new identities, concerns that virtually all working-class Americans, native-born and immigrant alike, share. When Mariela, a Mexican immigrant who earlier in the chapter shared her thoughts about ensuring the quality of black-market papers, leaves her home every morning to work at HiCap, she leaves behind her identity to occupy an identity that she had to construct to feed her two school-age children and send remittances to her elderly mother in Oaxaca, Mexico.

Racializing Illegality

The recruiter described the position: "They are adding a *new project* [her emphasis]. They [management] started with 'a team' on third shift, then with a team on second shift, and now they want to start a team on first shift and possibly add one more on third shift." She said she was having a hard time finding people to fill in the positions on the different shifts. I realized that she was talking about Hispanics when she said, "Ya sabes que mucha de nuestra gente quiere trabajar pero no tienen papeles buenos" (you know that many of our people want to work but they don't have good papers).

This exchange happened four weeks before I interviewed with Ms. Roberts, HiCap's human resources manager. Given bilingual supervisors' intermediary position between the agency and the company, most interviewed with Carla and Ms. Roberts.

Carla, the bilingual Mexican recruiter, talked to me in Spanish the day we met at Ready Hands, the employment agency screening bilingual supervisors for the job at HiCap. While the agency hired the bilingual supervisors, the company still had to interview these recruits and approve their hiring. Ms. Roberts was in charge of the interviewing and hiring after candidates have met with Carla. As I spoke to Carla, I noticed that there were white recruiters in the employment agency, sitting at desks nearby, making copies or delivering papers to in-box trays. Even though the employment agency was screening bilingual supervisors in an open space, the Spanish language made our conversation feel private and intimate, like having coffee with a relative at home. She looked at me straight in the eye before saying, "The factory is a rough place, and you are going to face resistance from some of the people that had been there for a long time. Many of them think that their jobs are secured." She paused and smiled nervously. "But . . . the company cares about the numbers and wants people that can be fast and highly productive. The company really likes hiring Hispanics." She smiled proudly: "They know that 'our' people are here to work hard. . . . They like that Hispanics are always on time for work and that they are rarely absent. . . . You know how . . . if they are going to be absent, they call and tell you straightforwardly why they cannot make it. . . . But they tell you. Hispanics are dependable and reliable, and the company likes that." She asked if I thought I was going to have problems with transportation since I lived in Jessamine. I told her that my car was getting fixed and I didn't expect to have any more trouble.

HiCap's Labor Queue: The Valorization of Latino Men

Employers at HiCap did not turn to immigrant labor overnight. When Roberto and I, the first two Latino supervisors on first shift, arrived, the plant was primarily Black and white. One day, I was sitting with Roberto in the cafeteria when a sixty-year-old white Cuban approached us. "Are you Mexican?" he asked with curiosity. He then told us that in the fifteen years since he had been at the plant, he had never seen "other Spanish people around" and that, in fact, the company did not even know he was Latino or spoke Spanish. Thus, even when the company hired the odd Latino, management had not shown the initiative to hire other Latinos.

At the start of the displacement, racialization of unauthorized labor had not crystallized. The initial logic used to justify race as a proxy in employment involved using deracialized hiring criteria such as "cultural fit." "Cultural fit" indicates that managers hire workers on the basis of a cultural match between new and existing employees in an organization. It also illustrates the tendency to portray organizations as race-neutral but open to purported cultural distinctions that have invidious consequences. Working as a human resources manager in a firm, Lauren Rivera found that firms use "cultural fit" as a schema deployed in hiring workers. In doing so, they deploy discriminatory practices.[12] HiCap used some of these strategies. However, while it selected undocumented workers on the basis of deracialized criteria, these criteria were culturally opposite to the attributes managers assigned to their current workforce—workers they perceived as "lazy" and "unmotivated." Using deracialized language, different interlocutors told me that the company wanted workers with "a good disposition." They wanted workers who "were energetic and [would] do anything [the company] wanted them to do." At HiCap, the workers it wanted had to be different from those already in the organization. HiCap showed no interest in benefiting from the variety of new ideas and talents that the hiring could introduce, as diversity arguments would suggest, but only in exercising power and control over the labor force.

The question of how employers get the idea of hiring unauthorized workers when employers had never worked in the factory points to a puzzle in studies on immigration and the racialization of organizations. Immigration research demonstrates employers' stated preference to hire immigrant workers, but how does this preference mesh with their ideal to appear unbiased, as shown in the literature on organizations?[13] Furthermore, with the stigma and ostracism directed toward Mexican immigrants in general and the undocumented in particular, why would any employer in the Deep South want to go out of its way to recruit these workers?

To an extent, mimetic isomorphism, the practice of following the managerial practices deployed by peers in other firms, brought immigrant workers to the attention of employers. To some extent, the wide use of temporary employment agencies, because "everyone else hired workers this way," shows why employers turned to immigrant workers. In the case of HiCap, globalization additionally contributed to the racialization of undocumented immigrants in the United States. As a transnational corporation, HiCap had set up shop in the Global South with subsidiaries in Mexico. When the company moved its Michigan plant to Monterrey, Mexico, it brought in a sizable group of managers and supervisors to train at another HiCap facility, in North Carolina. According to a company manager, "Unlike American workers, the Mexicans were always smiling. They never complained. They were the best workers we ever had." Keep in mind that these managers were comparing the cultural attributes of Mexican trainees in the United States with low-wage workers in the US South who had worked at the company for more than fifteen years performing monotonous, dangerous, dirty jobs day in and day out, with no mobility ladders. Additionally, the frame of reference from a worker in the Global South is considerably different in relation to wages and working conditions. When a foreign trainee in the United States sets foot in a US factory, they are earning dollars, not pesos. They are also learning state-of-the-art processes that they can carry with them when they return home. Even if they find the work or working conditions exploitative, the rewards can translate into higher human capital at home. To be working in the United States for a transnational corporation has "bling" on a Mexican employee's résumé and can translate to better job offers at home. I know this from talking to the groups of Mexican managers who came to visit the factory during the time I conducted research. Should I get tired of working at HiCap, I always had the business cards that managers gave me after we shook hands. Their introductions were backed by job offers.

Using cultural attributes of workers with notably different frames of reference, employers turned to immigrant labor after a year working with Mexican managers and supervisors. While it seemed absurd to use cultural attributes as a basis for hiring decisions, this type of selection bias played out in other firms. Unlike the cultural attributes in Catherine Turco's and Lauren Rivera's studies, however, the cultural attributes HiCap wanted were not those that aligned with the characteristics of existing workers.[14] Management decided to hire Mexican workers for their plant in the United States. What they liked about Mexican workers had nothing to do with skills but with a cultural perception of productivity.

Barbara, one of two non-Hispanic recruiters at HiCap, admitted, "To be honest, the best workers we hire are undocumented. . . . They want the jobs, and they are willing to work hard." Similar to findings from other studies, at HiCap the perception that the undocumented work harder and are "the best workers" derived from differences in tractability rather than inherent productivity.[15] The undocumented workers at the plant rarely reported injuries, rarely complained, often worked through their breaks, and were more willing to accept unrealistic demands coming from managers and supervisors. And as we have seen, most of the handful of documented Hispanics who did work at the company while I was there were "encouraged" to leave. By assigning them to the most undesirable jobs and reducing their hours, management drove documented Hispanics out of the plant to create vacancies for new and undocumented Hispanics.

Recruiting

Recruiting candidates for low-wage work is a taken-for-granted aspect of the hiring process that receives little attention in research or policy. In part, this is because this element of hiring is straightforward. Recruitment typically involves attracting candidates to the employer so that workers actually want to apply to work there. The hiring agent, a recruiter or human resources manager, should then find suitable employees from the pool of candidates who have expressed interest. Recruiting methods involve online, print, and word-of-mouth advertisement of vacancies, with the goal of reaching out to a large pool of reliable, dependable workers. Advertising open vacancies happens in the language used in the workplace, usually English in the United States. Recruiting is ostensibly a nonracialized process devoid of categories of distinction.

When targeting immigrant workers for jobs, however, recruiting turns into a racialized process. Recruiting immigrants involves tapping into ethnic and racial characteristics that would get immigrants to employers' door. Employers go out of their way to recruit immigrant workers through an infrastructure of bilingual recruiters, temporary employment agencies of shady morality, and supervisors. Additionally, employers use the language of the immigrant group to exclude non-immigrant applicants while getting the more exploitable workers they want. Using categories of distinction such as nationality and language, companies bifurcate recruiting along ethnic and racial lines to hire the workers they want for displacement.

At the start of this research, it baffled me to see the widespread and exclusive use of ethnic media in recruiting workers for "light industrial" (the misnomer for exploitative) jobs. As a result, I began examining whether want ads published in the Spanish-language newspapers had a counterpart in the English-language newspapers. I found that in the period between June 2005 and September 2006, only 20 percent of the jobs advertised in the Spanish-language newspaper had a corresponding want ad in Jessamine's English-language newspapers. Many companies advertised for crew leaders or assembly jobs exclusively in the local Spanish-language newspaper, *La Opinión*, and on local Spanish-language radio stations.

In *Recruiting Hispanic Labor: Immigrants in Non-traditional Areas*, the geographer Karen Johnson-Webb elaborates on the use of ethnic media in new immigrant destinations. She shows how employers heavily advertise in Spanish newspapers and radio programs to recruit Latino workers for job openings.[16] My observations confirm Johnson-Webb's findings, highlighting the importance of considering media outlets in "getting a job." In fact, in five of the seven jobs in which I immersed myself for this research, I got my job from advertisements in media outlets rather than through my social networks. And, even though the information for the other two jobs (HiCap and Sparks) came directly from my neighbor Lucy, the Spanish-language media was only one step removed.

HiCap employers used a complex model in which ethnic media produced immigrant workers. For example, Lucy, one of the most socially embedded immigrant women in the apartment complex where I lived, typically found employment information through newspapers, ethnic radio, or Spanish-language agency billboards. As it turned out, she, herself, had learned about HiCap through a newspaper ad rather than through her social networks. One night, she urgently knocked at my door, wanting to show me an ad she found in *La Opinión*. She opened the newspaper to show me a square with a job for a "Bilingual Leader" at HiCap (see figure 1.1). Lucy highlighted the position and two others with a yellow marker and singled out the small squares with a Post-It. "People don't need to speak English there because they are hiring *mayordomos* [supervisors] that speak Spanish. You can apply for the group leader. If they take my papers, we can work together there," she said hopefully.

NEEDED

Group leaders: Assist area managers in the supervision departments in Operations (assembly line). Applicants should have experience with managing people, be energetic and responsible and have worked in a production or industrial company. English and Spanish fluency required to train workers who do not speak English.

Assembly Line: Available to work in production on all shifts. Able to work standing for 8–12 hours. Have good work history, legal work status, pass drug and criminal checks and be available. The position may be temporary or permanent. Apply in person at: [Ready Hands contact details omitted].

Figure 1.1. Employment announcement in *La Opinión*

The medium here is the message. Immigrant workers at HiCap learned about the jobs in a Spanish-language newspaper, a practice that shapes the labor pool in favor of exploitable immigrants. Additionally, the ad listed assembly-line jobs just below the bilingual supervisor position. While the ad says it hires people with "good papers"—legal work authorization and no criminal record—the ad also suggests some flexibility in the matter, as the company still wants workers. It also hints at a "hard worker" expectation, as the company indicates that it wants people to stand for eight to twelve hours. In addition to listing the jobs in the local Spanish-language news media, HiCap contracted with Ready Hands, a local, independent employment agency with bilingual recruiters who assuaged the anxiety and fear associated with applying for formal employment in a new country and language. Signaling preference for immigrant labor, companies ensure that their advertising campaigns bring immigrant workers to apply for jobs.

The following excerpt from my field notes illustrates the effectiveness of racialized recruiting:

> Lucy and I drove by Ready Hands at least three times a week either on our way to Walmart or to the Plaza Latina, the strip mall where we bought fresh tortillas, cashed checks, or attended concerts organized by the local Spanish-language radio station. As we drove, Lucy invariably scanned the wanted ads and told me whether we should go to look for a new job. "Look! Laura! All the jobs they have for us. It shows that they really want us," Lucy exclaimed as we approached Ready Hands on Pioneer Road. Lucy read the job titles, spelled out in Spanish on the agency's billboard on Jessamine's outskirts. The billboard included the wages for each of the positions: "*Recepcionista* $9.00, *Operadores* $9.50, *Limpieza* $6.50, *todos los turnos.*"

The "they want us" theme reflected in the use of Spanish in recruiting is salient in this and many other examples in my data. It indicates that attracting immigrant applicants requires understanding immigrants' habits, hopes, and fears. Jobs need to appeal to the heart and mind of workers, and immigrants are no exception. Recruiting immigrant workers involves managing perceived deportation risks. While "good jobs," according to Arne Kalleberg, need to project stability and security, these terms have a different connotation in the immigrant lexicon.[17] Participants in my study expressed concerns about being caught with bad papers when stepping inside an employment agency to fill out an application. They also rely on agencies with branches in immigrant communities. Like three other temporary agencies in Jessamine, Ready Hands was strategically located in a Latino immigrant neighborhood. Its main branch was on Pioneer Road, the road with the most Latino foot and car traffic in the region. Pioneer Road also connected to Bristol Apartments, where many Latino immigrants lived.

Following tested practices in replacement, HiCap advertised jobs in Spanish on large billboards that captured immigrants' attention. It contracted with a temporary employment agency with a history of hiring and recruiting in the immigrant community. Its location mattered, showing how racialization transgresses firm boundaries. Additionally, listing assembly-line positions next to those of bilingual supervisors signaled interest in hiring Latino immigrants. The relevance of this signal merits emphasizing. It means that workers had access to a coethnic ally inside the organization. These trusted agents can alert and protect workers from backlash from American workers and from ICE raids, the Homeland Security agency in charge of holding employers accountable when they hire undocumented immigrant workers. Thus, using these recruiting strategies, HiCap not only attracted the immigrant workers it wanted as replacements for existing workers but also had access to a constant and continuous flow of immigrant replacements to account for the problem of good papers.

The Racialization of Hard Work

Two weeks before the displacement began in earnest, Jerry, a six-foot-tall Black man from the Motors Table, went on break to read the newspaper and smoke a cigarette during one of the two fifteen-minute breaks in his eight-hour shift. Five minutes before his break was over, Darius, the Front End supervisor, went to the break area to ask Jerry to come back to work.

"Hey, Jerry! Come back to work!" Darius commanded with the door to the smoking patio open. Jerry was sitting next to me reading the newspaper. He moved his eyes away from the newspaper for a couple of seconds.

"I ain't doing nothin'," he responded calmly between his teeth without looking at Darius, flipping the page of the newspaper resting on his lap while the cigarette rested on his lips.

"Back to work! There ain't no other loader at the table now," Darius urged him. With the door still propped open and everyone's eyes looking at both Jerry and Darius, Jerry reluctantly took a final puff of his cigarette and slowly put it out in a bucket filled with sand, where dozens of unfinished cigarettes evidenced the limited time workers had to finish a smoke.

"It ain't my problem," Jerry said as he grabbed his cigarette package and calmly inserted it in a pocket of his black sweatshirt and took another glance at the newspaper.

"What, now? Are you going to stay and read?" Darius raised his voice, reacting to Jerry's disinterest in urgently returning to the shop floor. Jerry did not answer, stood up slowly, grabbing the newspaper, and walked back to the floor with his eyes fixed on it, still waiting for the alarm to sound before gearing up to return to his job. When Darius and I joined Marcus, the section manager, after Jerry took his spot at the Motors Table, Marcus confronted us.

"What took so long? You're bringing the line down! We are losing units. We don't have enough loaders."

"What you want me to do? Jerry was on break," Darius answered.

"See what I mean? They feel like they own their time. They can do what they want with their time outside, but not here. Here they have to work," Marcus noted, ignoring that Jerry was smoking during his break time. Looking at the men working at the Motors Table, he remarked, "Those guys won't do anything else. You ask them to do something else, and they say, 'I ain't doing that. It ain't my job,' but we need to change that. . . . It's going to hurt them personally because they have been in that group for many years. . . . It's going to hurt them personally," Marcus commented.

In the era of work spaces as "playgrounds"—think Facebook or Google—when workers are encouraged to play at work to "unleash" their creativity, the idea of chastising workers for resting or enjoying themselves at work seems counterintuitive. Yet in low-wage industrial work, these behaviors are not only discouraged but penalized. These behaviors fuel stereotypes and generally trigger a desire from management to tighten their control over the labor force and, in the case described in this chapter, to change the demographics of the workforce along racial and gender lines. For managers at HiCap, resting between assemblies or playing games to pass time was viewed as "wasted time" or "idle time" and reflected a "poor work ethic," characteristics they associated mainly, although not exclusively, with Black men. With these beliefs, managers justified the means toward an end of shifting the workforce demographics, a shift that over the course of only two months transformed HiCap from having a primarily Black and white workforce to having a substantially Hispanic immigrant workforce.

The existence of the black market for papers meant that HiCap could hire undocumented workers without knowing for sure whether they were undocumented, but it also presented a challenge. If employers want undocumented workers but do not know if someone is undocumented, what do they do? They use race as a proxy.

* * *

At Jessamine, the new immigrant destination and city that supplied most immigrant workers for the displacement at HiCap, the origins of immigrant hiring started with attracting pioneers recruited in the 1970s. Textile mills, the main manufacturing industry in Jessamine at the time, sent a Cuban intermediary to Colombia to recruit the first immigrants to work at J. P. Stevens and Company, one of the textile mills flourishing in the region. When the Colombian pioneers were recruited, the hiring of immigrant workers had only weak connections to unauthorized status and to companies like HiCap. Manuel, one of the Colombian pioneers I interviewed to understand the arrival of Latinos at Jessamine, commented that the area's first immigrant cohort, of which he was a part, arrived with the legal right to work because the mills brought them to the United States. Not long after, employers attempted to hire more Colombians, but those groups were mixed in their documentation status, with many workers arriving with work visas that at some point expired. For the most part, the hiring of these undocumented immigrants—undocumented not upon arrival but upon settlement—remained well off the radar of immigration authorities and the public. Immigration status was simply not a salient characteristic. Before the Immigration Reform and Control Act (IRCA), employers bore essentially none of the responsibility of verifying employee status. They were essentially free to ignore documentation status while recruiting workers, even when actively using race and national origin in the selection criteria. This situation enabled Colombians, the pioneer group, to move into higher-status positions as they—along with their Mexican counterparts—eventually became part of the intermediary class that trained workers at HiCap and beyond.

But to use race and national origin in hiring required an infrastructure that HiCap did not yet possess. IRCA changed the rules on hiring, and the responsibility for workers being documented shifted onto employers. Companies needed ways to address the linguistic, cultural, and legal barriers that stood between them and a Latino workforce. The incorporation of the late-1990s cohort, hailing primarily from Mexico and Central America, shows the shift in the way firms hired and managed immigrant labor. Much of the racialized hiring occurring in the 1990s and later was facilitated by supervisors, labor market intermediaries, and temporary employment agencies. This is not to say that informal mechanisms such as network ties were not central to processes of immigrant integration in the labor market. Friends and acquaintances continued to play a central role in the employment of immigrant labor, but with a need to maintain access to a defense based on plausible deniability, the companies' reliance on temporary employment agencies and brokers became conspicuous.

Chapter 2 builds on the analysis of a racialized hiring process that changed HiCap's Jessamine plant from an African American workforce—with some white workers—to a workforce of approximately 80 percent Latino workers. I show the role that bilingual and bicultural intermediaries—temporary agencies and supervisors—played in the displacement that changed the color line in this southern manufacturing plant.

2

Enlisting Subcontractors and Intermediaries

How did HiCap change its four-hundred-plus employee workforce from almost entirely native-born to primarily unauthorized Latino workers? HiCap was entering relatively uncharted waters. It needed assistance in navigating the shoals and shallows of displacement, for which it turned to willing shipmates, a temporary employment agency and varied linguistic and cultural intermediaries. These partners, their biographies, and their behaviors constitute the social infrastructure of a racialized displacement. As such, this chapter looks at how intermediaries, that is, employment agencies and bilingual supervisors, created an infrastructure that worked through three central mechanisms: (1) providing plausible deniability for hiring undocumented workers, (2) hiding the extent of deliberate discrimination in hiring and firing, and (3) lowering barriers to incorporating an unauthorized immigrant workforce. These mechanisms show how, when changing the color line of the organization, HiCap managers and their intermediaries mediated a "match" between workers and employers at both the pre-hire and post-hire stages of the displacement process. From a racialization perspective, I illustrate how the match between workers and employers in displacement encourages the exploitation of immigrants and the exclusion of native-born workers. Intermediaries dilute legal liability and manage the cultural gap between workers and employers outside and inside the organization. In looking at intermediaries, I explore a social unit or "third" element, as it is known in sociology.[1]

The Employment Agency as a "Bridge" in Racialized Jobs

The waiting room at Ready Hands was cold and uninviting; a rectangular-shaped room housed a few metal chairs, covered with green fabric and lined up against opposite walls. Two framed posters with landscapes and flowers decorated the otherwise sterile space. The gray industrial carpet hid the stains from constant foot traffic. At the far end of the room looking toward the public entrance stood a metal desk under two windows. Sitting there, Ms. Johnson, a white receptionist in her early twenties, busily prepared clipboards with employment applications and answered the phone. The office opened at 9 a.m., but she must have left her home a little early to buy the cup of coffee and the bacon biscuit in a Chick-fil-A wrapper that she was enjoying while applicants filled out employment forms. This cold morning in December, a stream of "Spanish" job applicants had lined up outside the office long before Ms. Johnson arrived at her job with her coffee and biscuit in hand. Richard and Manuel, two twenty-something Mexican immigrants, were the first ones there.

"Hi, my name is Richard, but my friends call me Jorge." The shorter man introduced himself, preemptively addressing the questions that undoubtedly arise when an immigrant has to manage dual identities associated with working on "borrowed" papers. I shook hands with him and Manuel, and we talked about how we found ourselves waiting for the agency to open its doors on that cold morning.

They learned about the job from El Tio (the uncle), a man from their native Oaxaca who rented rooms in a row of three trailers housing immigrants from the same Mexican town. El Tio had worked with Carla, the bilingual recruiter at the agency, before he quit his job to run a full-time enterprise driving Mexican and Central American workers from Nogales, Arizona, and El Paso, Texas, to Jessamine, South Carolina. When Ready Hands hired Carla as its bilingual recruiter, she kept in contact with El Tio. He helped her with referrals of Hispanic workers to be placed in different light industrial jobs in the region. Richard and Manuel were trying their luck the day I met them waiting at the agency to apply for jobs at HiCap. They knew that some companies had strict requirements for good papers as a condition of employment, but they were not sure whether HiCap wanted only people with good papers and, if so, whether their recently acquired papers would pass muster. If Ready Hands let them down, they planned later that morning to head to a nonprofit agency managed by a Puerto Rican recruiter located in the Hispanic part of Jessamine. This was their backup plan, as the Puerto Rican was usually able to place people in a job, some job, even if their papers were not good. Richard and Manuel needed a job, and they woke up that morning determined to find one, even if the bike rides to get to the agencies were dangerous.

The night before, a rare ice storm had hit Jessamine. Locals claimed that they could not remember ever seeing anything like it. Freezing rain fell through the evening and night, and the chaos resulting from falling trees and power outages showed no sign of abating by the time Richard and Manuel got on their bikes to apply for jobs at Ready Hands. The streets were empty, and the absence of traffic produced an eerie silence; most businesses remained closed. The branches of the trees outside the agency all wore transparent sleeves of ice a full quarter of an inch thick. As the ice covered absolutely everything, the scene was both beautiful and frightening. When Richard and Manuel heard about the impending storm, they had no way of knowing what to expect, but they rushed to the supermarket to buy milk and bread, as that was what most everyone was doing. "I laughed when we got there, and the milk was already all gone; so we used the money we had to buy a flashlight. As it turned out, the flashlight came in quite handy when the power went off around 8 p.m. and the kitchen in the *traila* turned dark," Richard told me as we waited for the agency to open. The power was still out when they woke up that morning, and they had to shave using their new flashlight. It did not really matter, though, as they had already decided that nothing was going to stop them from finding work that morning.

As we waited, Richard leaned against the agency's glass door with his hands deep into his pockets to protect them from the cold, while Manuel smoked a cigarette under an awning outside the office. Every so often, Richard pulled his hands out to warm them with his breath. He kept his arms firmly tucked to the side of his torso, making a straight line that ended inside his jeans' pockets.

"Open soon, please open soon!!" Richard pleaded, like a small child, in hopes that Ms. Johnson would open a little early on this chilly winter morning.

"We'll have to wait until 9 a.m., Richard. You know how the Americans are with time," Manuel said, alluding to the punctuality that they had noticed since their arrival in Jessamine.

At 9 a.m. sharp, Ms. Johnson opened the doors, and I followed Richard, Manuel, and three other Hispanic men into the agency to fill out job applications.

"Espera aquí," said Ms. Johnson in broken Spanish, handing out clipboards with applications and directing everyone to sit in the green chairs. A few minutes after Ms. Johnson handed out the job applications, Carla, the bilingual recruiter, walked through the door and whispered inaudibly to Ms. Johnson. Taking her gloves off, she greeted those of us in the room.

"Good morning," she began in Spanish. "Please fill out the applications. When you are done, you'll come with me for an interview and a drug test. Does anybody have a problem with that?" she asked.

A Hispanic woman arrived, sat next to me, and then asked if I knew if they wanted good papers for the job. I told her I did not know. "Because the girl, the one that speaks Spanish, she didn't say anything about whether they are only hiring people with good papers, right?"

"No, she didn't say," I answered.

"Look! Manny, it's the same test. It has the math questions," Richard commented as he looked at a page filled with elementary school arithmetic problems: subtraction, addition, multiplication, and five sets of fractions.

"Quiet, Richard! I need to concentrate on answering the questions."

"*Chale*, Manny, they don't care if we get them wrong. I have answered them wrong on other applications, and I still got the job. The important thing here is for you to remember the name that goes with the Social you got. I think that they want people with good Socials for this job, and your name has to match the number, or else they won't give you the job."

Richard responded to Manuel's seriousness with a broad smile that made the solid-gold rim bordering four of his front teeth sparkle. At around 9:30 a.m., there were already eight Hispanic applicants filling out job applications when a white woman dressed in jeans and a heavy coat walked into the agency and went to Ms. Johnson's desk, slowly scanning the room and raising her eyebrows when she saw all the Hispanic applicants filling out employment forms. When she approached the desk, she asked, "Can I get an application for HiCap?"

"Sorry, but we have no job openings there at this time," Ms. Johnson told the woman.

"I know that HiCap is hiring. I need a job. I did good when I worked there two years ago. I was never late, and I never had no absences," she said to Ms. Johnson.

"I know you're a good worker, Lilian, but the plant only wants new people, people that haven't worked there before," Ms. Johnson explained.

"Why do they want only new workers?" the woman asked, surprised.

"They are starting a new project. I don't know why, but the company is only hiring new people right now."

"I really need a job," the woman insisted.

"I can give you an application in case something at a different plant opens up," Ms. Johnson said as she handed her a form.

The woman assented quietly. After taking the application, she sat next to one of the Latino applicants and filled out the form. As she completed the first page, Carla, the bilingual recruiter, came out of the office to call an applicant for an interview. The woman shook her head as she saw one of the applicants walking with Carla for an interview. After the white woman handed in her completed application and left, Ms. Johnson placed her application at the bottom of a pile lying on a thick folder off to the side of her desk.

As this vignette illustrates, reaching an employer when one faces linguistic and bureaucratic barriers—Richard and Manuel were Spanish speakers and were unauthorized to work—requires a "bridge" (the third element) to cross the structural hole that exists between workers and their employers.[2] In other words, while the black market for papers creates the conditions for immigrants to participate in the labor pool of workers searching for work in the formal economy, HiCap, a large global employer, would not go on its own to search for unauthorized Latino immigrant workers. Similarly, unauthorized workers like Richard or Manuel had dignity, pride, and fear. They would not go out of their way to approach a transnational company that could humiliate them or even deport them if they showed up at their door looking for work. To overcome these hurdles, managers and workers turn to subcontractors or labor intermediaries to facilitate the match. In Ronald S. Burt's conceptualization of structural holes, intermediaries (or the third element) in a social network "bridge" otherwise-disconnected others to allow for exchanges of services or information.[3] Under this deracialized interpretation, intermediaries (i.e., subcontractors) fill a market void when they connect employers with workers. From the perspective of racial capitalism, however, race patterns labor exchanges in the market. Thus, subcontractors such as employment agencies, act as the racializing bridge that connects employers and vulnerable immigrant workers in an exchange geared toward the exploitation of workers' vulnerability.

That HiCap relied on labor intermediaries to secure the immigrant workers it wanted is not surprising. Researchers have noticed the centrality of subcontractors and temporary employment agencies in immigrant recruitment and the fast-growing influence of these agencies.[4] Information from the US Bureau of Labor Statistics Establishment Survey, a data source that asks approximately six hundred thousand employers about their payroll records and annual, temporary, and contract employment, illustrates employers' broad reliance on the temporary employment industry. At the time of this research, the temporary staffing industry employed more than three and a half million workers. Additionally, the Establishment Survey indicates that employment in temporary help services grew on average 1.4 percent per year. For context, in 2006, there were fourteen million Americans employed in temporary jobs, which indicates that employment agencies brokered about a quarter of temporary jobs in the US.[5] The growth of temporary jobs suggests that positions brokered by employment agencies continue even in periods of economic expansion and historically low unemployment.

Although information on the size and growth of the local temporary labor market should give us a better idea of how Jessamine and South Carolina fit in the broad picture of labor mediation, unfortunately, data on workers hired and revenue are unavailable. Still, we can situate Ready Hands, HiCap's temp agency, as one of numerous temporary agencies in the region. Jean McAllister reports that the temporary labor market in Jessamine, HiCap's location, was healthy and thriving.[6] Additionally, the number of temporary employment agencies in Jessamine County grew by 500 percent in ten years, and "by the fall of 1994, jobs listed in the classified advertisements in the local daily newspaper were almost exclusively available through temporary service agencies."[7] HiCap was one of seven organizations I observed for this research. Each of these companies enlisted either temporary employment agencies or subcontractors to hire unauthorized immigrant workers.

Providing Plausible Deniability

If we consider that organizations protect their reputation and engage in ceremonial observance of equity norms and that the hiring of unauthorized immigrants is objectionable for many Americans, plausible deniability becomes a useful strategy for unethical companies avoiding public disrepute.[8] Plausible deniability justifies the act of withholding information from senior supervisors in efforts to shield top officials in case disreputable information becomes public. In the event that unwanted information becomes public, engaging in plausible deniability redirects the blame away from top business managers and toward lower participants in an organizational field. Thus, employment agencies and low-level supervisors can give companies a probable guise if their unethical hiring practices becomes public.

Furthermore, managers have an incentive to find ways to avoid the financial costs associated with hiring unauthorized workers. According to Title 8, § 1324a, of the US Code, it is unlawful for any person or entity to hire workers without verifying their eligibility for employment. In 2019, the federal government updated civil penalties to $22,927 per worker on a third-time offense.[9] Additionally, if HiCap was found consistently hiring unauthorized workers, the company could even run afoul of Title 18, Chapter 96, of the US Code (better known as the Racketeer-Influenced and Corrupt Organizations, or RICO, Act) and face much-higher criminal and civil penalties.

To minimize the risk of selecting immigrant workers who, by necessity, apply for jobs with bad papers and extract maximum labor input, HiCap managers contracted with Ready Hands, an independent temporary employment agency staffed with bilingual recruiters, to facilitate hiring and manage the flow of incoming workers. In doing so, the company transferred the liability for its illegal hiring practices to the agency. Since the wages at HiCap were competitive for the area and workers ranked these jobs higher in their queue—wages were double those in meat processing—the agency started by filtering out native-born applicants (as shown by the example of Lilian).

At that time, to avoid prosecution, the agency need not show that it verified eligibility; it only needed to show that it believed that employees were authorized to work. In this research, authorization meant verification that the workers they hired had good papers. The day I interviewed for the job at Ready Hands, Carla told me, "You know that many of our people want to work, but they don't have good papers." On a different occasion, I was talking to Diego, the night-shift supervisor, about whether the company was going to be hiring more Latino workers because the company was displacing native-born workers. The agency had told me that they could not find "heavy lifters" (Latino men) to fill the vacancies. "Carla [the bilingual recruiter and Diego's cousin] told me she has piles of applications from Hispanic men wanting a job, but they don't have good papers. We all know that the people that work here are all illegal, but we just play fools and ignore that they are. The difference is that these are people who found papers that work for the agency. . . . Carla can't tell them to find good papers. She said sometimes she wants to tell them, but she can't do that." On the one hand, Diego's answer indicated that the delay in filling vacancies was related to the agency's wish for plausible deniability. On the other hand, the example illustrates what we all knew at the factory, that the Latino workers the company hired were primarily unauthorized and that the agency was complicit in hiring them.

In the ethical game of blame transfer, the agency and the company had a "lower participant" to blame.[10] In the displacement at HiCap, when hiring unauthorized workers, the employers could blame the agency for not verifying documentation. The agency could blame the workers for supplying fraudulent documents. This would fit with the damaging perception that many Americans have of immigrant workers, and the most negatively affected would be the worker or their immediate supervisor—another immigrant. In Diego's terms, powerful actors "play the fool" by blaming others for engaging in categorical selection of workers using documentation status and race in hiring. Considering these examples, one could make the case that intermediaries facilitate plausible deniability to the company and to themselves under racialized displacement.

Hiding Deliberate Discrimination in Hiring and Firing

Additionally, enlisting intermediaries allowed the company to disguise the use of race and gender when engaging in deliberate discrimination in hiring and firing. As noted in chapter 1, civil rights legislation prohibits the use of race, gender, or nationality in hiring, and HiCap engaged in creative strategies to bend the law. To start, when hiring Latino immigrant men rather than native-born workers, the company deployed coded language and a logic of meritocracy. This involved developing a racialized ideology of the "hard worker," which favored unauthorized workers and confirmed the company's preference for the most exploitable workers.

For example, on one occasion, Barbara, one of two Ready Hands recruiters who was not Latino but on-site at HiCap, came to my section to "deliver" new immigrant hires for me to train. As she looked around, smiled, and called out to me, "Look! Laura, look how hard they work. They are not playing games like those loud people," she pointed first to a group of Latinos and then to a group of Black workers. "Sometimes they do. We like to have fun too," I commented. She disregarded my comment. Similar to what other studies have found, at HiCap the perception that unauthorized people work harder and are "the best workers" derived from differences in tractability rather than inherent productivity.[11] Unauthorized workers at HiCap and other organizations I observed rarely reported injuries, rarely complained, often worked through their breaks, and were more willing to accept unrealistic demands coming from managers and supervisors. Without clear evidence of increased productivity, what this suggests is that employment agencies, in their powerful structural position between workers and employers, reinforced stereotypes and exploitative hiring selection.

In addition to engaging symbolically in displacement by reinforcing employers' racialized ideology of the "hard worker," Ready Hands facilitated the use of race and gender in workers' selection and hiring. Several weeks into the displacement, I learned how HiCap used the agency in this type of practice. One afternoon, I was training Richard at the Transfer Corner when Marcus approached me. "Dave wants me to start with the project tomorrow," Marcus announced. "You should go ask the agency to get the people for us," he said in a relaxed voice. I asked Richard to take over and pulled out the notepad I carried in my back pocket next to the production schedule. "I want operators experienced with a screw gun," he started listing. "Heavy lifters, we want guys, we want," he hesitated for a moment, struggling to formulate his words. "Just tell them we want Hispanic guys. They'll know." Marcus had no apparent qualms about ordering workers on the basis of their ethnicity, but he clearly knew that it was not something to broadcast.

The engagement of the agency, however, became apparent after I talked to Andrea and Barbara, the agency recruiters. I found them in front of their computers at the Ready Hands office inside HiCap.

"Marcus asked me to tell you that he wants two workers for tomorrow," I said standing near their desk.

"Yes!" they exclaimed, as though they had been waiting for my request.

"What's your area?" she asked.

"The Front End," I responded, adding, "They need to know how to use the screw guns."

Andrea took a yellow pad from her desk and started taking notes. "Screw gun," she murmured under her breath as she finished writing.

"Heavy lifters?" she asked me, using the euphemism that managers and the agency used to refer to men in the plant.

"Yes."

"Hispanics?" she asked without lifting her eyes from her yellow pad.

"Yes."

"Okay, we'll have them here by tomorrow," she said, closing our conversation.

While Andrea finished her notes, Barbara pulled requisition forms out of her desk and started filling them out with the requirements. I returned to the line at HiCap, surprised at how the agency had clear knowledge of the displacement, surprised as well at how ordering workers on the basis of gender and ethnicity, although coded, was as simple and natural as ordering replacement parts at the tool crib. "Ordering" these two workers was the start of this episode in the displacement. Roberto and José Luis, two other bilingual supervisors, were already training as many Latino workers as the agency could find.

Market Makers and the Commoditization of Latino Immigrants

My interview with Gonzalo, a human resources pioneer/entrepreneur who collaborated with Ready Hands, provides context to the ubiquitous use of subcontractors and labor intermediaries in displacement. His interview highlights how temporary employment agencies played a central role in the racialization of hard work and employer-driven turnover in the labor force, all while reinforcing the script of Latino immigrants as the preferred workers. Additionally, Gonzalo's case illustrates how racialized recruiting evolves from the hiring of a handful of immigrants, as in most cases of ethnic succession and social closure, to the hiring of sizable numbers of immigrants, overhauling the demographics of the labor force in an organization.[12] The following descriptions and vignettes illustrate some elements of this process. Gonzalo told me,

> The first employment agency in Jessamine opened on Pioneer Road, just a few minutes northwest of the center of the budding downtown. Because of its location near some homeless shelters and areas of town without much economic activity, the agency focused on daily pay, daily work employees. Their main clientele were homeless people. At the time, there were not many Hispanics that applied for jobs because the agency didn't have people that could communicate with them in Spanish. Once I arrived, and the Hispanic workers found out that there was someone at the agency that could communicate with them in their own language, they started coming in to look for jobs.

Having someone who speaks the language of recruits, although a necessary condition, was not sufficient in and of itself to grow the influence of agencies in changing the demographic composition of the workforce in the region. That is, temp agencies still had to solve the issue of socializing and training workers. Although a handful of employers and supervisors believed that "body language does wonders when communicating with non-English-speaking workers," many companies, especially in light manufacturing, had complicated processes and procedures. If communication between workers and employers broke down, that could prove costly with regard to losses to capital equipment or even lives. Gonzalo described how this transition happened around Jessamine:

> We didn't immediately grow in the number of Hispanic workers we could place in jobs. The issue was that when we sent workers to jobs, they had problems communicating with the supervisors and their coworkers. We had a lot of problems with communication. I identified the problem, but

the temp agency wasn't giving me much room to maneuver. Then a national company that started in Chicago and moved operations to Atlanta bought our agency. This company had a long history working with Hispanics, and they knew how to place Hispanics. They contacted me and said to me, "Find out where the Hispanics live and where it's going to be easy for them to reach you. We are going to open a recruiting office where they are. We are going to place them in jobs."

The experience that large employment agencies acquired in traditional destinations like Chicago and the pressure to integrate the new immigrant cohorts influenced the commoditization of Hispanics as the ideal worker. The agency looked at the mismatch between the workers whom employers wanted (i.e., documented, English speaking, hardworking, and inexpensive) and the workers who actually existed. "The agency's corporate office examined the local economy and wondered how they could absorb the mass of Hispanic workers that was arriving in [town] in the 1990s. We were all scratching our heads on ways to absorb the Hispanic labor force. I did my research, and the company opened an office farther up Pioneer Road, near the apartment buildings where Hispanics lived. From there, I started making the connections between the companies and the workers," Gonzalo said, explaining how he formalized the relationship between workers and employers. His strategy was to connect workers with employers in a way that was sustainable and still met the demands of the employers. For instance, one company that hired mostly white workers was a company that made kayaks and canoes. It contacted Gonzalo. "They wanted me to send them fifteen workers, at once. I would tell them, 'We don't have them! There just aren't that many!' Then I told the personnel manager that the only thing that we have in large quantities is Hispanic workers. 'What you need are Hispanic workers, and these, I can supply to you,'" he announced, selling the workers to whom he had access and attaching ethnicity to the hiring process.

Clearly, employers are, at least to a great extent, rational actors, and the ability of the workers to communicate effectively enters in their calculus of evaluating the decision to establish a contractual agreement with an agency offering foreign workers. The companies' internal recruiters told Gonzalo, "I don't have people that speak Spanish here.

Who's gonna train them?" Speaking of the early introduction of large numbers of Hispanics in organizations, Gonzalo explained,

> I told them that if they wanted, I could send one, two, or three workers and see how they get integrated. I asked them to try the Hispanic workers and see for themselves. I personally went to the companies to translate for the supervisors. I would tell workers, "Look, you do this in this way. You do this in this other way, etc." I was the interpreter for them. I also interpreted by telephone. They'd call me, and the guys would ask me to tell their supervisors, "I would like to ask for permission to miss work tomorrow." So I had to call their supervisors to ask on their behalf. Well, those kinds of things took a little effort. But, they found that while one American would produce four kayaks per day, the Hispanic workers were making eight and nine kayaks each. Well, the personnel manager, the section manager, the plant managers, they loved that. Everybody loved that! Except, of course, the American workers that were already at the plant. They started to see the Hispanic workers as competitors. Still, what we did was to fill those fifteen vacancies with Hispanics. In fact, in the crew of fifteen that we introduced at the plant, we hired a bilingual worker, a man from Honduras, so that he could interpret for the other workers. I personally translated the operations manual, the employee policies, the orientation materials, and all those kinds of things needed to hire the workers. Then we used that model to go into other factories and to introduce Hispanic workers in other plants.

Although recruiters like Gonzalo acted in good faith (I know this because of Gonzalo's committed and positive involvement in the Latino community), organizational strategies that involve race in hiring can, and usually do, carry unintended consequences. In framing Hispanic workers as a valuable "product" that agencies sell and companies purchase, market makers commoditized the immigrant labor force. Additionally, language fluency in the hands of the bilingual recruiter or bilingual supervisors alters the organization of work, with implications for the relationship between managers and workers. When companies introduce a supervisorial layer in the hierarchy, the typically binary relationship between employer and worker turns triadic and companies transfer the power of managing workers to a loosely coupled agent (the interpreter) and, in doing so, detach themselves from the ability to and responsibility for applying corporate policies and practices in an equitable way. Furthermore, the legal status of the workers further complicated this relationship. From the outset, market makers like Gonzalo created a need for the workers by making it easy for employers to hire undocumented immigrant workers. They did this by doing their own research and then coaching the employers on how to review workers' credentials with the lowest level of scrutiny allowed by law. At the end of the day, immigrant workers were hired. They were still undocumented, however, and the consequence, intended for the employer and unintended for the worker, was that they were, therefore, vulnerable.

From a supply-side perspective, employers have traditionally contracted with temporary employment agencies to survive shifts in the production cycles related to seasonal shifts in demand or other macro-level market trends, including the introduction of new products or plant relocations, among others. In addition to these structural motivations to contract with employment agencies, however, employers engage with employment agencies for reasons involving sociocultural valuations and evaluations. When the need arises, employment agencies can be the actors that develop the scripts and narratives of the organization. One of the assumptions here is that employers, in the absence of intermediaries, would not succeed in overhauling a workforce. The reality is that, because of the legal risks, most would not even make the attempt.

As you read the biographies of labor market intermediaries, keep in mind that displacement is a racial project, one where employers want to reconstruct the workforce using ascriptive categories (e.g., gender, race, and legal status).[13] As such, the actors in displacement bring cultural and ethnic endowments that influence their attitudes and behaviors as they partake in the action. While I focus on the "backstage" and the actors, it is important to keep in mind that the actors are not performing in a vacuum. Institutions ensure that those inside behave in consistent ways. In *Asylums: Essays on the Social Situation of Mental Patients and Other Inmates*, Erving Goffman show us an extreme case. Looking at social behavior in "total institutions" like schools or mental hospitals, where patients are essentially trapped, he portrays the essential role of institutions in the "making" of a mental-hospital patient. The institution, rather than the illness, explains the patient's reactions and adjustments.[14] Because of the salient role of institutions, I borrow interactionist imagery (like Goffman's) to explain the structural elements of "backstage" activities using social networks arguments. In considering interactionist frameworks, the organizations examined, the stage, the audience, the script—all of these forces influence the act. The audience's response energizes the actors. An affirmative nod from the director encourages them. The flawless performance of each actor produces consistency and replicability in the act. Similar to the forces in Goffman's analysis of total institutions, the performances of intermediaries show how they influence and are influenced by the institutions. The cases of agencies like Ready Hands and supervisors like Roberto and Diego, whom we will meet soon, help us understand not only the backstage action but also how labor market processes and behaviors contribute to the "making" of an ethnic intermediary.

Lowering Barriers to Hiring an Unauthorized Workforce

The ubiquitous use of employment agencies in hiring unauthorized immigrant workers has transformed organizational roles and processes from racially inert to wholly racialized. Employment agencies hire ethnic recruiters and supervisors to match the racialized attributes of workers and facilitate hiring for employers. In racialized organizations, ethnic affinity—instead of skill—determines who hires, trains, and manages workers and, going unchecked, reinforces discrimination and hyperexploitation. This section shows how ethnic recruiters and supervisors often had no or limited managerial skills and that, in job displacement, attributes such as language and immigrant work ethic overpower subject-matter expertise. To illustrate the importance of ethnic recruiters and supervisors in job displacement, the analysis draws from the cases of Carla, Ready Hands' bilingual recruiter; Diego, the bilingual supervisor on HiCap's night shift; and Roberto, the bilingual supervisor who trained the replacement workers on HiCap's first shift. These three cases highlight how employers racialize the work of labor intermediaries in an effort to lower the barriers to hiring the vulnerable, unauthorized workers they want.

Carla: The Bilingual Recruiter

One of the central strategies that employment agencies use to facilitate replacement and displacement involves hiring bilingual recruiters and taking advantage of their ambition and ethnic affinity with new hires. Bilingual recruiters gain immigrants' trust and overcome linguistic and cultural limitations involved in hiring Spanish-speaking immigrant workers from outside the organization. Ready Hands hired Carla, a bilingual recruiter, to facilitate hiring and manage the continuous flow of immigrant workers into the displacement at HiCap.

A twenty-five-year-old blue-eyed Mexican, Carla was Ready Hands' bilingual recruiter. She had worked as an operator at HiCap and, when I met her, had moved to Ready Hands as a staffing specialist. I became acquainted with her when she interviewed me for the bilingual supervisory position at HiCap, and I later interviewed her for this study. The first time we met, we discovered that we both went to the same high school in Guadalajara, Mexico, and shared similarities in our upbringing. Our families were working class from modest means but with big ambitions for their daughters. We also discovered that we each had three sisters and transnational families. She talked to me as though, in her words, "we are sisters." This affinity helped build trust and camaraderie.

Carla first visited the United States in the late 1980s. Like many immigrants in supervisory positions whom I met at HiCap and other organizations, she came to the United States as a visitor, with no plans of staying. Her plan to return dissipated when Carla discovered how "companies really wanted bilingual people everywhere": "They wanted bilingual leaders to work with our people. Can you believe it! Everywhere, companies were saying we are hiring bilingual this and that." Carla's perception resonated with my observations, as I documented many instances in which companies were enlisting crew leaders to facilitate the management of immigrant workers. Unlike most crew leaders working inside organizations, Carla had ascended to recruitment specialist, a different position in the displacement infrastructure. When I asked her about her transition from HiCap operator to Ready Hands staffing specialist, she shared,

> I would have never, ever, imagined that I would be working in a factory when I came to the United States. . . . I had relatives in Miami and friends

in New York City. I wanted to travel and visit. My cousin Diego lived in Jessamine, and on one of his trips home, he invited me to visit him here. That got me thinking, and I applied for a passport and a visa. I was lucky, and I got the visa the first time I applied. I took a plane from Guadalajara and came to the US, to New York, but only to visit!

Carla had spent several months in New York City, but when the $500 she saved working as a paralegal at her uncle's law firm in Mexico ran out, she headed south to Jessamine to visit her cousin Diego. Diego had moved from New York to Jessamine and was working the night shift at HiCap when Carla arrived. When I interviewed her she told me,

> I had no money left. So, he asked if I wanted to work with him at the plant. The first thing I said, "Me? But I've never worked in a factory." I had also never worked the night shift, but I wanted to polish my English, and he said I could make good money and practice my English before going back to Mexico. I said yes because I wanted to buy things. You are going to think this is crazy, but I really wanted a pair of Nike sneakers, the white leather ones with the red swoosh, you know what I am talking about?

I knew precisely what Carla was describing. As a teenager in pre-NAFTA Mexico, I had wanted that exact pair of shoes myself. For Carla and other authorized immigrants or visa holders, conspicuous consumption and having the lifestyle of the upper classes in their countries of origin motivated emigration decisions. Carla started working as an operator, like Richard and Manuel. Unlike Carla, Richard, Manuel, and countless others who stayed in that job, the bilingual Carla moved out of an assembly-line job at HiCap into a job as a human resources specialist. Her bilingualism was a central attribute in her mobility into better jobs. "I started on the night shift, with Diego," she recalled.

> He was the shift supervisor at the Front End, and he got me the job. I was a production worker on the assembly line. My God, I hated that job. My whole body hurt from working there, and I cried every night. I never had a job that was as horrible as that job. I was so tired when I went home at the end of my shift. Then one day, Gary, the old guy [one of the managers] came to my section to talk to Diego when we were in the cafeteria.

I really didn't like that man. He was like eighty years old, and he'd ogle me and ask, "What's such a pretty girl doing here?" I just ignored him because I needed the job, but that day he asked me if I wanted to work at Ready Hands. I spoke English and Spanish, and the agency was looking for a bilingual recruiter. I went to the agency, and the next day Peggy, the agency's manager, hired me.

Bilingual recruiters like Carla enable displacement through agencies in particular ways. Carla was a secondary immigrant in South Carolina. Unlike many of the immigrant people she recruited to work for HiCap, Carla went to university and entered the United States with a tourist visa. At the time I met her, she had already shifted from starting at HiCap as an "unauthorized" worker to working at Ready Hands "authorized." She had initially entered the United States as a tourist visa holder, but the US government does not authorize tourist visa holders to work for wages. When she started working at the employment agency, however, she met a southern man ten years her senior at a cocktail party at the local chamber of commerce. They married six months later, and Carla gained legal permanent residency through marriage. This means that unlike the heavy weight that the mark of a criminal record imposes on employment opportunities for Brown and Black individuals, the "illegal" credential carries less of a burden. This credential we now know is more fluid.[15] Brokers like Carla, similar to other immigrants who are able to regularize their status, can go from unauthorized to authorized and divest themselves of the constraining effect that the "illegal" credential has on immigrant employment. Higher levels of human capital placed Carla in a position to manage workers while simultaneously deploying her ambition to move out of precarious employment through the management of immigrant labor. Additionally, having lived in New York City and South Carolina, she had gained experience with the immigration industry in both traditional and nontraditional destinations, which gave her a competitive advantage with employers. Carla helped the employment agency sort out different types of immigrant individuals and select those who fit the "hardworking" stereotype that her HiCap employers wanted.

The willingness of bilingual recruiters to cooperate in displacement emerges from a complex situation in which these brokers balance individual goals with a desire to see coethnics "do better." Their efforts elevate employers' valuation of the group. In displacement, it helps that immigrants working as bilingual recruiters aspire to a lifestyle incompatible with the wages and status of precarious jobs. Employers tap into these aspirations. However, while these recruiters cooperate with managers for individual reasons, they are willing participants in displacement because they want to aid coethnics. Carla commented, "[I] liked helping Hispanics and happily left the job on the assembly line at HiCap to work at the agency. I am better here, but . . . well, I think . . . somebody needs to help our people get jobs. Don't you agree? Many don't have papers. Who is going to hire them like that? We are all immigrants here, but not everyone wants to see that now. We have to help each other." The ethnic affinity that recruiters like Carla shared with immigrant workers places them in a unique position to try to do anything on their part to help people like them.

Additionally, Carla shared managerial beliefs that Latino immigrants work harder than native-born Americans do. For example, when I met her during my interview for the job at HiCap, she said with a sparkle in her eyes, "I just hired two Hispanic workers to start at HiCap! The company is adding a new project. The company wants to replace workers that don't want to work hard, you know, . . . like Blacks, with workers that do, like our people." I asked Carla about the white woman in the waiting room whom I had just heard being told that the agency was not hiring at this time. She responded with a subtle smile, artfully deflecting my question about the white woman looking for work. Once again, the logic of the "hard worker" lent itself to a colorblind framework that hid racism and white supremacy in many contexts.

Enlisting intermediaries for displacement goes beyond hiring a "staff" to manage immigrant workers. To recruit and hire large numbers of immigrant workers for categorical displacement, the jobs have to appeal to workers—the "job queue" side of the hiring process. "Job queues" refers to workers ranking jobs on the basis of valuations such as wages and working conditions.[16] In the case of unauthorized immigrants, job queues involve valuations related to more or less risk of deportation, more or less support to overcome linguistic and cultural barriers, accessibility with regard to closeness to immigrants' residency, and whether the job comes with a supervisor (or broker) they can trust. To this end, the employment agency needs to gain immigrants' trust.

While immigrants have agency and can navigate risk, some jobs carry more risks than others do. In an era of inhumane and rampant detentions, persecution, and deportation, agencies need to assuage fear if they want to hire immigrants and have their jobs rank high in the immigrant's job queue. Fear of deportation in the context of jobs at companies like HiCap is real. For instance, in 2005, ICE arrested thirteen hundred unauthorized immigrants at work sites. A year later, in 2006, immigrant enforcement more than tripled, with ICE making approximately forty-four hundred work-site arrests under Operation Wagon Train, the largest employment-site operation in US history. In interviews with community leaders, they described immigrant workers' barriers to employment, citing raids at Swift & Company. ICE agents detained about thirteen hundred immigrants working in six of Swift's meat-processing plants across the United States. The same year, ICE launched Operation Return to Sender, a nationwide campaign that resulted in twenty-three thousand arrests at work sites and other locations, including people's homes.[17]

The day I waited at the employment agency for the job interview at HiCap, I heard Latino applicants wondering if "'the staffing' would tell them about a raid" and asking, "[Do you think] ICE will be roaming around this plant?" About three months later, and after HiCap had hired us, I was helping Richard apply labels and screws in a slow run of twenty-five international air-conditioner models. He asked, "Laura, you and Diego are here to help us, right?" I was not sure where he was going with the question. "Of course I would help you, *en lo que pueda* [to the extent possible]." I qualified, because three days earlier, Richard asked if I could lend him $1,500 to buy a car to go pick up his sister at the border. "I am glad to hear that because I heard that *la perrera* [the kennel: the ICE van] is going around factories and arresting people. I don't want to get deported before my sister gets here." Relying on ethnic affinity and the interest of bilingual recruiters to help coethnics became part of the displacement strategy.

* * *

Displacement is a disruptive act that destabilizes work lives, a phenomenon in which employers push workers out of productive activity and potentially into unemployment or underemployment. Displacement disrupts the process of making a living, of building social relations around a common goal, and it heightens the boundaries between people of distinct ethnic groups, gender, race, and documentation status. All of this can make it difficult to hire workers, introduce them to the workplace, and have them stay in organizations where threatened workers push back. To minimize this risk, HiCap enlisted bilingual supervisors to bridge the gap between managers and immigrant workers and to address the symbolic and material needs of workers. In contrast to brokers like Carla who worked in an office outside the factory, supervisors worked inside. From a broker's perspective, the bilingual supervisors' main job was to train, socialize, and "buffer" immigrant hires. From management's perspective, the bilingual supervisors enabled them to exercise influence and control. In my research at HiCap, I found that once the company identified a section as "not making the numbers," managers tagged this section as priority for displacement. Managers then brought in bilingual supervisors to coordinate with a section manager for the hiring and training of Latino workers.

Diego: The Third- Shift Bilingual Supervisor

The night shift (third shift) was the first shift undergoing displacement. Diego worked on third shift and was the first Latino supervisor enlisted to facilitate the project. Additionally, Diego was Carla's cousin and the intermediary who brokered her arrival at HiCap. At twenty-six, Diego was younger than most Black and white supervisors. Management promoted him to supervisor, the first operator with less than five years of experience at the plant to be so promoted. Although Diego worked on third shift, I became acquainted with him because the company asked him to support the bilingual supervisors on first shift. Carla also asked Diego to help me. Every other day, he came to my section to "see if [I] was learning the jobs" and to tell me, "don't pay attention to the *morenos*"—the Black workers—"if they make your life miserable," and "do what Dave [the plant manager] asks you to do, and you'll be fine." He meant well. However, he never questioned the actions of employers and even shared their stereotypes about the work ethic of Black workers.

When the company promoted Diego, he had little experience managing workers. Like Carla, however, cultural and ethnic capital, more than production knowledge, placed workers like Diego on the path to management under displacement. Diego was bilingual and bicultural by virtue of an early arrival to the United States. His parents had a small retail business in Mexico City; but the Mexican economic crisis of the 1980s hit them hard, and they lost their business. Diego's parents moved to New York when Diego was still in elementary school in hopes of recovering financially.

Diego's parents' main motivation for migrating was for their children to learn English and have a better future. While in New York, his parents were keen to expose Diego to environments where English was the main language, but they remained convinced that he should maintain his Spanish. Being bilingual and coming from a working-class background and urban upbringing, Diego adapted easily to his new life in New York. "I had no problems making friends with Americans or Latinos at school or outside school," he told me when I interviewed him. This ability to straddle between English and Spanish and different cultural environments facilitated a seamless transition between the Anglo and Latino teams that Diego had to manage at the start of the displacement at HiCap.

As with many other secondary migrants in this study, Diego's family moved to Jessamine in search of good jobs and tranquility. Diego took classes in a community college technology program funded by manufacturing companies in the region. After his first year in school, he was lured by the aggressive recruitment of Latino workers that was conducted via the media, temp agencies, and social entrepreneurs in Jessamine.

> One day, I went to Walmart and saw a bunch of cardboard signs along the parking lot advertising jobs in Spanish at a good company. I wanted a job where I could use Spanish and English, and the ads got me thinking. . . . After I left the store, I was driving home, and I heard an ad for the same jobs on Radio Fantastica! So, I said, "This is it!" I called the number, and they asked me to come in for an interview at 9 a.m. the next day. I went, filled out an application, took the drug test, and started working right after that. I was happy to get a job at a good company and one that I didn't need to pay to get in.

Diego was alluding to companies at which immigrants have to pay coethnic intermediaries to get them jobs. He explained further, "The supervisors at *la pollera* [the chicken-processing plant] were charging $100 to get you into a job at that company. That's because people don't have good papers. It bothers me that people abuse us. I didn't want to work at a company where this happened."

While Diego had limited managerial experience, he had a good understanding of the production process. He worked as an operator at HiCap for two years before the company promoted him to supervisor, and he became involved in the company's displacement project. When I asked how he started at HiCap, he shared, "I was the first Hispanic on the night shift. There were no other Hispanics. The plant, in general, was all *morenos* and whites. . . . Well, the night shift was all Black. They had a hard time hiring whites that wanted to work the night shift, so they'd hire whatever they could find. I don't mean ill, but it is hard to find good workers for night shift."

"What makes you say this?" I asked.

"I've seen it, and Carla tells me they can't find people for this shift. They come, but they don't even last a single shift. If they do, it's because they hide themselves behind the boxes and sleep!"

"So you were saying there were no other Hispanics at the plant when you started?"

"There was a Puerto Rican guy on first shift that had worked at the company since it opened, but he spoke to me only once, when we saw each other during the shift change a few weeks after I was hired. But that was it. The agency knew I was bilingual, so they would call me every time they hired people that didn't speak English to translate for them. Then, Marcus, the Black supervisor at the Front End, asked me to train the 'Spanish' workers—that's how he called us—because the Blacks on the shift didn't want to do it. So, that's how I started training people."

According to Diego, with Carla and others who started on night shift at HiCap, the Latino group started to grow gradually. Following well-established social-network mechanisms that sociologists have come to expect, Diego recommended friends and kin to the agency. Technology also played a role, as Diego used his Facebook account to invite friends and relatives to join him at work. Roberto was one of the friends who saw Diego's posting on Facebook and was hired within days of arriving at Jessamine. Roberto later posted openings in his WhatsApp account. But for the displacement to happen on a large scale and within months, formalizing the role of bilingual supervisors was needed. When I interviewed him, he shared, "I was called to meet with Arthur and Dave [plant managers] in the main office. Arthur started talking about bringing in a group of Hispanics to work under my supervision. Dave said they wanted to start a 'new project,' to weed out workers that didn't want to work hard. They said they wanted someone that could do all the jobs on the line, and, well, I was good with that. They wanted someone to work with Hispanic people. And I guess they saw that people listened to me. I trained the people that didn't speak English, and we worked as a team, and I guess somebody noticed. They said they wanted me to build a team of hardworking Hispanics on third shift. They asked if I wanted to be a supervisor. I said, 'Okay.' They asked me to work with *el estáfin* [the temp staffing agency] to bring in the people that I needed. I started my section with a group of twelve people, all from Mexico."

"How did the non-Hispanic workers react?" I asked.

"A few people got mad at first because the Hispanic group was growing fast. But with time, they got used to us. Then other managers saw that we were working very well, and they started doing the same in other areas."

"Who were the workers that left? Their race?"

"They were all *morenos*."

After the company promoted Diego from operator to supervisor on third shift, they promoted other bilingual operators, as the displacement plan moved to second and first shifts. The company moved Jaime, a Mexican man who worked as an operator in the Back End, from third shift to be a supervisor on second shift. What this meant was that displacement contributed to the movement of a handful of bilingual Latinos into better jobs—those on second and first shift—but the vast majority of the Latino workers remained vulnerable to exploitation. A month after the company had replaced about two hundred native-born workers with Latinos, the company promoted Roberto, a bilingual supervisor from third shift, to be a first-shift supervisor. A month after that, I arrived to HiCap and went to first shift as well.

Roberto (Beto): The First Latino and the First Supervisor on First Shift

> I was the only Hispanic there. The vast majority were African Americans, and, well, the environment was very different. They [African Americans] have a more relaxed work ethic than Mexican workers. They don't like people telling them what to do, and it was a small section with about sixteen employees. Thank God they asked me to focus on production and wait for Hispanics to arrive.
>
> —Roberto, bilingual supervisor at HiCap's Back End

Several years before Roberto told me how HiCap enlisted him for the displacement, he fled Mexico to come to the United States. He boarded a plane, wishing to forget his impending marriage. Distractedly playing with a fine gold chain hanging from his neck, he told me about his desire to move on. His fiancée gave him the chain by the door of her parents' living room when he went to say his farewells. She wanted him to wear it as a reminder of their engagement. The shiny metal felt out of place, as out of place as his thoughts of marrying his eighteen-year-old fiancée felt in his head. He was only nineteen years old. He had just finished his second semester in the engineering program at the Universidad Autónoma of Guadalajara. He wanted to travel the world. He hated the idea of ending up like his father, and it haunted him. His father married and had children at a young age because of social convention. Beto said he loved his fiancée. But the idea of marrying the girl because he got her pregnant was driving him crazy. He wanted to leave Mexico to sort things out, and things did sort themselves out by happenstance; his girlfriend decided not to have the child. They lost contact when she moved to Los Angeles. Almost two decades earlier, his father escaped similar circumstances to work the fields of California after marrying his mother. Beto was now escaping to the Bronx.

His cousin called him that morning to tell him to wait for him outside the baggage claim at La Guardia in New York.

"Beto, you do have a visa, don't you? Otherwise *la migra* won't let you in," he remembered his cousin warning, thinking that he was only half joking.

"You think I am stupid? I am not new to this!" he snapped at his cousin.

Beto wanted to say that he was no stranger to the United States. He had visited Disneyland when he was ten years old. He had a costume from the "Pirates of the Caribbean" that he wore proudly on Halloween. Secretly, he sang the lyrics of "It's a Small World After All," even as he pretended to dislike the ride in efforts to avoid being bullied at school. When he was a teenager, Beto spent two summers working with his father in the fields in California. His father took him to Universal Studios and for ice cream on Santa Monica Boulevard as a reward. Before he met his fiancée, he traveled with his mother to Los Angeles on a couple of shopping trips. In spite of his familiarity with Los Angeles, Beto was never fond of California.

"I never got along with my family in California," he told me as we ate hot dogs in a small diner a few miles from HiCap.

"They're involved in gangs, and I don't want that life for me or my kids. I don't talk to them, and I don't see much of my father either. He drinks. It kills me to see him destroy his life. My uncle in New York is a good man. When I needed to leave Mexico, he invited me to come and stay with him and my cousins. I told him I was going to visit for a while and go to school to learn English. I was interested in learning more about computers. If I got married, at least knowing English and something about computers would help me get a better job, so I came to the United States with that idea."

"Did you go to school and study English in New York?"

"Funny that you ask. I have been wondering about that because I didn't. I kick myself for not doing it. My cousin was a waiter in a restaurant and found me a job as a busboy. Before I knew it, I was waiting tables. I started getting good tips, and you know how it is. You start making money, and when you are a kid, even a meager wage looks like a lot of money. If you don't have rent to pay and food to buy, it looks like even more money. When I arrived in New York, there were so many things I dreamed of buying. I was in one of the best cities in the world, and I wanted to buy everything! I wanted to buy Converse All-Star basketball shoes, Milky Way chocolate bars, Spam, baseball gloves. . . . I wanted new things. I wanted to go to bars and dance with blond girls. I wanted to be looking up to the sky when the big ball with the hundreds of tiny mirrors dropped down into Times Square in Manhattan on New Year's Eve. I wanted to empty my lungs shouting in a Van Halen concert in Madison Square Garden." Beto stopped to catch his breath and leaned forward. Lost in remembrance, his eyes gained the sparkle we are used to seeing in the eyes of a child unboxing a long-anticipated toy. But the vivacity was gone with a sip of sweet tea as a different thought brought a cloud that eclipsed the sparkle. He leaned back in his chair, shaking his head, disapproving of his train of thought.

"It sounds ridiculous and banal, doesn't it?" he asked with concern, taking the reflective stance that many immigrants adopt when they examine the beginning of their migratory journey years later. Like Beto, they use the lens of responsible citizenship, in which conspicuous consumption is limited, work is precarious, and trite desires lay buried under a harsh fiscal reality.

"No, it doesn't. I grew up dreaming about having so many of those same things," I genuinely reassured him.

Beto represents a new generation of immigrants and a new brand of workers acting in racialized employment contexts that involve a complicated system of laws, motivations, and family structures. Beto was born in a mixed-status family. After working unauthorized for more than a decade, his father obtained US residency during the IRCA reforms of the 1980s. By the time Beto's father was able to acquire his US citizenship, he had a new wife and children and had settled in Los Angeles.

Beto's household was transnational. He remembers missing days of school when his father, uncle, and cousins came "home" to Guadalajara on vacation and spent a whole month partying during the Christmas holidays. Beto soon found that extended leisure periods carry costs. The workplace was the "bank" where immigrant workers stored hours of hard work so they could withdraw hefty periods of leisure once or twice a year. There was little rest in between. In spite of the heavy toll that work had on immigrants, they spoke about the good in their work lives, rarely about the ills. These experiences, as Beto saw it, influenced how he acted at work.

"We were neither rich nor poor," Beto told me, examining his class standing in Mexico. "My mom worked in a government office, and my father managed a construction crew in Los Angeles. We had our own home, food, TV, and a telephone with long-distance service. My father sent money for me to go to school. We had what we needed. You could say we were middle class."

This class standing partially contributed to Beto's cosmopolitan views and aspirations. Many of the intermediaries or brokers (e.g., bilingual supervisors, team leaders, and interpreters) working with US employers in the management of immigrant labor arrive with similar backgrounds. When they get to positions of authority, these actors have more to lose than their more disadvantaged counterparts do. As is the case of bilingual recruiters like Carla, in their desperate efforts to pursue their dreams of advancement, brokers often comply with the demands of employers, even when those demands are patently unreasonable. They engage in behaviors that challenge the ethics acquired in the home country and are constantly in search of *la cora extra*—the additional quarter per hour of pay, or the best next opportunity. They are ambivalent about issues of race and fairness as practiced in the US workplace. Because workplaces provide few opportunities to improve workers' human-capital endowments, this situation feels more daunting to people with greater ambition, like the brokers with a middle-class point of reference. But the rhythms of immigrant work and immigrant life are what some, like Beto, know from an early age. Others adapt upon arrival, sharing the same motivation. Most want to go beyond the often-repeated cliché that "it's better to be poor in a rich country than rich in a poor one." When Beto got on a plane that day bound for New York, he had a hunch that settlement in the United States was inevitable. Summarizing his experience, he told me, "I wanted to get to know America, to see with my own eyes what everyone talked about. If you don't know America and remain in Mexico, you are doomed. You will always live with the inkling that you want to come here and see America with your own eyes. I didn't want to live like that. I came for a short period of time to visit my family, and, before I knew it, I had been here several years. . . . I was staying."

Where Beto's journey would lead him, however, was less certain. Following part of his dream, Beto married a blond American woman he met dancing at a club in the Bronx two years after he arrived in the United States. He divorced a year later. "She walked out on me. The woman took everything I had, including the refrigerator and my laptop computer," he said, upset. "From then on, I have been living with other single immigrants. I have been working two jobs and killing myself to pay the rent and child support. Now I realize how stupid I was. Why did I even come here?" he asked rhetorically, fundamentally questioning his American dream. Before he answered, he got lost mixing mustard, tabasco, and ketchup with a white plastic knife on the red tray, where the hot dog patiently waited for the first bite. "I could only think that I did it in an outburst of stupidity. I was about to be married, and I was scared. So, I left. I was looking for an easy way out. I didn't want to work hard in my country, and I came here only to find out that you have to work even harder here. But once you are here, you're stuck. You don't want to go back and tell everybody that you didn't make it. You don't want to be the one who failed. . . . So, I stayed. I have been killing myself working ever since."

Beto's move to Jessamine after his divorce was not foreordained, but after the company in nearby Yonkers, where he was working as an assembly-line operator, moved its operations offshore, he had an incentive to make a big change in his life. For Roberto, this was a good thing. A week after he left the Bronx, he was working the night shift at HiCap. "Finding work here was easy. *Los estáfins* were going crazy hiring Hispanics. If you worked hard, companies promoted you. I had friends that were operators in Yonkers, and here, they were working as supervisors. The apartments were new and nice. The rent was cheap. I could see having a better life here."

At the start of the displacement at HiCap, the general manager transferred Beto to first shift. He had already learned all the jobs on the assembly line and was the first bilingual supervisor on first shift, where he trained the Latino workers brought into the workforce at the Back End. A year later, six months after I had left HiCap, Beto quit the factory. I interviewed him for a second time, and he reflected on how the company enlisted him for the displacement.

"Actually, African Americans didn't like reporting to a Hispanic supervisor. They didn't like a Hispanic giving them orders. It was difficult getting started. Like I told when we worked there, I'll tell you again now. I got the feeling that African Americans live with a slavery complex. Because of this, they don't like that anyone gives them orders or manages them. You know what I mean? When they sent me to the Back End, it was a difficult situation because they [African Americans] didn't like to work. And more than anything, the company had that record, they had history, that problem for a long time with them. So they hired me to change things. But in these companies, this is a process that takes a long time. You were there. They brought in the Hispanics. I was not willing to go forward with the full project."

"What do you mean?"

"My salary was not that great to deal with such a problem. They wanted me to abuse my own people."

"In what way?"

"They sped up the line. They got smart and wanted one person to do the job of three people. They did it in your section too, and they kept at it. They wanted more and more. They wanted cheap and perfect. No mistakes. They thought Hispanics are superhuman. They aren't. We are not superhuman! This problem was in my head all the time. I went home, and I could not think of anything else. I fell into a depression. So I started looking for work in other places."

As this quotation illustrates, supervisors like Roberto were cognizant of the racialization involved in displacement and eventually fell ill from it—in one way or another. Reinforcing their employers' views, they were also aware that their "niche" was with the Latino workforce and not in managing African Americans. Further evidence of the racialization of the workforce was Roberto's attitude toward the one white worker on his team. In his section was a young man called "Elvis" because he danced on the conveyor belt and dressed like Elvis. Although this type of behavior violated company policy and was the subject of discipline ("write-ups") or termination, in my time at HiCap, I saw only one white worker disciplined—after several write-ups and after the agency found out that he was selling drugs in the company's parking lot. Elvis stayed on as support staff (a "floater"). In spite of Elvis's eccentricity, Roberto rarely acknowledged his existence. Given the small numbers of white workers on the shop floor, managers and supervisors rarely mentioned them in displacement.

Roberto and others had their own biased and racialized perceptions of African American workers and showed discomfort in assignments that involved them, but the manifestation of racial attitudes was selective. While Roberto did not resist the replacement of African Americans, ethnic affinity with Latinos drove him to leave the plant before engaging in further exploitation. Still, the Back End, Roberto's section,

was the first section to change from having a majority of Black workers to a majority of Latino workers. The change to full displacement at
the Back End was possible because the section was in a small and isolated area staffed with about sixteen temporary operators. Workers at
the Back End performed a set of relatively simple industrial processes
that new employees could learn in a matter of hours. Consequently, replacing native-born workers with Latino immigrants at the Back End
happened as fast as the temporary employment agency could terminate
native-born workers and hire new workers. When I asked Roberto about
his involvement in the displacement, he told me, "Overnight, the managers told me that I was going to start firing people, most of them Black,
and that I was going to bring in Hispanics to replace them."

"How did people react?"

"People didn't like the change at all. They moved the white supervisor
that was in my department to a different area. . . . What happened is that
the company was in the red. I think management wanted to outsmart
everyone else and decided to bring Hispanics because they know that
Hispanics work hard for little pay." Roberto found himself involved in
displacement because of his promotion.

Training and Buffering Displacement Workers

After the agency sent replacement workers, labor intermediaries
deployed different strategies. Because existing employees refused to
train Latinos, the bilingual supervisor had to figure out a way to train
the new workers on the assembly line to avoid disrupting the production process. Supervisors generally trained workers, but many bilingual
supervisors were inexperienced themselves. They needed the cooperation of native-born workers to train the Latino operators. Yet the degree
of power that the bilingual supervisor had over workers depended on
whether they shared authority with the native-born supervisors. For
example, simpler operations, requiring only one supervisor, went from
having exclusively Black and white teams to having primarily Latino
teams when management replaced the native-born supervisor with a
bilingual supervisor and kept power concentrated in the same structural
position. This was the case in the Back End. Conversely, in more complex operations requiring more than one supervisor (as in the case of

the Front End, where I was assigned), only one native-born supervisor was typically replaced with a bilingual supervisor—risk to production would be too high in these complex operations to completely replace the leadership with newly hired and inexperienced foreign-born supervisors. Because of the fragmentation in the authority structure along racial lines, native-born and bilingual supervisors had to negotiate power among themselves. Furthermore, the ability of supervisors to command respect from their workers led to two important outcomes. On the one hand, sections where supervisors commanded respect from their workers could focus on improving productivity and possibly avoid the entire displacement process. On the other hand, sections where authority was weak or fragmented could not sidestep the displacement, and native-born workers chose to focus on sabotaging the work of the new workers, becoming even more prominent targets for replacement.

Additionally, the degree of influence that supervisors had over the hiring and firing of workers varied in relation to the degree of complexity of their sections and the importance of their sections to the production process. More complex sections typically required a larger number of workers, and sections with more workers involved more supervisors. Sections with less than fifteen to seventeen workers and low levels of complexity, for example, typically involved only one supervisor, while sections with more workers typically had multiple supervisors. This resulted in a concentration of power in the supervisory role in smaller and less complex sections of the plant. Supervisors in these sections had more autonomy in personnel decisions, as their decisions had less influence on the production process. Decisions about firing workers in small sections were typically made on the recommendations of the supervisor, whereas in larger sections, replacement decisions resulted from the inputs of multiple supervisors as well as floor managers. In larger and more complex areas of the plant, supervisors also relied on social bonds to maintain a degree of control, as workers could influence the production process and undermine the authority of the supervisor by bringing scrutiny to supervisors' efficacy. For example, workers could bring a complex operation or line down if they chose, causing their supervisor to lose face with co-supervisors and managers.

In supervisors' role as mediating agents between managers and workers, they had to comply with management directives and balance these directives with the power that workers had over the production process and with the power of co-supervisors. One strategy that supervisors employed to comply with the replacement process and still maintain authority was to rely on social bonds and group affinities. Because of the ethnic segmentation prevailing outside and inside the plant, group affinity was usually developed along racial lines. Most workers used their breaks to spend time with members of their same ethnoracial group, ate in the cafeteria with members of the same ethnoracial group, and tended to talk to members of the same racial group on the job. Yet, racial affinity between supervisors and workers was somewhat influenced by gender. Black male supervisors generally maintained relationships with Black male workers, and white male supervisors generally maintained relationships with other white male workers. Female supervisors, however, typically maintained social ties with women workers regardless of race. In my time at HiCap, it appeared that, in the case of female supervisors, church activities and the presence of children in their home created opportunities for Black and white women to develop social bonds.

In small and less complex sections, reliance on social bonds was not a determinant of survival, as the supervisor could more easily spot workers' attempts to undermine authority and remove those workers without impacting the production process. In sections with a distributed authority structure, however, supervisors had to rely on social affinity. It was in the best interest of supervisors to protect workers with whom they had strong social bonds as a form of securing their authority and standing. In general, female supervisors found that female workers challenged their authority less than did male workers. Male supervisors, on the other hand, were disregarded by female workers and received more cooperation from male employees. Consequently, supervisors relied on the strength of their racial and gender ties to maintain their authority. In the presence of a displacement threat, the supervisors typically saw the situation as a zero-sum game, and for them to maintain their power, someone else would necessarily need to lose theirs. When the efforts of supervisors failed—more often than not due to sabotage—the company demoted the supervisors and created an opening for an "enclave" for a bilingual supervisor to manage. The arrival of Latinos to fill the power void further fragmented the weak social bonds that existed between some workers and supervisors. Following a "divide and conquer" strategy, segmentation along racial and gender lines occurred in complex production sections at the plant.[18] Black supervisors were generally overseeing the work of Black workers (mostly men), white (mostly women) supervisors were managing the work of white and Black women, and Latino supervisors managed the work of Latino workers. Power divisions along racial lines challenged the gendered group cohesion existing before the displacement and created the conditions for some replacement to occur.

In racialized organizations, "matching" workers and employers in jobs goes beyond economic goals. Displacement, a racialization project, works because labor intermediaries deploy symbolic and material strategies to advance the goals of powerful employers. In showing how intermediaries and agencies—actors conspicuously missing from (or euphemistically disguised on) organizational charts—cooperate in organizations in displacement processes, we see the ubiquitous influence of these actors on racialized hiring processes and the employers' ability to skirt the law and, even more important, distance themselves from the legal and business risks that blatant discriminatory employment practices should generate.

This hiring infrastructure involves three distinct types of intermediaries working in concert to absorb risk for an employer: a temporary employment agency, a bilingual recruiter, and a team of bilingual supervisors. Analytically, I conceive of this infrastructure as a form of brokerage, bridging the distance between otherwise-disconnected others.

In displacement, labor intermediaries bridge the distance between unauthorized workers and employers. Under this framework, agencies and bilingual recruiters are external "brokers" because they connect employers and workers from outside the organization. External brokers are a company's eyes and ears in the larger organizational field. In the sociology of organizations, employment agencies function as on-the-ground agents, in this case as a representative of HiCap. Because they are often embedded in communities, they are closer to the pools of workers and their dynamics and, as such, are more capable of learning and adapting their hiring practices to employ workers whom they considered a better "fit" with their hiring expectations. Agencies and recruiters understand the dynamics of migration, immigrants' vulnerabilities, the labor market, and the common practices of their business competitors. Bilingual supervisors, on the other hand, are "embedded" brokers because they connect employers and workers inside the organization and at times inside the community. The distinction between embedded and external brokers shows that agencies and bilingual recruiters are engaged in different stages of displacement. Companies enlist employment agencies and bilingual recruiters for the pre-hire stage of the process, while they hire bilingual supervisors for the post-hire stage.

Finally, large organizations, while interested in the control that having a primarily unauthorized and vulnerable labor force confers on them, rely on intermediaries to avoid the costs in reputation and legal fees associated with directly engaging in recruiting and hiring unauthorized immigrant workers. Because immigrants face a threat of deportation and must trust employers and companies in applying for jobs, HiCap and similar companies enlist labor intermediaries, which have an entrepreneurial advantage in shielding firms from legal risks and reputation loss. They provide unauthorized workers with jobs while simultaneously enabling the production of exploitative conditions for vulnerable workers.

3

Creating Job Vacancies

A month into the displacement, it was unclear how HiCap would introduce the Latino operators to the shop floor. The company had enlisted the cooperation of the employment agency, Ready Hands, to recruit and hire Latino immigrant workers and had trained the bilingual supervisors. Still, there were no open vacancies for the incoming workers. All the positions on the assembly line had an operator performing the job. Furthermore, other than the displacement "project," the company had no plans to increase production or innovate with new products, which might have justified additional workers. Yet with no apparent reason for adding new workers, how would the company produce vacancies for Latinos to fill?

The key difference between displacement and replacement is in *the process* of vacancy creation. Paying attention to departures—not solely arrivals to an organization's workforce—will provide scholars and policy makers with a clearer understanding of racialized displacement. Companies use different approaches, but the key to differentiating displacement from replacement lies in creating vacancies. At HiCap, managers jump-started displacement with small teams of temporary workers. Yet to employ large numbers of immigrants among more than four hundred employees, the company had to remove workers from their jobs while avoiding resistance and disruptions to production. To this end, HiCap engaged in a series of experiments that ultimately prompted permanent hires to leave the company. The outcome was empty slots in the labor queue for managers to fill with unauthorized immigrants, the most vulnerable workers.

The Easy Route

Creating the first vacancies for the teams of Latinos on first shift involved identifying a small number of workers targeted for displacement.

"Floaters" were the easiest to replace. Originally, the floaters were a group of cross-trained workers who would "float" from section to section to maintain production levels as efficiently as possible. They were expected to serve as backups when a worker was injured or fell ill, as an emergency team if parts needed to be preassembled rapidly, or as a utility group to make multiple repairs on a given day. In practice, floaters at the plant fell short in meeting managerial expectations, making it easier for management to replace them.

Undervalued in the "employer's queue," the floaters proved disposable because the group had devolved into what many workers at the plant referred to as "the tourists." Therese, one of the white women at the Baseboard Table, coined the term to capture the sentiment of frustration the women felt when they saw these young workers walking around the factory. I asked Therese how the floaters gained the "tourists" moniker. "Look at them! They don't work; they come here like they're on vacation." Therese was referring to a group of nine to eleven young men (Black and white) who traveled on short assignments from section to section, dressed in hip-hop garb. The men in the floaters group, in general, saw the jobs as temporary and irrelevant. They accepted the threat of a write-up or losing the job without resistance. "I got better things to do with my time. It don't matter if you fire me," one of the floaters told Marcus, the Black floor manager. Furthermore, because the floaters' work ethic and short-term contract were at odds with those of others on the shop floor, floaters clashed with permanent workers and temps assigned to specific tasks. Floaters walked around the plant drinking sodas and wearing tinted safety glasses—both prohibited on the floor—passing their time chatting and teasing operators. Like Therese, most workers resented them, because they shared few work expectations or aspirations. In the words of Rusty, another white female operator, "They don't work. They're here just playing and hanging out."

Because of the floaters' low status in the employer's labor queue, they turned into easy targets for vacancy creation. The shop-floor supervisors labeled the floaters' lax work ethic as "laziness." They also experienced the floaters as disengaged in work. One day with a busy production schedule, Darius, the section manager, discovered two of the floaters sleeping on a bed of stacked cardboard boxes and yelled, "These are the laaaaziest of all!" waking them up to the laughter of their friends.

The floaters were unmoved by warnings or disciplinary write-ups, challenging the managerial desire for more control. On a different occasion, James, a high school graduate working only until he made enough money to purchase a gold cap to cover a pristine white tooth, grabbed Tasia's golden hair extension and pinned it onto the conveyor belt. The incident disturbed her to the point of tears and caused the blockage of a safety guard at the Transfer Corner in the assembly line, disrupting production. When Marcus asked James why he should keep him on the job, James playfully responded, "Because I get bored at home, man!" and went on laughing and fiddling with his baggy jeans.

Although white and Black men worked as floaters, managers and supervisors racialized the group on the basis of their dress style and work ethic, suggesting that categories of distinction pattern the process of dismissing workers. On repeated occasions, managers generalized the behaviors of a handful of young workers, both Black and white, to support the stereotype that native-born workers (and especially Blacks) "don't want to work hard" and the perception that Blacks have an "attitude." In addition, managers often used a blanket racial stereotype when the typically lower engagement of native-born temporary workers was taken as evidence of a lack of commitment and work ethic on the part of Black American workers in general, particularly vis-à-vis their unauthorized immigrant counterparts.

It is tempting to adopt the stance that floaters were undeserving of the jobs and, subsequently, deserving targets for displacement. HiCap workers certainly believed it. We should keep in mind, however, that productivity evaluations mask structural inequalities emerging from organizational hierarchies. HiCap had a hybrid temporary/permanent labor force structure, with over half of workers permanent (also known as "plant employees"). The remainder were temporary workers. Indeed, permanent workers got more work done than their temporary counterparts did but only because they were also more experienced and found creative ways to counteract the boredom of assembly work without disrupting production. Even on hard days, permanent employees found motivation in job stability, higher wages, and company benefits, which temporary workers lacked. With permanent and temporary workers, the company had an unequal structure in which managers and the employment agency deemed temporary employers "inferior." By virtue of these workers' contingent contract, the managers and employment agency referred to them as more easily disposable. Thus, managers created the first vacancies by comparing temporary to permanent workers.

To create vacancies for the first unauthorized immigrants, the company called Ready Hands, the employment agency, to terminate the floater assignments. "Your assignment with Ready Hands has ended, but we'll call you when something else comes up" was the typical message workers received when their contract with HiCap ended. Since the temp agency had been interviewing Latinos over the preceding two weeks, Ready Hands used some of the Latino recruits to fill floater vacancies.

When Marcus introduced the Latino workers filling the vacancies, he approached me with my first assignment: to train a small group of unauthorized Mexican workers from the states of Chiapas and Hidalgo. "Ms. Sanders, see the guys there by the pallets, in preassembly, playing with the grommets?" Marcus asked in his standard formal style as he talked to me on the opposite side of the conveyor belt, carefully leaning on the edge so that I could make out what he said. He spoke softly and skittishly.

"Yes, I see them."

"They're heavy lifters. Dave wants me to start the 'project' and wants the interpreters"—Marcus called the bilingual supervisors "interpreters"—"to start training these guys. I want you to get ready to start training."

"Where do you want them trained?"

"Start them as floaters. Give them something easy. Show them how to add grommets. Then coordinate with Kesha and Darius to take jobs on the assembly line. I am making some major changes here." He pointed with his head to the assembly line without fixing on any point.

"Are Darius and Kesha okay with this? We don't have positions on the assembly line."

"You let me worry about this. They'll be on board. They'll be on board. I'll work on that," he muttered and disappeared quickly, before I could ask more questions.

The exchange with Marcus suggests that managers viewed vacancy creation as less problematic when it involved temporary workers, but, as I discuss later, the process still required supervisor buy-in. Temporary contracts eliminate the higher costs (legal and financial) involved in hiring and firing workers. When dealing with temporary workers, companies use active terminations to create the vacancies needed to bring in workers ranked higher in their labor queues. All it takes is one phone call, and without assuming any legal responsibility at all, the employer using the right employment agency can replace one group of workers with another, even when using race, gender, and nativity in the request. Consequently, while companies avoid the risk of firing categories of people, the increasing prevalence of temporary employment enables companies to bring in the workers they want and maintain legal compliance or at least the perception thereof.

As I was watching this series of coincidences unfold, it became clear that I was not observing the results of random hiring practices but a well-orchestrated production. A little more than four weeks after Marcus moved from third to first shift to lead the displacement, about fifteen sections at the plant already had from three to five Latino workers working as "backups"—covering for workers who called in sick or had what Darius called "the Monday flu." About ten other Latino workers walked around the plant as floaters, taking the place of the team that, prior to the displacement, included seven to eight Black men and two to three white men. "Make sure your guys know all the jobs on the line. Tell Marcus that I want him to bring your people two at the time until you have a solid Mexican enclave here," Dave instructed me when Richard and Manuel arrived at the Front End to work.

Cover Your Legal Bases

How does a company scale up displacement when it wants to create hundreds of vacancies? How do employers assess the legal risk from displacing a group of people in a protected category (e.g., race, gender, or nationality)? While the legal prohibitions are the same with respect to using race or other protected categories in deciding to hire or fire employees, the risk to employers of these two illegal actions are significantly different. Most managers and employers are well aware that they cannot use protected categories as criteria for employment decisions, so it is rare that even the most discriminatory employer will tell a candidate that they are being hired or fired because of their race, sex, religion or nationality.[1] In the absence of clear-cut evidence of discrimination based on disparate treatment, lawyers usually use statistical patterns to argue cases of discriminatory employment practices, even when the case pertains to an individual decision.[2] It is the determination of these statistical patterns that make discriminatory terminations and promotions riskier for employers than discriminatory hiring.

When a plaintiff is evaluating a company's employment practices, the plaintiff must show that the employer selected a decidedly nonrandom set from a qualified applicant pool.[3] In the case of promotions and terminations, this pool can be known with near certainty, as it consists of all current employees or some easily measurable subset of current employees. For example, if a company lays off 10 percent of its production workforce, those who are eligible would be defined as the total pool of line workers currently employed. If the assembly-line workers are 90 percent Latino, then we should not be surprised if close to 90 percent of those who are laid off are Latino. If, on the other hand, the workforce is only 30 percent Latino yet 90 percent of those who are laid off are Latino, then there would be a solid argument that the criteria used to create the layoff list disparately impacted Latinos. Likewise, if assembly-line workers are 90 percent Latino, but promotions are given to white or Black workers 90 percent of the time, the criteria would also be called into question.

This situation is different on the hiring side of employment decisions. Most unsuccessful job applicants, such as the white job seekers I witnessed the company turning away as it hired Latino workers, have no way of knowing anything about the applicant pool. Usually, the unsuccessful applicant will not even know how large that pool was. However, even if a plaintiff somehow gains access to the complete demographics of the pool of applicants, the task of ascertaining which of the applicants were qualified would prove to be nearly impossible. Therefore, if a company hires 90 percent of one racial category, even though that racial category only represents 10 percent of the local population, in the absence of hard data on the demographics and qualifications of the applicants, there is no evidence that the process was discriminatory. It is entirely possible that 95 percent of the qualified applicants were members of the hired racial category. Given the pattern of recruiting and hiring by tapping into the social networks of existing employees in some industries, this might even be suspected in some contexts.[4] The uncertainty surrounding the characteristics of the baseline pool shows that employers face considerably less risk in their hiring practices than they do with respect to promotional and firing practices. The net result is that in a rational world where employers seek to minimize risk, we can expect to see more discriminatory practices related to hiring than firing.

My study of hiring managers at HiCap and other manufacturing companies complicates the argument of rationality. Indeed, some managers made the distinction that hiring decisions require little to no supporting documentation, while terminations usually involve pages and pages of supporting notes, signed and witnessed written warnings, and multiple visits to the human resources department. Still others, at HiCap and elsewhere, pointed out that they had never seen corporate legal counsel review a hiring decision but that every layoff roster (with the possible exception of a roster based purely on seniority) receives such a review prior to implementation. Similarly, some of these managers told me that while there is clearly no company hiring policy reflecting this, they feel that the level of scrutiny that they give a candidate is directly related to the difficulty that they will have terminating the employee. Their articulation why, however, reveals the influence of both reliance on a temporary workforce and cultural frames in their decision-making. For example, one manager from a midsized manufacturing company told me,

> If I am hiring someone as a temp, I check to make sure that they have some skills and won't be an obvious problem, but, knowing that a single phone call will make them go away with no questions asked, I don't look very deep. On the other hand, if I am hiring to fill a permanent position, I have the person talk to quite a few potential coworkers to make sure the *fit* [my emphasis] with the overall team will be good. There are things that make firing some employees even more difficult than others, and these make the hiring decision even more critical. Examples of this might be if the candidate has family who work for us. I hate firing a flaky cousin of a great worker and losing them both because of family loyalties. It happens. Also, if an applicant falls into a protected class like race, age, disability, whatever, . . . that makes it harder to let them go if they don't fit. Let's face it, hiring isn't an exact science, so we all make bad hiring decisions on occasion, so hiring anyone that is going to be difficult to fire is always risky.

Another manager summed it up this way: "If someone is easy to fire, then they are easy to hire." He continued, "It's that simple, and the opposite is also true." Even in the absence of all other labor queue dynamics, this single perception of risk is likely to create a meaningful queue, one that Barbara Reskin and Patricia Roos describe as "low intensity."[5] But even if the queue only serves as a tiebreaker when two applicants are essentially equally qualified, the results will be consistently biased toward the lower-risk candidates in most organizations. Thus, as managers gear up to create large numbers of vacancies involving protected categories of people, we can expect them to find ways to avoid risks by disguising their illegal practices.

Getting Buy-In

While white managers were the architects of displacement at HiCap, they delegated the responsibility of hiring and terminating workers to floor managers and supervisors. HiCap was staffed with large numbers of women and Black individuals in supervisory positions. This meant that managers of color and women were responsible for displacing groups of people with whom they shared not only categorical affinity (i.e., by race and gender) but also social affinity.

While other studies illuminate how managers rely on coethnic mediation to meet their organizational goals, my research extends prior work by demonstrating how coethnic affinity works in organizations, changing along intersectional categories of race, gender, and unauthorized immigrant status.[6] Considering coethnic mediation not only shows how companies avoid the appearance of hiring bias but also, as I show in chapter 6, allows us to understand how changes in attitudes and immigration policy influence displacement.[7] At HiCap, vacancy creation involved disrupting bonds of solidarity based on race, gender, employment authorization, and other social affinities. To get the buy-in of minority managers and supervisors, white managers (1) misled them and (2) gave them a language in which they framed displacement under the logic of efficiency.

Mislead Them with Colorblindness

When white managers, almost without exception, talked about decisions involving vacancy creation, they used colorblindness and preemptively dispelled any potential concerns regarding unequal treatment. Colorblindness, a strategy that powerful white individuals sometimes use to deploy racial frames while sidestepping race altogether, was the strategy managers favored at HiCap.[8] The type of colorblindness deployed in displacement, however, rather than involving denial under an accusation of discrimination or racism, involved a deracialized narrative that the decisions to replace workers were to save jobs. Before anyone at the plant had an opportunity to question the racialized departures occurring at the plant, or when confronted with questions about racial selection, managers issued proactive statements. "We are not targeting anyone here," "we treat everyone the same here," and "we are only weeding out people who don't want to work hard and bringing in people that do want these jobs" were common and culturally powerful tropes.

Unlike HiCap managers, the employment agency justified the displacement using legalistic tropes. When referring to hiring unauthorized Latino workers, recruiters emphasized legal compliance. "We have strict procedures about the legality of the workers," and "we only hire workers with documents." Managers and recruiters countered any suggestion of discriminatory treatment on the shop floor by reiterating their commitment to equal treatment. Claire, a white trainer, talked about the difficulty implementing vacancy creation at one of the plants in the North because the plant was unionized. "The union didn't want us to make any changes. When we had the workshop [to identify targets for displacement], we had to bring everybody from all three shifts and talk to everyone. The corporate lawyer was constantly following us around," she told me as we washed our hands in the employees' bathroom next to the Front End. I asked how she was going to convince people to cooperate in the displacement. "It depends," she responded without hesitation. I found her eyes in the mirror. "Sometimes I tell them they are going to lose their jobs to China. Here I will tell them about Mexico—whatever fits." Dave, the general manager, used the same threatening strategy. "Our jobs are bound for China or Mexico if our numbers stay as bad as they are!" he unhappily announced at a meeting. While it might be possible that the jobs were going to other countries in the long term, the company used these justifications to convince workers in the short term, misleading by creating the perception of a crisis.

I recorded other instances in which the company tried getting buy-in by appealing to the communitarian ideals of working-class factory workers: "We are eliminating a few jobs but saving hundreds," even when the goal was to populate those positions with more vulnerable workers. In South Carolina, a right-to-work state, the company implemented the changes without a union, but they brought what they learned in that environment to bear, asserting equality at every opportunity. HiCap's rhetoric of equal treatment prevailed even though the company clearly had legal concerns.

It was not enough to simply *talk the talk*; employers also had to *walk the walk* by enforcing workplace standards and rules uniformly across the board. To list a few of the many examples in this study, when Latino workers were absent two times in thirty days, the company ended their employment, just as it would for white or Black individuals. When the agency ran a background check and uncovered a criminal record, employment was terminated regardless of race or nationality. And when the company implemented a program called 5S, if anything, the Latino workers were expected to clean more, not less, than the native-born. The policies had a disparate impact as the demographics shifted in favor of unauthorized immigrant workers and against native-born Americans and authorized immigrants, but under the framework of colorblindness, disparate treatment was nowhere to be seen.

Give Them a Language

In racialized organizations, powerful stakeholders hide illegal and morally dubious practices to avoid legal discovery or financial risk to themselves or their organizations. To this end, displacement, a process contributing to the racialization of organizations, relies on coded language to avoid discovery and protect a company's reputation. We can think of language as the veil that masks biased practices when managers use authorized and unauthorized statuses to shift the racial and gender makeup of an organization. As such, racialized displacement operates under the pretense of colorblindness, plausibly denying any discrimination all the while protecting powerful white actors. At HiCap, managers preemptively blocked perceptions that their hiring, firing, and promotion practices carried biases based on race, gender, or citizenship. Instead, managers framed the displacement project with "efficiency," "hard work," and similar terms when their practices were questioned.

Managers used coded language to discard people under protected categories (e.g., women, Black persons, employees legally authorized to work) and acquire workers from even more vulnerable categories (unauthorized workers). Under displacement, managers convinced workers to cooperate by telling them that the company's focus was on improving productivity and keeping only those employees who were "willing to work hard." To add legitimacy to these claims, the company engaged in two experiments in improving productivity before scaling up displacement. One, the Lean Manufacturing Initiative, or LMI, forced many workers to leave.

"They need you at the cafeteria. Something like a class that you have to go to," Kesha, the Black female supervisor at the Front End, told me without a hint of emotion on a cold morning in January. We had just returned from a weeklong plant closure, and the announcement of the class came unexpectedly. Leaning her head on the radio clipped onto the shoulder of her top, Kesha explained that the company was asking Darius and Jacob (two Black supervisors), Ron and Sam (two white supervisors), and me to go to "a class." She avoided commenting that management had not asked her to attend the training workshop. Kesha's exclusion, I learned a few days into the workshop, was necessary to facilitate the racialized displacement. Kesha's removal caused the exit of several women, as they no longer had anyone with enough power to advocate for or protect them.

Up until this point, management had not invited bilingual supervisors into the typically white spaces at the plant. In displacement, the "us" versus "them" boundary still patterned interactions. The offices, training rooms, and a private cafeteria were out of bounds for most shop-floor supervisors and, even more so, for the Latinos, who were segregated in a cafeteria at the back of the plant. Consequently, when the supervisors entered the clean room, with clean worktables and cushioned chairs, they exchanged curious gazes after they adjusted their eyes to the brightness of the room. In silence, also adjusting their hearing to the quiet of the room, which contrasted with the noise and darkness of the shop floor, the supervisors waited for the training to start.

As the displacement process was under way, supervisors wondered about their own jobs. I wrote in my field notes that everyone looked older and tired under the bright lights in the seminar room. Darius removed his do-rag, and the light revealed some signs of gray in his curly hair. Sam, a tall white manager from second shift, had dark circles under his eyes, which he attributed to staying up late to watch his kids. He finally broke the silence. "I wonder what management is up to?" Sam asked, mostly to himself but loud enough so that the question reached everyone's ears. "Are we really here for training, or are they just calling us in to tell us we're fired? We haven't had any training in years." Darius concentrated on chewing tobacco and did not say anything. He opened an empty plastic Dr. Pepper bottle and spit into it when Henry and Claire, two white trainers directing the seminar, burst into the room.

"Why are you here?" Henry asked rhetorically, opening his arms in our direction.

"You're here because you're the smartest people in your section!" he said, increasing the pitch of his voice while simultaneously bouncing across the room as he paced back and forth. Sam turned to Darius and rolled his eyes, silently questioning management's intentions.

Henry was no taller than five foot two. He had a neat goatee that he touched every few seconds nervously. He contrasted in height and grooming with all the men sitting in the room. Unlike the skeptical and tired supervisors watching him attentively, Henry was full of energy—partly sustained by a large thermos of coffee that he drank like water throughout the day but probably also by the fear of failing to get supervisor buy-in. He told me over the course of the training, "If I don't meet corporate's benchmark, I can kiss my job good-bye, and nobody else will hire me for a job like this now." This type of fear was a common motivation to carry out displacement. Dave, the general manager, often mentioned during management meetings, "We need to improve our numbers. If we don't hire workers that want to work hard, headquarters will close the plant," or "We are this close to kissing our jobs good-bye [dramatically showing a small space between his thumb and index finger] if we don't give the jobs to people that want them," he would say when supervisors ask about the turnover. White managers, in general, unified around the script that displacement was necessary to save jobs.

Henry and Claire represented everything that those who were working the line feared. They were middle managers, perceived as having little understanding of the production process yet full of ideas on how to change it. Sam, the white supervisor from second shift, told me later that day, "These are the people management sent to avoid facing us. They know nothing about what we do but want to come here and make all kinds of changes in the name of making things better." Sam was partly correct. The training managers represented a layer of intermediaries, and their task was to convince supervisors that any changes were for efficiency's sake.

As I observed the managers and the disaffected supervisors, I wondered what the trainers wanted to achieve with the superficial remark about the intelligence of a clearly marginalized group relegated to following orders. And why did the company call the bilingual supervisors to this "class"? The response to my questions came sooner than I expected. The company was making its way to degrading the jobs to push some of the existing workers out of the organization and create vacancies for the replacement workers. Without looking at notes, Henry wrote on a white board, "sales − costs = profits." He wrote some company-specific numbers related to sales and said, "The company needs profits to go up, and the only way we can do it is by looking at things that we have control over." He paused before he continued energetically, "Productivity and efficiency of labor . . . We are going to train you on the Lean Manufacturing Initiative, L-M-I," he wrote in bold letters on the white board. LMI involved a 5S program to "eliminate waste" and included "balancing the line," programs the company told us would increase productivity. "With LMI, you will increase profits for the company. The company has to lower costs to compete and to save our jobs. We are going to reduce costs by eliminating waste in process, idle time, body motions, etcetera," Henry explained, almost agitated, as the caffeine from his coffee coursed through his veins.

5S is a quality-focused methodology that originated in Japan as part of the lean manufacturing movement. The five s's are *seiri, seiton, seiso, seiketsu*, and *shitsuke*, roughly translated as organization, orderliness, cleanliness, standardization, and discipline. The objective, according to the American Society for Quality, is to create a workplace that is clean, uncluttered, safe, and well organized and thereby optimizes productivity and reduces waste of materials and effort.[9] This kind of program could improve employee morale, reduce costs, utilize better equipment, and improve product quality—in essence, turn a bad job into a better one. While there is not much to dislike in a program so described, and while 5S is widely used throughout industry to make work easier and more efficient, the HiCap version of 5S would have been more accurately called 1S, as it focused almost exclusively on *seiso*. *Seiso* is translated euphemistically by American industrial engineers as "shining." This is the closest word beginning with an *s* in the English language that describes the actual activity that so many workers find particularly distasteful: "cleaning."

To convince workers, the company used the language of efficiency. Managers instructed supervisors to have workers "eliminate waste" in all areas of the plant. But the instructions and the focus demonstrated that the fundamentals of 5S were clearly lost: the elimination of waste in materials and effort that is central to the 5S methodology was replaced with the elimination of waste in the form of physical trash. At the Front End, supervisors were asked to engage workers in eliminating clutter by prohibiting behaviors that contributed to waste accumulation (e.g., trash on the floor, food and drinks at workstations). Supervisors arrived with buckets of soapy water, rags, brooms, and other cleaning supplies. Without explanation, they instructed workers to clean remnants of food under workstations and asked them to remove clothing left for weeks, if not months, hanging out of broken lockers and sometimes even on machines. Although most workers removed clutter during their shift, many blatantly refused to cooperate. It was clearly one of the most undesirable tasks for many workers. Adding a 5S program, especially one focused almost exclusively on *seiso*, to their job descriptions fundamentally changed the nature of those jobs for many.

Employees refused to cooperate in this initiative because they perceived cleaning to be a degrading and racialized activity, an activity for people at the bottom of the labor queue. When managers requested that workers clean between machines and work overtime on cleaning tasks, some of the native-born openly complained that cleaning was outside the scope of their jobs. Barbara, a Ready Hands recruiter who worked at HiCap, said that operators had gone to her to complain that supervisors were asking them to sweep at work. "I wasn't hired to sweep," an operator told her. "You should be glad that you get paid to sweep the floor here," Barbara responded and sent the operator to continue with the cleaning task.

To compensate for the lack of cooperation of native-born operators, Marcus asked the Latino operators at the Front End to work overtime and on weekends and brought in Latino workers from third shift to help complete the tasks. The Latinos washed the floors between machines where nobody ever cleaned, floors that had accumulated years of dirt and assorted production residue. They repainted the safety lines that had faded from the floor and touched up the paint on machines and broken-down lockers. Within two weeks, they transformed the plant, and Marcus credited the Latinos for their contribution, emphasizing the contrast between the reluctance of native-born workers and the attitude of the immigrant new hires. "These guys are God-sent people. The place already looks different," he commented proudly.

Changes to work expectations and activities increased as cleaning extended beyond the two weeks of in-depth restoration involving operators. Cleaning became a more salient task in the jobs as supervisors asked workers to sweep regularly and to leave their sections in pristine condition before a shift change. One afternoon, we were near the end of the shift, and production had slowed down. The floor was dirty, and Marcus asked the supervisors to get the floor cleaned for the workers coming in on second shift. Latino workers grabbed the brooms and started cleaning without any issues. After seeing that the Hispanic workers were cleaning, Darius asked Tasia, a Black operator, to clean, and he handed her a broom. "Here. You are going to clean," he instructed. "No. I ain't cleaning. I'm going to do wiring," she responded. Darius looked at the Latino workers, then said to Tasia, "Everyone else is cleaning." "I ain't cleaning!" she shouted and shook her head. "Come on, clean around here," Darius pleaded with a big smile. Tasia grabbed the broom and started sweeping begrudgingly. After a few days of frequent quarrels with Darius about cleaning, Tasia left the job. But Tasia did not leave HiCap on her own. Chloe, a friend and coworker whom Tasia drove to work, was left with no way to get to HiCap and was forced to leave as well.

Degrading Jobs

The preceding example highlights two important aspects of vacancy creation when employers use the strategy of degrading jobs. First, if given the choice, the immigrant workers would have rather engaged in more stimulating activities than cleaning, as almost any other worker would. Their need for jobs, however, made them less resistant to this activity than their native-born counterparts were. Consequently, the vulnerability of the replacement workers clearly influenced the ability of employers to have workers who could and would meet their demands. A second, but no less important, point is that changes can have a multiplicative effect based on network dependencies, which can influence the number and rate of vacancies created. For example, even if Chloe had been willing to comply with managerial requests and meet the new expectations of the job, her reliance on Tasia for transportation to work tied her exit to Tasia's. This interconnectedness contributed to the rate of vacancy creation and the degree of change in the demographics of the labor force due to job-queue shifts. Specifically, Tasia and Chloe's departure created vacancies for Wendy and Rosa, the first Hispanic females on the Front End assembly line. The entry of Wendy and Rosa and their subsequent placement at the Capacitors Table disrupted the in-group dynamics at the table and pushed those remaining workers a bit closer to the "exit door."

The process of vacancy creation illustrates the continued relevance of the labor process on labor market stratification. Many researchers have paid attention to the complex relationship between the degradation of jobs and workers' experiences.[10] Following Harry Braverman's *Labor and Monopoly Capital*, published more than forty years ago, studies on jobs going bad focus on "deskilling" or on whether skilled labor has been "dumbed down" to remove control from workers.[11] In contrast to these studies, the case of HiCap shows that jobs, rather than the labor process per se, are degraded so that incumbents will exit them. At HiCap, managers degraded jobs not so much to control the labor process but to control who carried out the labor process.

After enlisting the cooperation of supervisors, HiCap managers focused on degrading the jobs to "motivate" even more workers to leave. In low-paid jobs, changes need not be major for some workers to feel a disruption in their work lives and cause them to exit jobs that no longer meet their goals. Changes can range from increasing worker surveillance to restricting social aspects of the job. Subtle and not so subtle changes to working conditions can generate vacancies and enable a gradual shift in the demographics of a labor force. The key in degrading jobs was to "motivate" workers to leave rather than firing workers and increase the risk of discriminatory hiring accusations. As companies redefine jobs to reclaim vacancies for the unauthorized workers they wanted, they (1) speed up the assembly line to force workers to quit and (2) deploy an isolation strategy.

Up the Speed

"Balancing the line" refers to a reorganization of work assignments so that every step in a process takes the same amount of time for workers to perform. Managers adopt this type of reorganization in the belief that if they can define every step of a process to require the same labor input, then no labor resources will ever be idle. On the surface, this seems to make sense, but as I learned from discussing this with an engineering consultant specializing in manufacturing—and reaffirmed by reading Eliyahu Goldratt and Jeff Cox's classic *The Goal*—balancing the line was a bad idea from the start.[12] The logic supporting a balancing of the line, it turns out, completely ignores that all process steps vary in their performance. What this means is that as soon as one process has a hiccup and loses a small amount of time, not only does that process step lose time but all of the processes that feed it or are fed by it also lose time that can never be recovered. As different process steps have their natural hiccups, this lost time keeps accumulating until the newly balanced line sets new records for inefficiency and low productivity.

Although many companies understand that balancing the line is not an effective means of optimizing throughput and productivity, others attempt this approach. Just as HiCap's implementation of 5S did not fit with the standard implementation, its implementation of balancing the line was also somewhat nonstandard. Rather than focusing on optimizing a process flow, the focus was on extracting more work from each worker. From the start, balancing the line introduced anxiety-generating practices, overtly transforming the shop floor into an observation laboratory and workers into lab rats.

Surveillance and policing workers' actions at HiCap changed the working conditions, and jobs lost value in the job queue for workers with other more attractive options. As I sat with Darius and other supervisors in the balancing the line course, the trainers, Henry and Claire, asked that to reduce "waste," we observe workers and identify people with "the wrong attitude." "Today we are going to work on balancing the line," Henry announced. We are going to "weed out people who don't want to work" and "people with the wrong attitude." He instructed the supervisors on how they were going to participate in the "Front End Trial" and assigned Darius to lead the project. Claire walked into the training room with clipboards for each of the supervisors, a stopwatch, and a video camera. She demonstrated how to use the stopwatch to measure production cycles, instructed the group on using the video camera, and distributed clipboards. "Y'all will get a turn," she told us. Henry and Claire escorted the group to the Front End and asked us to take notes. The group started observing the Baseboard Table, taking notes as instructed. We moved through sections of the assembly line taking turns timing the operators and videotaping. "Look for 'waste,' like idle time and areas to improve productivity," they reminded us, adding, "Pay attention to places where two or even three jobs can be combined into one." As the group walked through different areas, the workers' anxiety, brought about by the intrusion, was palpable. "Did you have fun? Filming people, timing people, making them feel nervous?" Janine confronted the supervisors when we returned to work on the assembly line after a morning in the training room. No one responded; everyone was in role. For many workers, however, the presence of supervisors and managers with stopwatches and video cameras on the shop floor raised serious concerns about job stability.

News and rumors of upcoming changes in the workplace traveled fast across the assembly line, feeding workers' concerns. Given the local history of textile mills and other manufacturing operations relocating overseas, many, if not most, of the workers had direct experience with layoffs and plant closures or at a minimum knew someone who had been affected directly. Several workers called their supervisors to communicate their fears. On my way out of the factory one evening, I ran into Kesha. "People have been calling me. They're worried about losing their jobs. They tell me, 'Kesha, don't let me lose my job.' Today I'm gonna take my phone off the hook," she continued, sounding weary and tired. "Do you have new people starting with you tomorrow?" she asked wanting to find out if the company was still hiring Hispanic workers.

"Yeah, I think they are sending two new operators tomorrow," I said.

"Some Hispanic temps do a better job than plant people." Kesha repeated what she had said on other occasions, her comment reflecting her agreement with management's preference for the Hispanic workers she supervised over the course of my study.

The logic of efficiency served to foreshadow further changes to the job queue. In the training room, the supervisors watched the video footage to identify "bottleneck" areas and jobs with visible idle time that they were going to transform. Claire pointed out that many people were "idle, joking, walking around, standing, doing nothing" in several sections, including the Baseboard Table, the Inductors, and the Tape Dispenser sections. Henry talked about opportunities to reduce "labor-hour waste" in those areas. Claire suggested that we watch the video footage one more time, taking the opportunity to time the different jobs to determine the bottleneck priorities and change the labor maps. Henry asked that we "work as a team" to decide how to "balance the line." Ray and Darius took the lead. On a large representation of a labor map posted on the wall, Darius crossed out jobs with X's on the paper. He marked the jobs that were going to be lost as "–1" or a "negative one." He then moved to a labor map with a third fewer people, including two supervisors instead of three, for the more complex units. For the manufacture of simpler units, Darius wrote down that only half the current number of people were needed. Since some of the changes collapsed three jobs into one, the plan came to be known as "3-for-1."

Darius, Ron, and Sam walked back to the Baseboard Table, the workstation at the beginning of the line and one of the most critical to the Front End. Henry was talking to Therese, Tara, and Leah, when Ron took their position on the assembly line to show how a three-operator job could be done by one operator. The combined job included securing a clamp with a screw, straightening and fastening cables inside the clamp, and attaching the ground wire with a second screw. Claire timed the cycles before and after Ron took over. Ron was having a hard time keeping up with the combined jobs at eight seconds per cycle. Darius took over, but he, too, could not combine the three jobs. They settled for combining two of the three jobs in one and had two successful demonstrations out of seven attempts. They asked Tara to try the combined job. Henry was videotaping performance and "attitudes." The group watched Tara trying to keep up with the combined jobs and failing, creating gaps on the line.[13] Tara gave up after several failed attempts, picked up her purse, and left for the day. The supervisors asked Leah to give it a try. Leah, too, had a hard time with the combined job. The supervisors then decided to try it from the other side of the line, to see if it was easier. Darius secured the power-cord clamp and the ground wire and asked Leah to try it again. She shook her head, pursed her lips, and grabbed the screw gun from Darius begrudgingly. Her perfectly styled hair had come out of place, and her mascara was dripping under her eyes as she started sweating. "I can't do this!" she yelled after trying for a few minutes and letting go of the screw gun. She ran to the bathroom, and Darius stepped in, still only able to combine two jobs instead of three. Leah came back with red eyes and a runny nose. She grabbed the screw gun from Darius without saying a word. "Uh-oh, they are getting mad. Look at Leah. She is very mad," Claire told Henry as she continued to time the cycles with the stopwatch.

If openly treating the workers as laboratory subjects and asking them to meet untenable standards was not enough, comparing their "attitude" to that of Hispanic immigrants moved some native-born workers even closer to the edge. In an effort to demonstrate how the combined jobs could be done with "the right attitude," the trainers called Ramon, one of the most seasoned Hispanic operators from third shift, to demonstrate the relative disposition of immigrant workers to adjust to the new expectations. "It can be done. It can be done," Ramon kept saying about the combined 2-for-1 job that Leah and Tara resisted. Although Ramon made mistakes when he tried the job, he was determined to succeed. As Ramon trained on the combined job by the Baseboard Table, Darius told Henry, "Yeah, it's all about the attitude. These guys have the right mind-set," confirming what Henry said during the training sessions. For several days, Sam and Ron, the second- and third-shift supervisors at the Front End, had their Hispanic workers trying and succeeding at the combination, and they were not shy about telling workers that "*the guys* [Latinos] *on second and third shift can do it.*"

Having vulnerable Latino immigrant workers, who were willing to comply with any expectation, enabled the managers to use these workers as their reference group. In so doing, they racialized the notion of hard work and demonstrated to native-born workers that others were willing to work harder than they were. Without explicitly repeating it, they also proclaimed that if workers lost their jobs, it was "because they didn't try hard enough." This trope was echoed by many of the people whom I interviewed for this study, even many who never worked at HiCap. Although HiCap managers generally warned workers about losing their jobs to competitors in other countries if they did not work hard, when they brought in a worker, as in the case of Ramon, it was done not so much to threaten them but rather to show them that the new standards were, indeed, possible to meet. In racializing hard work, the management used a colorblind meritocratic logic to preemptively counter any possible claims that an ex-employee might be able to make about unreasonable expectations.

"Things are bad. I used to like this place, but now I'm sick of it! I can't wait to get out of here," said Tara a few days after she had walked off the job during the "balancing the line" exercise. Upset by the changes, she called in sick to buy time and look for another job. When she returned, I asked, repeating what I heard from Kesha, "I haven't seen you at the plant for a few days. Did you take a short break?"

"I wish I could take a long break," she said. Her smile faded, and her pale skin turned red with anger. "Like many people here, I have given the plant [many] years of my life. I regret it. I hate this place. It's bad to have people in a place everyone wants to leave," she said, visibly upset and fighting back tears. "The changes with balancing the line are real bad," she continued. "Combining the jobs is bad. It's very hard to do two jobs at the same time. The supervisors are not helping! All they say is, 'Third shift is doing it. These other workers are doing it' [referring to the Hispanic workers]. I can't stand being on this job anymore!" she said, clearly frustrated.

"What are you going to do? Are you looking for a different job?"

"I wish there was something else, but I don't know. I am going to keep looking," she responded.

Shortly after this conversation, Darius lectured her as she refused to do the combined job. Tara left the factory soon after. Tara, a single mother with a child in high school, thought hard before leaving the job, but she reached her threshold of tolerance when the standards became untenable and her performance was compared to workers with options even more limited than those available to her.

The Transfer Corner was one of the toughest jobs at HiCap. Workers on this job had to transfer a fifteen-pound inductor assembly with a sensitive circuit board from one side of the assembly line to the other every few seconds. The constant twisting strained operators' backs, and they ran the risk of having wires trapped in the conveyor belt as they made the transfer. More than once I used the E-stop, a large red button that stopped the entire production line, seconds before operators had their fingers crushed while trying to release entangled wires at this station. Operators were generally willing to work the Transfer Corner, provided they were free to negotiate a swap with another worker on standby for relief and as a backup.

During the balancing the line exercise, supervisors rotated Richard into the Transfer Corner position. Richard, the man we met at Ready Hands in chapter 1, was five foot tall but stout, a man who had worked as a bus driver before migrating from Mexico to the United States. He wanted to buy a car and bring his sister to South Carolina from Mexico, which in part drove his unencumbered disposition to "want to work real hard." "Please, give me a lot, a lot of work. I want to be here working, not at home," he said during his first week at HiCap. Seeing Richard perform the job without using the backup operator led Darius to suggest the elimination of the backup operator at the Transfer Corner altogether. That Richard was able to do so without the backup operator immediately set a new standard for this job, at least temporarily.

After working at the Transfer Corner for two days, Richard was reassigned to work in the loading area. Darius then assigned Janine, a woman always cracking jokes and teasing others, to the Transfer Corner. Riley, a woman Janine knew from church and from her previous job at a now-shuttered mill, worked next to her. "Darius doesn't want me to help Janine anymore," Riley noted. "He said that if Janine only kept her mouth shut, she could do the job." Janine made an effort at the Transfer Corner but quickly expressed her desire to be moved to a different job, one where she would be able to socialize and move around. She told me after trying the job for a couple of days, "I want you to get someone to help me because I am very tired. My hands hurt, my arms hurt. This is not a job for one person. You're gonna have to have someone rotate with me." I helped her out for a while and talked to Darius about having her rotate with Riley. But, knowing that Richard had no issues working the Transfer Corner solo, Darius ignored Janine's pleas for relief. Janine was clearly upset. "I can't keep going. I am going to the nurse's office. You tell Darius where I went," she announced, walking out of the area. When she came back, she was wearing a wrist support. "I'm fine. I just need to wear this for a while," she told me in a disheartened voice. Several days later, Janine quit, but not alone. Shared transportation proved, once again, to be an issue that multiplied the number of vacancies created in this process. Riley, it turned out, relied on Janine for transportation to work. They both commuted from a neighboring state every morning, and the only way that Riley could afford to keep the job was by carpooling. In spite of her reluctance to leave, as she "couldn't afford being without work again," when Janine quit, Riley was left with no choice but to quit herself.

The company continued to identify "bottlenecks" and "labor inefficiencies," promoting the exit of native-born workers and bringing in more Hispanic workers as vacancies were created. One of these areas involved three jobs in the midsection of the conveyor belt and three operators. Shantelle, a quiet Black woman studying psychology at a local community college, worked in "the tape dispenser job." Quinn, a Black man in his twenties, an aspiring hip-hop singer and record-label entrepreneur, worked in the "clamp and screw job," fastening a screw using a hanging screw gun. Bryanna, the third operator in the section, worked in a support capacity, most of the time plugging cables into an assembly and preparing a clamp for fastening to the circuit board. Quinn used the time between cycles to tease Bryanna and joke with the men at the Assembly Table. Outside HiCap, Bryanna was "working on getting [her] cosmetology license," and it showed. She wore colorful wigs and scarfs that some workers admired and others used as a source of teasing and playing. She often sparred verbally with the men at the Motors Table about this and other topics. Despite the teasing, she said, "I don't mind the job because it's easy." Indeed, her job was not as difficult as the other two jobs in her section. The hanging screw gun required many weeks of experience just to develop rudimentary proficiency, and it could also easily twist an operator's arm to the point of injury. It also took several weeks for workers to learn how to use the automated tape dispenser, and even though it required slightly less skill than the screw gun, its effective use also involved the possibility of injury, as workers could not use gloves and the tape peeled the skin off their fingertips, forcing them to stop to apply a bandage. Operators were always also responsible for replacing the rolls of tape to keep the dispenser functioning. They often fell behind when working the job alone. In the process of balancing the line, Darius eliminated Bryana's job and asked Shantelle and Quinn to combine the three jobs. "They ain't paying me to do three jobs," Quinn told the group of supervisors and walked off the job. Marcus asked me to bring Gabriel, a Hispanic worker who had just arrived from Mexico to South Carolina, to replace Quinn. When neither Kyra nor Gabriel could do the three combined jobs, he asked them to try combining two jobs. Kyra stayed on the job for a few more days until Belinda, one of the Hispanic new hires, learned the combined job of the tape dispenser and the clamp. Once Belinda learned the job, Marcus decided that Kyra "was too slow" compared to Gabriel and Belinda and that he wanted to bring in "all Hispanic workers to the section." With the changes he had already made, he was well on his way to meeting that goal.

We can juxtapose the raw and blatant nature of the discriminatory hiring with the indirect, contortionist-like approach that the company took to dismissing employees whom it no longer wanted. An example of one of the strategies to degrade the jobs was to move native-born workers to areas where they had no friends or social relations. I wrote in my field notes,

> Darius told me that Marcus had sent Pontraine (a Black woman) to third shift. He said, "He didn't tell me nothing, he just moved her to third. Pontraine used to do the job Richard is doing now." I told him that she is a good worker. Darius agreed that she was, and he did not understand why Marcus sent her to third shift. I asked what happened to Dora (a Black woman). He stood up straight and looked to a point in the distance. "Marcus also sent her to third shift. That makes three people that he's sent off to third [shift] this week."

The company went to great lengths to get people to quit, but apart from attendance problems, I never saw them fire a single permanent employee. The discrepancy between the way the company hired and fired workers who could question the legality of HiCap's actions forces us to look deeper for an explanation. While the company had secured a few vacancies, the question of how they filled other positions to bring hundreds of unauthorized workers remains open.

Producing Vacancies

As illustrated in the preceding examples, having immigrants available to show what was possible allowed the company to shift the job queue. This shift drove both temporary and permanent workers to leave their jobs and opened more vacancies for the agency to fill with Hispanics, rapidly transforming the demographics of the labor force. To create vacancies for Hispanic workers at the plant without creating the impression of targeting employees by ethnicity or gender, managers routinely and strategically deployed the logic of efficiency and equal treatment, which preemptively dissipated any potential accusations of hiring bias.

When managers veil racialization under the guise of efficiency to create vacancies, they play directly to the popular idea that as long as you are not treated differently, you are not being targeted for discrimination. Using language and practices that appear colorblind, they implement untenable standards by using vulnerable and desperate immigrants to "prove" that the standards can be met. When native-born workers eventually quit from HiCap, they did so knowing that, like Tara and Janine, they hated their jobs. Both "voluntarily" quit their jobs, neither realizing that management manipulated them into doing so. They could not have known that the new standards were, largely, untenable even for the immigrant workers. That the immigrant workers could meet the new standards for some amount of time, and do so without major complaints or resistance, was not proof that the job was tenable; it only showed that that they were willing to try. Ultimately, immigrant workers themselves needed to rotate out of the most difficult jobs, or they, too, would end up injured and unable to work.

These examples illustrate how in exploiting the vulnerabilities of immigrant labor, companies implement untenable standards that produce vacancies for new hires. At HiCap, these standards were not just impossible for Black individuals but were untenable in general, but they resulted in Black workers losing employment opportunities. Essentially, the employer deployed a rhetoric of efficiency to mask exploitation and discrimination. At every chance, it repeated the trope, "If you lose this job, it's because you are not working hard enough." Eventually, even the displaced came to believe that it was true.

4

Shifting the Labor Queue by Race and Gender

"Your first guys for the Front End are waiting to get started," announced Marcus, the Black HiCap floor manager. He pointed to an iron post at the back of the Front End where two Latino men were standing and talking to each other. We approached the two men, and they introduced themselves in Spanish. "My name is Richard. He is Manuel," said the shorter of the two, extending his right hand to greet me in a firm handshake. "Tell them that you are going to be their supervisor," Marcus instructed me in English before walking away. We started getting acquainted, talking in Spanish. Richard looked for ways to place me in his memory. "You look really familiar to me. . . . You didn't come by our trailer with the Jehovah's Witnesses a few nights ago, did you?" I smiled and put him at ease. "No, I think we met a couple of weeks ago at the Ready Hands Agency—the morning after the big ice storm." "Oh, okay, that's good! Now I remember," Richard said flashing his gold-rimmed smile. "I don't speak English, and I've never worked at a factory like this before, but I work hard, really hard," he said looking at me in the eye.

Richard and Manuel are cousins from the Mexican state of Chiapas. Richard is about five feet tall, while Manuel surpasses him by seven inches. Manuel grooms a thin mustache above his upper lip and has a silver rim outlining his front teeth. He carries himself with confidence and talks only if you ask him a question. He rarely smiles, but when he does, he shows only a half smile. His appearance is almost impeccable, wearing clean and well-cared-for jeans, a polo shirt, and white tennis shoes. Richard is more casual in the way he carries himself and in his clothing preferences. He can wear a wool hat or a black "NY" cap with a flat visor facing back. He switches between carpenter jeans and camouflage pants, long shirts with logos and messages that he still does not "know what it means" when you ask. Once he wore a T-shirt that he bought on a Sunday at the flea market with a Confederate flag printed on the front and "I love Dixieland" printed on the back. "The Black guys are staring at my shirt. Is it dirty?" he asked me as we strengthened the wires of an air conditioner in the repair's table. He knew almost nothing about the history of the South, and his innocent question reflected it. He tried hard to fit in with the native-born workers at the plant. Like Richard and Manuel, other undocumented immigrant men in this research were eager to adapt in the way they carried themselves, and, as many of their peers in new immigrant destinations, they wanted to work hard, making the HiCap job a preferred one in their "job queue."

Before joining HiCap, Manuel had worked in a now-defunct textile mill where he learned some English working with Americans on the loading team. His prior experiences and his interest in moving out of the lowest paying and hardest jobs convinced him that he needed to work with native-born workers. "If you can, please place me with English-speaking people so I can continue learning the language," he said, sharing what became a common request from many Hispanic new hires at HiCap and other jobs I encountered in this research. These types of requests, however, quieted down when native-born workers resisted their entry into workplaces organized along Black and white racial lines. Richard and Manuel experienced this unwelcoming reception sooner than most.

As I stood talking to them on their first day at the plant, a heavy wooden pallet crashed down against the concrete floor, just inches behind us. Richard, Manuel, and I all jumped at the noise. Manuel stumbled sideways and tripped on a cardboard box of parts. He grabbed onto a corner of the conveyor and just missed catching his hand on the running conveyor belt. We turned around, and one of the Black men from the Motors Table was walking back to his workstation with a satisfied expression on his face while his friends watched, laughing. Marcus was also watching the scene. He looked at me, concerned, and shook his head from side to side. He then turned to Darius, the Black supervisor at the Front End, and told him that one of his people dropped a wooden pallet on the floor, nearly hitting us. "What can I tell him?" responded Darius, lifting his shoulders and hands up at the same time. Marcus looked at us apologetically and walked away. As the arrival of Latino workers, like Manuel and Richard, became evident in the racialized displacement at HiCap, native-born workers responded to their presence with some veiled, and some not so veiled, forms of intimidation and resistance. The displacement triggered a sense of threat that generated different responses from men and women. Before assigning Richard and Manuel to a job, I walked them to meet Kesha, the Black female supervisor running the assembly line with Darius, and thought to myself, "Welcome to HiCap."

Racialized and Gendered Labor Displacement

Under racial capitalism, racialization and gendered labor turnover in some organizations can steer an outside observer to believe that once employers set their minds to overturning the labor force, they enlist workers' compliance to achieve full demographic change. Research on organizations generally supports the idea that employers exercise control over the labor process and, in the absence of unions or other institutional bargaining forces, coerce supervisors and workers to cooperate in implementing their preferences. While this argument suggests that racialization and gendered managerial mandates can transform the demographics of the workforce wholesale, arguments highlighting the informal power of supervisors and their networks suggest that worker resistance can influence the kind and degree of forced racialized turnover in organizations. Extending arguments about worker response to employer-driven vacancy creation, I ask how the embeddedness of individuals in gendered and racialized social networks influences resistance to displacement and its subsequent influence in the racialization of organizations. I focus on how the introduction of a third group (Latino immigrants) unsettled existing racial and gender dynamics and the power supervisors exercise in displacement.

I use the case of HiCap to illustrate how organizations change from a Black and white to a triracial demographic (Black-white-Latino) when managers introduce undocumented immigrants as a third group in a racialized organizational hierarchy. As shown in chapter 2, at this factory, employers wanted to replace Black and white native-born workers with "enclaves" of Latino immigrant *men*. These shifts, however, failed to align perfectly with employer desires. At the start of this research, the composition of the labor force at the Front End of HiCap had a Black and white biracial composition. That is, 21 percent of the workers were white, and 79 percent were Black. With the exception of the Back End, an isolated section of the plant and production process, there were no Latino workers on first shift at the plant. Two months after I started conducting observations at HiCap, the composition of the labor force had shifted from a Black and white to a triracial composition. Most workers were Black (about 60 percent), while whites and Hispanic immigrants represented 20 percent each.

At the rate of demographic change I saw initially, and based on my observations at other factories, I expected that five months later, when I left the research site, the workforce would be 60 percent Hispanic (male) with about 20 percent Black and close to 20 percent white. When I left the site, however, the company had a composition at odds with my expectations. The company's ethnoracial composition was 90 percent Black and Latino, divided roughly equally between Blacks and Latinos (primarily women), with about 10 percent white. While changes in the temporary workforce were significant, a full third of the permanent factory employees had also left their jobs. In the process, the Front End became 47 percent Hispanic, again, being mostly women. In essence, the composition of the labor force shifted in the direction of Latinos, the category of immigrant workers the company wanted, but away from men and toward women, who were not the preferred group. How did this shift happen?

My main argument is that gender, race, and legality—both as a "mark" and as a bureaucratic barrier—overlap with how workers, supervisors, and upper management relate to employment insecurity. Unlike arguments that view gender in association with the type of work employers sort workers to perform, gender in displacement often works in concert with a complex network of social relations and organizational practices that intersect with race. That is, the primary effect of gender on shop-floor dynamics does not come as one may expect from job-level gender segregation or solely from large-scale discriminatory hiring practices. Rather, the relational intersection of race, gender, and legal status (broadly defined to capture the experiences of Black men and undocumented immigrants) is central in explaining shifts in the demographic composition of the labor force of organizations.

Furthermore, how embedded racially and gender-bounded subgroups are and the extent to which ethnic and gender affinity exists determines the degree of racialization in organizations. Managers adjust their expectations as they come to accept workers (immigrant women) from categories that were not at the top of their labor queue but satisfy their need to control the labor process through racialization. That is, as native-born women left the plant, managers filled those vacancies with undocumented Latinas when they could not secure Latino men. Workers' "job queues," however, intersected with employers' "labor queues."[1] In depressed industries like manufacturing, retaining a job ranks high in workers' preferences, and some workers fight hard to keep their jobs. Workers with limited options, such as Black men who disproportionately bear the burden of criminal records, older workers near retirement, managers without credentials, workers with health dependencies, and undocumented workers find themselves at the juncture of compromising their moral boundaries—harassing and intimidating peers and engaging in racial and gender discrimination—or losing a job.

Refusing to Train as a Form of Native-Born Resistance

Managers, who characterized native-born men as "not wanting to work hard" and identified their work groups as targets for displacement, wanted Latino men. It then follows that, at the start of the displacement, native-born men, the group in direct competition with Latino men, were likely to feel a more heightened sense of threat than women. Furthermore, given that the majority of men were Black, Black men reacted most directly to the threat. The first response occurred at the Motors Table, where native-born Black men sought closure against Latino workers. It was at the Motors Table that workers enjoyed a fair degree of autonomy and stability prior to the displacement. Workers there (John, Carlos, Tyrone, and J.T.) were all good friends with Thomas, the assistant supervisor. In fact, when Thomas was not working as an assistant supervisor, he worked at the Motors Table. The closeness that workers achieved in these workstations resulted from the homogeneous configuration of the group along racial and gender lines.

Key to protecting group boundaries was resisting the introduction of Latino men in their teams. Unfortunately, for the group, during the Lean Manufacturing Initiative (LMI), managers identified the Motors Table as a challenge in their efforts to regain control of the labor force, and they decided to disband the group. The strategy to break the social cohesion of the Black men at the Motors Table involved bringing Ramon, an experienced immigrant worker, from third shift to work on the team of Black men.

Darius agreed to move Ramon to first shift to help train the Latino newcomers. Not everyone agreed. When Darius told Thomas, his assistant supervisor, he was bringing Ramon to the Front End, Thomas opposed it. "No way!" he said immediately. Darius doubled down: "It'd be great if Ramon moves to first shift so that he can train the other guys [referring to the other Latino workers]. They can learn from him because people here don't want to train them," acknowledging that opposition to train the newcomers was a form of native-born resistance. "No way! The guys are not gonna like it." Thomas refused again, concerned about a potential negative reaction from the men at the Motors Table if Ramon made it to their workstation. Darius closed the exchange: "I want to get rid of some baaad apples here. I heard Henry is telling Dave that we haven't done anything we've said we were going to do in LMI," explaining his desire to show management his willingness to cooperate and his genuine seriousness toward work.

In spite of Thomas's refusal, Ramon moved from the night shift to the day shift. Marcus, ignoring his order to Thomas, placed Ramon at the Capacitors Table, with the goal of having him learn all the jobs before bringing other Latinos and displacing the women at the Baseboard Table. Ramon's job involved attaching a ground wire to the baseboards using a screw gun. The wires usually come bent in a U shape trapped inside a plastic sleeve. Without pulling the wires out of the sleeve and straightening them, operators had difficulty attaching them. A seemingly simple motion, the operator screwing the wire to the baseboard had a hard time adding it to an already difficult task. Darius asked Tyrone, one of the Black operators from the Capacitors Table, to straighten the sleeve for Ramon so that he could complete the wire. I wrote in my field notes that I thought that there were no issues, but that was not the case.

I heard Ramon yelling my name and found him frantically chasing baseboards, trying to attach a screw in missed units. I hurried to where he was, thinking he was hurt. "Laura! I am falling behind, and it's not my fault!" Ramon cleaned a few drops of sweat from his forehead with the side of his arm, still chasing units. "The Black guy [Tyrone] doesn't want to straighten the wires for me. I asked him to do it, and he got mad and is dropping the baseboards, as he wants to hurt me. He said, 'You didn't ask nicely.' I don't know what he wants me to do. Is his job! He is leaving the white sleeve all crooked. This is making me fall behind! I have to spend time straightening the wires, and I now am falling behind!"

"Okay, let me ask Tyrone to help you straighten the wires." Tyrone looked at me, dropped a baseboard loudly, straightened the wires with force, and gave us both a defiant look. He pulled the wires from a couple of more sleeves, still dropping them loudly on the conveyor belt, signaling that he was going to do it but not willingly. Ramon yelled my name again.

"Laura! He is doing it again! Once you left, he did it again. He is giving me that evil look and leaving the wires tangled. I don't want Marcus to fire me because of him!" Later that day, he talked to me more calmly: "Can you move me to a different job?" he asked. "I can't work with Tyrone. He always leaves me to do more work. I have to do more than he does. My hand is tingling. Look! It's trembling [he showed me a shaky right hand] from pushing the capacitors because he doesn't want to do that. My thumb is hurting. I think what's going on is that the *moyos* [Black people] are trying to make me fall behind so that I don't take their jobs."

Ramon repeated a common perception that Latinos had that Black people opposed their training because they feared replacement. Marcus had observed the interaction and moved Ramon to the Motors Table without talking to anyone about it. He asked him to rotate with Carlos, a Black operator in his early twenties. Three days later, during the morning break, Ramon told me that the workers at the Motors Table were making his life miserable. "They don't want me here. They are making fun of me," he added.

Before talking to Marcus about it, I went to the Motors Table to observe how the native-born men worked with Ramon, but I saw everyone working and behaving with civility. Ramon placed the starters on the motors, then pulled the plugs out and placed the screws on one of the rows of motors on the table. J.T. unloaded the motors from the crate, placed the starters and the screws on the next row. John loaded them, and Carlos used the gun to screw them to the baseboard. They worked in a coordinated fashion. I did not see any hazing or mocking. After an hour observing the men work, however, Ramon moved to the more difficult job of screwing the motors. Suddenly, his jaw tightened, and his face turned red in anger when one of the men "accidentally" pushed him while reaching for the screw gun. With his head low as he was loading a motor before adding the screw, Ramon spoke to me in Spanish.

"They are not going to say or do anything while you are here. They'll start talking after you walk away. The skinny *moreno* is going to start making fun of me."

"What are they doing to upset you?" I asked in Spanish, trying to help but knowing that Marcus would want something more concrete to advocate for him with Darius.

"They are saying that I am slow, that I need to hurry up, that I am doing it wrong, and I don't know what else. . . . I don't understand what else they're saying. . . . After the tall big tall *moreno* [J.T.] says these things to me, he laughs with the other two. They don't let me do my work."

I spoke to Ramon for several minutes, and since he stopped working, J.T. signaled Thomas to come to their workstation.

"What's up?" Thomas asked.

"This guy is a baby, he has an attitude!" J.T. said preemptively.

"Ramon is having some problems with Carlos and J.T.," I defended Ramon.

"They are telling me that he has an attitude," Thomas said, shaking his head.

"They are making fun of him and getting upset because he is falling behind! Who should we believe?" I responded, aggravated, and fell into the pattern that other bilingual supervisors described, advocating for Latino workers facing intimidation.

Deferring confrontation with the men at the Motors Table, Darius asked me to persuade them to train Ramon. When I asked Carlos to show Ramon how they load the motors, he responded condescendingly: "Yes, madam," sucking a lollipop, but he walked away without training Ramon. Ramon was right. The native-born men did not want the Latinos on the shop floor, and resisting their training was their way of showing it. Their opposition continued in both overt and subtler forms of resistance.

The men at the Motors Table wanted to prove managers wrong about their belief that Latino workers were better than their Black counterparts. Manuel was the second Latino worker, after Ramon, whom the Black men at the Motors Table rejected. At Marcus's request, I assigned Manuel, one of the Mexican men introduced earlier, to the Motors Table. His experiences with the men at the table were similar to Ramon's. "They don't help me. They left me on my own loading motors. The *moyos* were right there, but they were not helping me. They're a bunch of slackers, and the supervisors don't tell them anything. They wait until we fall be-hind and gap the line before they say, 'Go help him.'" As Manuel noted, the native-born men resisted him.

What these cases illustrate is how, in racialized displacement, the native-born opposed cooperating with management in the training and integration of Latinos and pushed managers' preferred workers out of the organization. Additionally, acts of resistance to managerial direc-tives result in Latinos' understanding of Black men as "lazy," which did not help in blurring the boundaries of distinction between Black men and Latinos. Manuel and Ramon believed that the men were not help-ing them in part because they were afraid of losing their jobs. Yet, they, and many others, associated a lack of cooperation with Blacks having an inferior work ethic. Consequently, the Latinos felt that they were more deserving of higher spots in the labor queue. More generally, Latino immigrants identify the sense of threat that the Black men experience. Casting aside any possible structural explanation, however, they inter-pret their reactions as data supporting a racial stereotype. After several days of contentious exchanges with the Black men, Ramon quit the job.

It is possible that the resistance that native-born men demonstrated with the arrival of Latino men illustrates a general response to newcom-ers, independent of racialization. The cases of Freddie and the team at the Motors Table, however, indicates a racialized response. In contrast to Ramon's treatment, when Marcus assigned Freddie, a young Black man, to the Motors Table to replace Ramon, the men gave him the sim-plest task. They asked him to pull plugs off, while Carlos, John, Tyrone, and J.T. did the rest. When Freddie moved to mounting motors, Carlos added the screw to attach the motors to the baseboard. Even more in-formative was finding that after the trouble the men created for Ramon for not removing the trapped wires before mounting the motors, Fred-die began mounting motors on top of the wires without even making an effort to move the wires. After about ten baseboards went down the line with wires pressed under the motors' legs, Marcus asked the supervisors to fix the problem in the defective units. Thomas came to the Motors Table to fix the problem and was working next to where I was standing. Without even the slightest complaint, he helped Freddie by straightening the wire harness from under the motors so the loading met engineering requirements. It was clear that the men mounting the motors on first shift did not use a different technique than the men on third shift, where Ramon was coming from. Every operator needed help straightening the harness. The case against Ramon was purely a pretext aimed only at driving him away from this work group or the first shift entirely. The issue that the men at the table had was not about competence; it was clearly about race-based boundaries.

Sabotaging the Work of the Latino Men

Latinos, as a group, share the perception that companies pay them less than the native-born and work them more. "We are the ones always working hard, and the *morenos* are always talking," one immigrant worker noted. In the view of Latinos, managers and supervisors discriminate against them when they assign them to the worst jobs. Although I did document instances at other sites where I worked in which employers pay Latino immigrants less than the native-born, HiCap paid all temps the same wages. Thus, the data provide no evidence of wage discrimination among temporary workers at this plant. This is not the case, however, if we factor in the level of effort immigrants invested in these jobs vis-à-vis the native-born for the same wages. What I saw was native-born resistance to doing more work without increased pay, which played into immigrants' perception that managers extract more labor from them than from the native-born. Native-born men engaged in behaviors that support these characterizations as they fought to protect in-group members from the threat of displacement. Consider the situation with J.T., a Black man about fifty years of age, working at the Motors Table at the Front End. J.T. was in charge of taking off the plugs on the motors and adding the three screws inside the holes in the motors' legs, the job assigned to Ramon earlier, when he started to fall behind.

"Gimme a screw!" J.T. yelled as he moved down the line trying to catch up. "Sam! Stop the line!"

The line stopped and then restarted. A few seconds later, the same drill.

"Screw! Gimme a screw!" J.T. yelled and extended his hand to Tyrone, who took a couple of seconds to give him the missing screw.

"Sam! Stop the line!" J.T. yelled again.

Shortly thereafter, J.T. asked Sam to stop the line a third time because he was falling behind. Thomas stood up from the other side of the line and yelled.

"J.T., whatcha doin', man?!" He was frowning and had his upset look. J.T. started yelling at him about him coming to do this job for a change. The line went on, and J.T. kept missing screws until he stopped chasing units.

"I ain't taking anyone without screws no more. I am here to make a living. I ain't killing myself for nobody."

J.T. proceeded to focus on screwing down the motors and let all the motors without screws go down the line. Darius came and started backing up J.T. with a screw gun. He kept looking down at the screws, the gun, and the motors but did not say anything. We moved on to a different model, and I moved away from the Motors Table. When I came back, I noticed that Thomas was at the Motors Table. He had taken J.T.'s job, and J.T. went to build motor subassemblies to "cool off." What surprised me in all this exchange was that they never actually said anything to J.T. They moved him away from the job so he could "cool off." Darius and Thomas showed concern that I had witnessed J.T.'s resistance to comply, which, had it been Latino workers, would have engaged Marcus in writing up the worker or, if a temp, terminating the worker. Furthermore, when the men at the table asked Marcus to remove Ramon and Manuel, J.T. had nothing but negative comments about the Latino men. "He has an attitude. Take him out of here! He's like a baby," he told me. When I asked him to train Manuel, he said, "He's sloooow! I need someone with muscles here. Bring men that can do this job. These are babies." Rejection and teasing, in this case, served to draw a bright boundary around Latino men and pushed them out of the jobs.

In displacement, driving the preferred group to make mistakes constitutes a dominant form of resistance. At HiCap, three months into the displacement, the native-born men managed to push out more than twelve Latinos assigned to the Front End. Richard was the exception.

But even though Richard was acceptable to his Black coworkers, the native-born men continued to sabotage Latino men to prevent managers from using undocumented immigrants as replacements. As noted earlier, when asked to train Latinos, the native-born workers often drove them to make mistakes, challenging the managerial narrative of immigrants as the ideal workers. Mistakes resulted in "gaps on the line," which meant losses of thousands of dollars for the plant and shattered the perception that immigrants were superior workers to Blacks. One day, Tyrone, a Black worker, refused to work on a rotation at the Dust Pan Station. Richard, on his own and on a job designed for two men, was constantly missing screws, and the dust pans fell from the units. As they fell, the line had to stop, causing multiple gaps. The men at the Motors Table made fun of Richard. I asked them to stop. An hour later, Richard yelled my name, calling me to his workstation. I found him frustrated, frantically struggling with the Makita gun. "Laura, there are gaps because those guys [the Black guys] switched the new screwdriver bits for worn-out bits when I went on break. . . . They want me to have problems. I asked Darius for new bits, but he just gave me more worn-out bits."

When I talked to Darius about Richard's observation, he dismissed the immigrant worker. "I have no idea what he is talking about," he responded. At the end of the day, Marcus asked me to bring Richard to quality control to show him all the units pulled from the assembly line with screws missing. He told Richard that he would not tolerate more mistakes. I changed the bits for him; but every time he left his station, he returned to find worn-out bits in his gun, and this caused him to miss more screws. After two days with repeated gaps on the assembly line because of missing screws on the dust pans, Marcus came to talk to me, infuriated. "I am not sure 'the project' is working," he told me and asked that I stop "ordering Mexican heavy lifters until we could see if things got better" with my team members. The native-born men created situations like these to push Latinos out and ultimately led to the displacement not going exactly as management had expected.

Native-Born Women Resist Latinas

> ROSA: We are back to being all women, almost all Hispanics. The
> women are winning. . . . When Wendy and I arrived, there were only
> men. Wendy was the first one, I was the second one, and now we
> are only women. Well, with Richard, *un bendito entre las mujeres* [a
> blessing among the women]. We women showed them that we can
> do it. At first, we didn't like working here because we didn't have any-
> one to talk to. Not even Wendy and I talked to one another because
> she was in one corner and I was on the opposite side of the line.
> MARIELA: But you speak some English. You could have talked to
> people.
> ROSA: Yes, but when you are new in a job, it's embarrassing to arrive
> and start talking with people because nobody wants to talk to you.
> The women didn't want us here, but now people talk to us, we play
> games. We are even liking this job.

Rosa and Mariela, two of the first Latinas arriving at HiCap, here describe how the women incorporated as the Latino men left the plant. Rosa's allusion to a welcoming reception, however, refers to the Native-born men's response, rather than a unified native-born reception. My data show little indication that the native-born women warmed up to their Latina counterparts. In part, this was the case because removing the female supervisor in a situation of gendered authority relations resulted in an increasing number of vacancies that the native-born women left for immigrant women to occupy. This outcome, however, emerged only after a series of efforts on the part of native-born women to protect their jobs. As native-born men felt a racialized sense of threat and "pushed" the Latino men out, native-born women experienced a gendered sense of threat when the Latinas arrived. The native-born women expressed their resistance to the Latinas in multiple ways, including intentional gapping, resistance to training newcomers, and boycotting the efforts of bilingual supervisors.

Racialized and gendered displacement processes have the potential to work against management desires not only with respect to labor but also in relation to productivity. In particular, displacement triggers a sense of threat from targeted groups, which generates reactive behaviors that can translate into production loses. At HiCap, "gaps on the line" represented successful efforts at bottom-up resistance.

The company was running copper tops, a simple model of air conditioners produced by the company, when I saw some gaps on the line in the segment between the Baseboard Table and the Transfer Corner. I put my gloves on and went to help Rosa, the Mexican worker at the Transfer Corner. Rosa was running nonstop to pick up baseboards and close the gap. She was upset because the women at the Baseboard Table were making her work harder. Native-born women, Black and white, joined forces to make the Latinas fail. These efforts to resist heightened racialized Latino views of Blacks and fragmented boundaries along gender lines. Rosa told me,

> I just realized that those women are gapping the line intentionally. They have been doing it all morning. I know they are doing it to give me extra work because when I was running to close the gap and transfer the baseboards, I caught *la gorda prieta* [the fat Black woman] laughing with *la flaca prieta* [the skinny Black woman] every time they saw me running to get the baseboards at the beginning of the line. This last time when they did it, I stopped and stared at them, and they stopped laughing. I know they are doing it intentionally because they stopped laughing when I looked them straight in the eye.

Given that employers consider that undocumented immigrants work harder than the native-born, women at the Baseboard Table were in a vulnerable position, and the displacement affected them disproportionately. As the displacement was ongoing, Darius placed Mariela and Barbara, two Latinas, at the Baseboard Table for training. He replaced Janine, the cheerful Black operator, with Rosa, a bilingual Latina. Riley, a white woman, eventually left her job to Lola, and Darius assigned Rosa and Norma to a rotation at the Platform Station to replace Sandrine and Nana. As management assigned the Latinas to jobs that native-born women had held, the remaining native-born women—typically permanent plant employees—resisted. Similar to the strategies deployed by native-born men, native-born women resisted by creating gaps on the line and setting Latinas up to fail, seeking to tarnish the image of immigrants as ideal workers.

Immigrant women, however, often tired of workshop abuses. As in the case of Rosa, at times they broke their self-imposed rule of ignoring native-born aggression to avoid trouble. Instead, they subtly confronted the native-born using nonverbal harassment such as staring at each other in a sustained and intense manner—what some scholars have described as the "hate stare."[2] Exchanges between the native-born and immigrants often led to hate-stare matches, with the native-born wanting to intimidate Latinas and the Latinas trying to fight the women's efforts to undermine them. When immigrant workers reported the intentional gapping, bilingual supervisors often confronted the native-born. In the case just mentioned, I spoke to the native-born women at the Baseboard Table, but the workers denied having anything to do with gapping the line. To successfully resist, native-born workers surreptitiously sabotaged production or derailed the work of the immigrant replacement workers. Black workers with seniority and few alternatives felt threatened. Consequently, they engaged in impression management to give the appearance that they were cooperative and hardworking, two traits managers valued and two conditions that kept some native-born workers employed.

Consider another example. Five months into the displacement, Darius was standing next to the Baseboard Table talking to Therese. He asked me to join him as he moved forward with assigning Latinas in jobs that native-born women had. The displacement drove a man like Darius to make decisions that compromised his moral boundaries and that he did not take lightly. Since he defined himself as someone who "didn't like talking," he let his body speak for him. In talking to the women at the Baseboard Table, he bounced on his feet, shifting his weight from side to side. Then he took his hand to his chin, and in his characteristic mood of discomfort with an impending decision, he moved his mouth from side to side and opened his eyes widely while he looked in the distance at Brenda and Lola, two new Latina workers. He was standing next to Therese.

"Do any of the ladies back there speak any English?" he asked me, anticipating communication with the women at the Baseboard Table to be an issue if he assigned only one of the Latinas there.

"I am not sure, but I can ask," I answered.

Therese rolled her eyes before pulling a baseboard to screw a ground wire.

"I want one of them to do the rotation at the table," Darius said hesitantly, knowing that he risked raising the ire of the native-born women but knowing that, if the Latinas survived, he could give managers immigrant workers and protect his male friends in the process. Viewed from this perspective, workers were a commodity to be traded, and managers and supervisors often framed them as such.

"What you need is to have Mariela train here and have the other lady do the gun. Mariela is already trained," Therese said, singling out the quietest and most conflict averse of the Latinas on the shop floor.

Mariela was a single mother still paying her border-crossing financial and social debts, and she could not afford her emotions getting in the way of her employment. She was in the process of moving with her two young children from a rental trailer home—located in one of Jessamine's worst neighborhoods—into an apartment. She was saving to purchase a car, as she depended on *raiteras* (i.e., coethnic transportation before Uber and Lyft) for transportation to jobs and services. The conflict-averse gendered behaviors that Mariela displayed were situational but informed Therese's perception and recommendation. Darius still hesitated because, in his words, Mariela was a "good worker and wanted to avoid the women pushing her out if he assigned her to their team." Rather than asking the women at the Baseboard Table to train the new Latinas, Darius asked me to have Mariela, who indeed had trained at the Baseboard Table, train Lola, a single mother from the Mexican state of Guerrero, at the screw gun.

Confident in Mariela's skills, I left Mariela training Lola and went to do some translations at an office inside the plant. The company often asked me to interpret for Latino workers when their bilingual supervisors were absent in other sections or sent me to do translations. The day Mariela trained Lola was one of the days the company pulled me into the office to do extra work. When I returned to the shop floor, Sarah, a white supervisor, quickly searched me out.

"Something bad happened when you were not here."

"Is anyone injured?" was my first reaction.

"No, but close. Therese almost hit Lola and yelled at your ladies. You gotta go talk to them."

Everyone on the shop floor had a somber and quiet look, the kind of look that comes at the end of a crisis. The Latinas looked emotionally bruised. I found Lola back at the Tape Station rather than at the Base-board Table and Mariela next to her. Lola's face was red, and her eyes swollen as if she had cried all morning. I asked if she was okay.

> I'm enraged! The women were gapping the line intentionally! I had to stop to tape my fingers because I had blisters, and I missed the little wire because my fingers were hurting. They said they couldn't keep going be-cause I missed the wires. Therese yelled at me, cursing, and told me rude things in English. We both said bad words. I don't want to repeat them, but we both were at it for a few minutes, and then she took one of the baseboards and sent it flying, trying to hit me in the head, and you know how those things can hurt you because they are sharp. She missed me and took another one. I got scared. I started crying, and I yelled, "Here is your job! I don't care if I get fired!" I don't remember what happened after that or what she said, but I went to grab my lunch bag and my jacket, and then Darius was calling me. "Lola, don't leave. I need to talk to you!"

According to Lola, and everyone else who witnessed the incident, Therese started cursing at Lola when she missed the assembly. Darius never mentioned the issue, but others talked about it for a few days. I learned that Marcus pulled Therese and Lola aside and asked both to be nice to each other. While managers intervened to quash the con-flict, the incident illustrates acts of violence (e.g., trying to hit or hitting workers with assembly parts) that occurred on several occasions toward Latino immigrants. As noted earlier, displacement processes disrupt em-ployment stability and can drive workers with fewer options to uncivil behaviors, with implications for gender and race relations. When I in-terviewed Lola, and we talked about the incident outside the shop floor, she labeled it as one of the worst experiences she had with white workers (in the context of race relations) and at work.

> LOLA: Therese wanted to hit me, to hurt me! Then she said that I started it. How would I be the one that started things? I didn't speak English. Even if I did speak English, I would not have said all the bad things she said I said to her because I knew she could report me to the supervisor. Marcus, or whatever his name was, he was fair. He told me that if I did anything to her, that they were going to fire me

and that if she said anything to me, that they were going to fire her. This woman had more time with the company, and she is American, but he treated us fairly. He didn't fire me.

LAURA: What do you mean?

LOLA: After all that, they were nice to us. They saw they were not gonna get away treating us badly. . . . We knew the women didn't like us there. They often said bad things about Hispanics. "Pinchis Hispanics," "motherfucker," and a bunch of other insults. They just didn't do it in front of the supervisors. . . . They didn't want us to learn their jobs because they knew that if they trained us, they were going to lose their jobs. They didn't want to train us because they are racists.

Lola's response speaks to the complexity that the displacement introduced into the relationship between the native-born and immigrant women. The native-born women were willing to make concessions with Latinas who, for structural reasons, fit the submissive stereotype in some workers' imagination. Lola challenged the stereotype and resisted the women's efforts to intimidate her. In situations where immigrants rank higher in employers' labor queues than native-born workers do, as in the case of HiCap, the immigrant workers remained employed, and immigrants interpreted the permanence as an act of fairness. While Therese stayed because her ill husband relied on her health benefits, Lena and Rhonda left. Furthermore, given that the Latina immigrants ranked higher in the labor queue than native-born women did, even the more experienced permanent workers relied on the protection of supervisors and managers, which the women on the Baseboard Table no longer had.

"Doing Gender" and Resisting Displacement

It is easy to associate the image of "labor femininity"—well-dressed, heeled, and made-up women in climate-controlled offices—and women's managerial aspirations with white-collar occupations. Yet gendered labor images also prevail in other organizational contexts. In manufacturing jobs, women also "do" gender—the process of constructing and reaffirming sex categories.[3] Despite the high temperatures, the demand to be on their feet for nearly eight hours straight, the sped-up assembly lines that end up making any worker sweat, women (and men) "play the game" of binary gendered labor. The women in my study adopted feminine props such as wearing makeup, sophisticated hairdos, and long, sparkling nails to assert their identities. Some tanned their bodies, others read the Bible, and many brought and shared the food they cooked at home for friends and colleagues at work. They wore perfume and feminine clothing and shared stories and pictures of their children or pets with one another. In engaging in these practices, women constructed identities that reaffirmed their sense of self and challenged managerial control. Managers wanted them exclusively focused on work, all eight hours of it, and, as an aside, "not pregnant." Women opposed it, maintaining a sense of who they were.

Men, too, entered the stage of the workplace wearing masculine-gendered selves. In a contemporary version of what men ought to be, they stepped onto the shop floor showing their muscles in tight, sleeveless shirts when weather allowed for it. They wore attractive golden jewelry on their necks, diamond-like crystals in their ears, and turned-around baseball caps on their heads. They teased women and caused trouble, generally behaving like the "lads" the theorist Paul Willis describes in *Learning to Labor: How Working Class Kids Get Working Class Jobs*.[4] Like the women, the men fought to protect their selves from management's efforts to erase their identities.

In the nearly two years I observed the racialization of workplaces in the South, I found that we cannot study shifts along racial lines without taking into consideration how workers "do gender" when their jobs are at stake. To begin, workers default to gendered constructions in part because the institutional environment of the shop floor pushes for homogeneity, challenging the gendered binary of labor femininity and labor masculinity. In matters of self-presentation, some companies require that women and men wear steel-toe shoes; leather holsters hanging from their hips to keep their tools; personal protective equipment (PPE) including safety glasses, shields, and masks; ear protection; hair nets; uniforms or smocks; gloves; and Kevlar sleeves to protect their arms from burns and cuts. Most low-wage, exploitative, jobs deprive workers of having or using artifacts (e.g., a purse, a phone, a computer) that symbolically ground workers with their societal identities while at work. In their place, companies introduce artifacts that symbolize a productive woman or man rather than a person. For example, in some cases, companies give men and women a large rolling toolbox—a home away from home to be dotted with pictures—and gadgets and tools. While it is true that women feel empowered when entering jobs that men have traditionally occupied and, as a result, embody the productive self of managerial dreams, the industrial environment removes many of the key symbols of gendered representations.

Industrial jobs homogenize men and women with uniforms and PPE and tools. Thus, workers make every attempt to maintain a sense of who they are with their own clothing, makeup, perfume, and jewelry, and in their efforts to resist managerial control, they reproduce gender. Furthermore, managerial efforts to control labor contribute to the emergence of work subcultures that pattern the gendering act. In efforts to resist boredom, workers play games or engage in pastimes. Through these practices, and ingrained gender socialization, men exercise dominant behaviors such as the act of starting and/or choosing the game to play or verbally sparring, teasing, and touching women. Consequently, managerial strategies that unsettle the social organization of work—such is the case of displacement—activate gendered behaviors.

As I observed men's and women's behaviors under the threat of losing their jobs, I came to realize that displacement influences the construction of "gendered labor" and workers' decisions related to vacancy creation. In adding a new category of workers, Latina/o workers, employers unsettled the taken-for-granted social constructions of being a woman or a man in the US workplace. This is particularly the case when displacement involves a transition from a biracial to a triracial system of stratification involving an immigrant group. In these cases, the presence of a new group and its own gendered practices can unsettle the preexisting relationships between men and women. At HiCap, the arrival of Latino immigrants highlighted distinctions in gendered behaviors involving a heightened sense of threat for women and the opposite for native-born men. The key processes at play here are bottom-up claims for equal treatment and symbolic boundary making fueled by attraction and linguistic appropriation.

A Hot Chili Pepper: Attraction and Racialized Boundary Making

"What's that girl's name?" J.T. asked me, pointing to a dark-skinned, petite woman from southern Mexico on a March morning at HiCap. Workers at the Front End were building a new model, and managers were moving forward with the displacement. I was not sure where J.T. was going with that question. Janine was standing next to me preparing the wires for a motor that J.T. was about to mount.

"Which girl?" I asked, although I imagined he was asking about Hyacinth, since her arrival caused more excitement on the floor than the announcement of the week off that management mandated three days before.

"He wants to know about the one that looks Black, the one with the curly hair," Janine intervened eagerly with the happy tone that characterized her voice when things were going well for her, subtlety commenting on the interest Black men had shown toward the Mexican new hire.

"That's Hyacinth," I responded.

"Ah, Hyacinth, that's a pretty name," J.T. answered, repeating her name without effort. "It doesn't sound Mexican. Ain't that a flower?" he asked, turning his head upward and missing loading a motor on a baseboard. I avoided telling him the story behind the name, fearing that Janine and others would tease her.

"He thinks she is a hot chili pepper," Janine said musically, making everyone smile as she danced to the rhythm of some imaginary gospel song. "He thinks she is a hot chili pepper," she sang, laughing and dancing, moving her arms between assemblies but keeping pace with the conveyor belt.

"I said what?!" J.T. asked, raising his voice over the honking of a forklift that was dropping motors near the assembly line. "A HOT CHILI PEPPER," Janine shouted this time, enunciating each word clearly. J.T. gave her a half smile, turned his head up and to the side, and dismissed her comment.

Hyacinth represented not only a preferred worker in the employers' queue but also a preferred coworker in the native-born men's job queue. In displacement terms, native-born men acted favorably toward and sought to include Latinas in permanent jobs, Latinas whom they found nonthreatening. Low levels of threat contributed to more fluid symbolic boundaries between native-born men and Latina women than between native-born men and Latino men and more fluid than between native-born men and native-born women. Attraction, in particular, was a tool of inclusion that played a role in the gendered nature of displacement.

Managers wanted to replace native-born workers with immigrant men, who were both difficult to find and difficult to retain. In place of the men, the company introduced Latina immigrants. Although native-born men antagonized the Latinos, pushing some of them out, they achieved a truce with the Latinas. How did this happen? My data indicate that attraction blurred group boundaries and contributed to the growing numbers of Latina women in the organization. Importantly, the vacancies that the Latina women filled were created by the departure of native-born women who had been working at the plant for many years.

After Latino men left the shop floor and the temp agency filled their position with Latinas, the sense of threat that native-born men experienced with the arrival of Latino men lowered. The men showed little objection to Latinas. In fact, they moved from displaying antagonism toward the Latino men to expressing attraction toward the Latina operators. Attraction involved personal closeness and a blurring of boundaries along racial and gender lines.

I documented many instances in which native-born men behaved in unique ways toward Latinas and asked personal questions about them that they never asked about the Latino men. Some of the operators asked the supervisors to place them in jobs near the Latinas so they could "talk"—using body language and some Spanish words—and play games with them. Others asked me to translate declarations of romantic interest and invitations to go out. Questions ranged from asking women about their marital status (most Latinas wore no wedding bands, prompting the men to inquire about their availability) to whether they like going to parties or drinking. Native-born men acted in many different ways, but for many, their ethnoracial attraction drove their interactions with Latina workers and fed into conflicts with native-born women. For example, on one occasion, Darius stood around looking at the Hispanic faces growing visible in the Front End. When his eyes found Rosa and Norma, who chatted affably while at work at the Transfer Corner, he wondered incredulously, "Are they all Hispanic? . . . I mean, . . . is Rosa, is she also . . . Hispanic?" Darius asked me.

"Yes, they are, . . . she is," I responded.

"No?!? Really?? Is Norma . . . Hispanic too?

"Yes, she is."

"You're kidding. Are they all Mexican? Do they speak other languages in Mexico? . . . I mean Spanish. . . . Do they also speak . . . Mexican?" Darius asked me hesitantly, and, like others at HiCap and the different plants I observed, he wondered if Mexican and Spanish were the same language.

"I thought Rosa was Colombian, . . . and I thought Norma was . . . from some other place like that. They look, . . . I don't know. . . . I didn't think they were Hispanic. Barbara and Hyacinth, they look like . . . Black."

Inquiring about ethnic origins might suggest that racialized physical characteristics were the basis for the attraction and subsequent boundary making. While I must admit that when I saw the men's response to Hyacinth and Barbara, another dark-skinned woman from El Salvador, I initially believed that the Black men were mostly attracted to the women because some of them, in their words, "looked Black." A closer examination of my data, however, drove me to look for other explanations. Rosa, for example, had light skin and light-brown eyes. She colored her hair with honey highlights, making her skin look even lighter. Norma's skin tone was even lighter than Rosa's but close to Mariela's. Norma had intensely black hair, the same color of her eyes, and often talked about her French and Spanish roots. Hyacinth and Barbara shared that their parents were "dark" skinned, and Rosa and Norma teased them for, in their words, being "*prietitas, prietitas* [really dark] like the Black women at the plant." The range of skin tones among the Latinas and the interest of native-born men (Black and white) in them, regardless of skin tone, suggests ruling out attraction as based solely on perceived Afro-descent.

The attraction leading the native-born men to view the Latinas as complements rather than competitors, my observations suggest, involved a degree of emotional affect and an interest in a relationship beyond that of coworkers. Consider the following example.

A week after Norma's arrival to HiCap, Norma and Rosa were laughing quietly and chatting while we were on copper tops—the simplest units. They were talking about the several men interested in going out with the Latinas.

"He wants to talk to me in the cafeteria," Norma said about Terry, the white loader.

"Do you have many admirers?" Rosa asked her, and they both chuckled.

"Some men I met here want to see me and talk to me. I guess I do," she responded.

"Are they Hispanic?" Rosa inquired with curiosity, knowing that Norma favored white Americans.

"No, why do you think that? They are American!"

"Are they Black? Because the Blacks were flirting with Wendy and me all day yesterday," Rosa noted.

"No, no, not Blacks!" Norma said and paused for a minute. "I only go out with Americans. I didn't think Black men were interested in Hispanics. . . . Are they?" she said pensively.

Norma, like most Latinas, was surprised to find Black men showing interest in them, particularly in the context of the tense relationships they had with Black women. The answer to Norma's question came several days later when Darius volunteered to help her at the Loading Corner. He stood behind her, covering her petite figure with his tall body and casting a single shadow on the floor. Not realizing that I was nearby helping Lola, Darius was openly flirting with Norma, talking softly to her about her hair, using simple linguistic constructions for her to understand.

"How long is your hair?" he asked.

"Long," she responded, using some of the words she knew in English. She proceeded to touch the bun holding her hair and then her lower back.

"Can I see it? . . . Please?" Darius asked and moved to the side to let Norma show him her hair. She took the pin holding her hair in a bun, and her hair cascaded down her back. She moved her head side to side to show her hair.

"What's she doing? Does she think she's in a shampoo commercial?" Lola murmured in my ear waiting to see if they ever noticed us watching them.

"Nice," Darius said as Norma moved her black, long, curly hair, and then he touched the end of her hair. Norma rapidly moved away and noticed that Lola and I were standing nearby looking at them. When she saw us, she quickly pinned her hair back up in a bun.

"I couldn't rearrange my hair back with the gloves, so I had to redo it," Norma said, embarrassed and trying to justify what we had just seen.

While skin color might have played a role in Hyacinth's case, the interest that Darius and Thomas, two Black men, had in Norma, Rosa, and Mariela, the women with the lightest skin color, points to other factors explaining the attraction.

Gender stereotypes carried weight in the attraction that the native-born men showed toward the Latinas and in the fluidity of their boundaries with members of this group. Workers and managers generally stereotyped Latinas as acquiescent and blissful, "always smiling." Drake, a white operator, once said, "I need their smile to make me get through the day." Another man said, "Mexican women [the blanket term used for Latinas] don't complain." A third noted, "Spanish girls are nice and are always smiling, not like American women." As these examples illustrate, native-born workers deployed stereotypes to understand how race and gender intersected, and supervisors and managers contributed to their construction. When I asked Sarah, the white supervisor, if the company hired Hispanics because they thought they were more productive, she deployed racialized and gendered stereotypes of Latino men and women as acquiescent and submissive.

> No, it's not because they are more productive. It's because of attendance, because they come to work every day. Mexican men do what you ask them to do. They work hard, and they don't complain. They focus on their work. Mexican women are . . . [she paused] different from American women. American women are foul-mouthed. I shouldn't say "American women." I wasn't brought up like that. I should say southern, southern women are bad-mouthed. Mexican women are different. . . . They don't speak up, . . . and even if they say something, the supervisors don't care because they don't understand them.

Although Sarah ties the stereotype of Latino submissiveness to nonromantic attraction, the quote captures a generalized notion that Latinas "are different" from American women. In classifying the women in the factory as "southern," Sarah also engages in a process of "othering." Othering in the context of queuing processes allows workers to evaluate worth vis-à-vis a reference group. In Sarah's view and that of other white managers, "Black southern" women were "foul-mouthed," an attribute they considered objectionable because it challenged gendered notions of femininity. Thus, the welcoming behaviors expressed toward the Latinas and their growing numbers on the shop floor, my analysis suggests, resulted from the "acquiescent" stereotype vis-à-vis the "rowdy" that a process of "othering" created.

The romantic attraction that the native-born men expressed toward the Latinas involved similar patterns of interaction associated with "otherness." Native-born men contrasted the Latinas' behaviors to those of the native-born women. Native-born women were the group that complained about the teasing and harassing and responded to them, shouting, "He aggravates me" or "Shut up! Shut up! You think that you are big dog, but you ain't." Theoretically, the contentious reaction derives from the introduction of a new group of workers in a dyadic system of social relations that creates cleavages in the dyad, common in "third element" types of relationships.[5] However, from the perspective of the native-born men, the Latinas did not challenge them but rather made their work and their lives easier. Acquiescence, in this sense, led them to prefer Latinas and blur outgroup boundaries. Still, the hurtful stereotype of "domesticated women" obscures gendered and racialized behaviors grounded in a sense of fear and vulnerability that is triggered in displacement situations.

Attraction influenced displacement through protective measures showing men's dominance. For example, the native-born men repeatedly used protective behaviors to insulate Latinas from excessive demands. During the LMI, when the company implemented the 2-for-1 and 3-for-1 program, the men overtly and paternalistically challenged the supervisors when they asked the Hispanic women to do more than they thought was reasonable. On several occasions, masculine chants of "You're killing them!" resounded from the Motors Table as Black men took a protective stance and resisted the exploitation of Latina women. Conversely, native-born men were silent when the company implemented the 3-for-1 initiative with native-born women at the Baseboard Table and the Transfer Corner, both of which were visible from the same Motors Table, the all-men station with the most power on the shop floor.

Attraction and Blurring Boundaries through Language

Aside from the protective strategies that native-born men deployed to keep immigrant Latinas working and weaken native-born women's power, symbolic processes supported the truce. As noted earlier, native-born men showed their resistance to displacement through flirting, but they also bridged the social distance that separated them from Latinas using linguistic closure. Some of the men gained women's trust via efforts to speak Spanish. HiCap workers, in general, used the expression "I took Spanish in . . ." high school or college. Thus, Spanish served both as a bridging and as a control strategy in native-born men's efforts to interact with Latinas. Four months into the displacement and with Latinas having now replaced nearly all the native-born women on the assembly line, supervisors Thomas and Darius started teaching themselves words and phrases in Spanish. Native-born men wanted to learn some Spanish for two reasons: to signal an affective interest to Latinas and to acquire simple communication skills. How they did so, especially in their choice of worthwhile vocabulary, reflected their power and limited linguistic curiosity. In contrast, management, for the most part, was happy purchasing linguistic expertise (i.e., hiring bilingual intermediaries).

On one occasion, Sarah and I were finishing the paperwork for the shift change when Darius approached us.

"Hey Laura, how do you say 'you are beautiful' in Spanish?

"Why do you want to learn that so badly?" I asked, balancing the desire to teach Darius Spanish and resisting the increasing categorization of Latinas as "beautiful women" rather than as committed and hard-working operators.

"I just wanna learn," Darius answered, sensing my hesitation.

Fortunately, we were busy, and the subject quickly turned to the more mundane task of accounting for that day's gaps on the production line. Darius, however, clearly saw the advantage of learning some Spanish, and my reluctance to help him flirt with the Latinas did not dissuade him entirely. Later that week, Darius approached me with his Spanish vocabulary list at hand. He asked, "How do I tell workers to stop the line in Spanish?" I told him, and he said it was hard to pronounce. He took notes of words and phrases that he wanted to learn. Thomas came and looked at the list. He asked how to say "good morning." Darius responded with a quick "buenos días" and smiled proudly. Thomas looked at me, and I repeated it. "The two of you are saying it very differently," he noted, before trying again. "Buenos diaz. . . . Man! That pronunciation is difficult." Of note is that when Latino men were on the floor months earlier, native-born men signaled no interest in learning Spanish or getting to know the immigrant men better.

In contrast to the neutral or sometimes distancing role that language played in the way native-born women responded to the Latino men, native-born men used language more intentionally. Expressions like "mamacita" (hot mama; as in English, this objectification has nothing at all to do with anything motherly) and "muchacha bonita" (beautiful girl) were some simple, albeit not terribly romantic, examples that men used to attempt to get closer to Latina women. Men frequently learned these expressions from other men who worked on the line. With this, native-born men adopted stereotypical and sexist language in their attempts to interact with Latinas.

As a cultural tool to manage conflict and competition, workers' language use weakened protective boundaries. From the perspective of critical feminist theory, expressions like "mamacita" are forms of oppressive masculinity by which men establish power through objectification of women in relation to attractiveness. From an organizational perspective, concerns with the enforcement of sexual harassment policies patterned workers' reactions. In most situations, the women expressed discomfort with the teasing. Yet, when I told the Latinas that I would talk to the men, they asked that I say nothing. "Don't tell them anything. We just ignore them, and that way it doesn't bother us. We don't want problems." When I talked to Norma about reporting a man harassing her, she responded, "I don't want to report him. I just ignore him, and I am fine." Rosa, Norma, and other women deployed a protective stance characteristic of many undocumented women (and sometimes even men) when they are the source of harassment and mistreatment in organizations.

In general, immigrant women neutralized harassment—and other forms of injury to their dignity—through dismissal. This was particularly the case when they associated expressing grievances with job insecurity. As we saw in the case of brokerage, some women did exercise voice through a third party (i.e., a temp agency or a coethnic supervisor). Unfortunately, however, most asked the supervisors to "leave things as they are." Neutralizing harassment through dismissal only fed the stereotype that Latinas were better than native-born women because they did not complain or because they smiled and cooperated—feeding the "acquiescent" stereotype. Consequently, the reproduction of gendered job queues and their importance in displacement relied on the vulnerability of female workers.

Women's Resistance as a Corollary of Attraction

From the start, native-born men welcomed and flirted with Latinas, and, in contrast to their more contentious relationship with the Latino men, their behavior indicated a complementary relationship rather than one based on being substitutes. This type of complementary relationship, however, had gendered and racial undertones. Contrary to the Black men, the native-born women perceived their Latina counterparts as a threat rather than as a complement. That is, the welcoming response that the mostly Black men expressed toward the Latinas exacerbated the bantering, teasing, and "aggravating" directed at native-born women.

Consider an example of how gender, race, and symbolic boundaries influenced the nature of displacement in favor of Latinas but against native-born women. Felisha, a Black woman studying psychology at a community college, and Norma, a Mexican woman who completed two years of a bachelor's degree in mathematics prior to migrating to the United States, found themselves caught in the crossfire of the gendered struggle to protect their jobs. Specifically, supervisors and women at the Baseboard Table used the company dress code to keep or discharge workers. On one occasion, Sarah and Darius called Felisha to the side. Sarah wanted Felisha to go home and change her pants. Felisha was wearing dark Lycra tights, and according to Sarah, Felisha "was overweight and shouldn't wear clothes like that." She added that some of the women considered Felisha's clothes to be "too revealing," but I never heard anyone else complain. Felisha worked at a job where she was required to sit on a stool to bend copper wires. Sitting on the high stool, her pants sagged somewhat, revealing her hips and the tops of her underwear. "I'm sending Felisha home," Darius told me before asking me to place Norma at Felisha's station. When the women at the Baseboard Table learned that Darius had sent Felisha home to change her clothes, this poorly managed personnel issue turned into a queuing issue. Felisha talked to Therese. "I'm lookin' around right now, and I see the people on second shift arriving. Look at them with tight clothes and sleeveless, spaghetti-strap blouses. Look! The woman in my place [Norma] is wearing spaghetti straps, and nobody says nothing." A few minutes after Felisha talked to Therese, Thomas called me to the Baseboard Table.

"The shirt Norma is wearing is not acceptable for work," he said in front of Felisha and Therese. At this point, and after the company demoted Kesha, Thomas had become an ally of the native-born women.

"What's wrong with it?" I asked. "It's pretty hot today, and other women are wearing spaghetti straps."

"She should go change. We're supposed to be all the same here, and spaghetti straps are not part of the dress code." Therese interjected that she felt that the company was disproportionately targeting native-born women.

"I don't see a problem. She looks fine to me," Darius said, dismissing the comments.

Darius's matter-of-fact dismissal of the issue, given his interest in the Latinas, left me wondering if he was commenting on the appropriateness of the blouse or the way the petite Norma was wearing it. Darius's stance on the matter resolved it from the perspective of the supervisors, but the native-born women were vocal for the remainder of the day. "The ladies at the Baseboard Table are upset because the Latinas get their way with everything, like the spaghetti straps," Thomas told me later that day. In seeking fairness, the women affirmed that if supervisors sent Felisha home because her clothes were tight, then they should also send Norma home because she was wearing spaghetti straps. After the incident, native-born policing of Latina attire and behavior increased, with an emphasis on "we are all the same here." Unsatisfied by their supervisors' response, the women at the Baseboard Table started complaining about the length of the women's blouses and even the embroidered rose on the back of Rosa's tight-fitting jeans. For several weeks, the native-born women complained, and for the entire time, the Latinas talked about the issue on our ride home. The Latinas were learning their new jobs well, and the managers wanted them to succeed; so the native-born resorted to emotional pressures as a last-ditch effort to create a hostile environment for the Latinas.

While these situations might appear trivial to an outside observer, the conflict that they generated was palpable to the workers and influenced the gendered response to displacement. Native-born women made every attempt to stay in their jobs and "push" the Latina women out. Because native-born men had no rigid boundaries against the entrance of Latinas, in part because the women represented a lower threat than the Latino males, they did what they could to keep the Latinas, including trading native-born women for newcomers.

Displacement and the Gendered Nature of Alternatives

"Nice Christmas present," remarked Kesha sarcastically as workers started to pile up to read the 8½-by-11 sheet of paper posted on the glass-door entrance of the shop floor at HiCap. Kesha's body was nearly touching the glass door as she attempted to resist the force of the growing crowd.

"Back off! I can't breathe!" she shouted, taking a red and white velvet Santa hat off her head and gasping for air. "I'll read it to y'all. 'Due to lower customer demand, first shift will be off next week.' That's it, we're off!"

The workers broke from the gathering silently, most lost in thought, as though figuring out how to deal with a week off without pay. "At least they're not closing the plant and sending it to Mexico," Therese said, showing a sense of optimism that was rare in the crowd. The workers then walked away to get into gear to start working first shift. Most struggled with the reality that their pay for December would be 25 percent less than they had expected. The company closed one week in December and another week in January and yet another week at the beginning of March. The Hispanic workers were among the first to react, demonstrating their lower tolerance for the change in work hours. When the company announced the January closure, Ricardo, a man from Durango, Mexico, approached me voicing the concerns of others. "How often are we going to be off? Can you tell us so that we can look for another job? We were off a week last month, and if we are going to be a week off every month, that just won't work," he said and then explained that he took care of his ill dad and that he needed to earn money to pay for doctors' visits and medication. I asked around, but neither Darius nor any of the other supervisors had any real insights to share. In some traditional destinations, like California, painting, landscaping, and construction were seasonally predictable; but in the Carolinas, weather was a transient phenomenon, and inclement weather frequently caused immigrant workers to lose pay. The predictability of factory work, therefore, was one of the few positives that many saw when they compared light industrial work to other available jobs. Plant closures were a direct assault on that predictability, and that threatened to move HiCap down the collective job queue, especially for the immigrant men.

Shifts in production cycles remind us how organizations have overlapping processes that influence labor force turnover. In this case, a reduction in product demand prompted managers to implement a policy that diametrically opposed their desire to keep and grow the labor force that they wanted. Although weeklong plant closures were demotivating enough on their own, the company followed up by occasionally reducing workers' hours on short notice. That is, unstable demand for the product caused labor needs to be assessed daily and in relation to the production schedule. If the company was scheduled to produce at a lower level, managers instructed supervisors to send workers home. Permanent plant workers were somewhat accustomed to these changes, as the company had a history of cyclical ups and downs related to seasonal product demand, but the Latino workers were taken by surprise.

My interviews with Latino workers revealed that many were willing to accept the lower wages and hard work typically associated with factory work when that work came with paycheck stability. In fact, some left the relative cultural comfort of jobs in the ethnic economy or the flexibility of informal job arrangements to seek a reliable paycheck. Consequently, when companies failed to meet the expectations of stability, their positions weaken in the immigrant job queue. This change led many Latino immigrants to reevaluate the calculus surrounding job choice, a calculus that intersected with decidedly gendered job queues informed by current options (e.g., existence of other light industrial work, demand for construction labor). As a result, Latino men's elasticity with respect to the stability parameter was lower than that of the immigrant women in my study. In other words, that immigrant men had more options made them less tolerant of schedule instability, and many chose to seek opportunities in other industries.

* * *

This chapter focuses on the intersectional influence of race, gender, and legality in displacement. It addresses why labor force turnover does not always go in the direction managers want and how the displacement shifted from Latino immigrant men to Latina immigrant women. Resistance as a mechanism worked in an environment where structural conditions configure different group perceptions of alternatives. When Black workers feared losing their jobs, they engaged in same-sex antagonism against out-group members. This form of coordinated resistance contributed to the exit of the Latino men at the plant. Similarly, native-born women, following the pattern of same-sex out-group antagonism at play in other contexts, pushed back against the arrival of Latinas. Gender influenced the response of men and women to displacement because native-born men, rather than joining forces with native-born women, deployed welcoming behaviors toward Latino women. In fact, attraction contributed to the complementary relationship that developed between native-born men and Latinas, ultimately creating a demographic shift that locked Latinas into and pushed native-born women out of bad jobs. Men's acts of sabotage contributed to native-born women's exit. The men weakened the power of women in efforts to maintain their dominant position and save their jobs.

Although Black men were able to exclude Latino men to a large degree, some native-born men *were* displaced by Latina women. And importantly, the native-born men who were "displaced"—they typically left on their own rather than being forced out—were actually the native-born men with the most market power. As we saw in chapter 1, the native-born men who stayed were, arguably, not so much "protected" as "left behind" (because criminal stigma reduced their exit options). Thus, in the end, management got a dependent workforce not just by replacing native-born workers with vulnerable immigrant workers but also by leading the native-born workforce to self-sort, so that only the most vulnerable native-born workers remained behind. Of course, to some degree, this is a generic process in any oversupplied labor market: when there are more workers than jobs, employers can lower working conditions and still fill their labor needs.

The chapter expands on the classical organizational ideas that focus on the behaviors of workers.[6] Studies focused on the human-relations tradition emphasize the need to pay attention to the emotional needs of workers. Extending this research, the chapter accounts for embeddedness, relational inequality, and cultural processes. In support of this approach, Heather Haveman and Rachel Wetts note that while research on the human-relations tradition considers workers' woes and pleas, a careful analysis of this research reveals a conceptualization of workers as mere "tools" that employers use to achieve organizational goals.[7] A more fruitful approach departs from the commoditization of workers by paying attention to the culture of organizations. Taking into account the importance of rituals and practices that bind members together, such as playing games and symbolic and social affiliations, this chapter also considers the agency that occurs within and constitutes group boundaries.[8] Taking some steps in this direction, the chapter introduces key mechanisms that explain how racialization unfolds when organizations introduce a "third group" (Latino immigrants) into workplaces with a binary (Black-white) racial structure.

Unlike other studies that explain changes in the ethnic composition of the labor force using social networks and employer preferences as the main mechanisms, the chapter suggests that labor displacement happens because race and gender intersect in queuing processes and because power, resistance, legality, and alternatives influence labor turnover. These mechanisms, however, respond to political forces. Chapter 5 covers how political forces shaped, and frequently disrupted, some of the displacement dynamics.

5

Show Me Your Papers!

E-Verify and the State's Influence on Racialized Displacement

"Our lives have gotten so tough. Before, jobs could be found easily. Good jobs were all over the place. But now there is no work. Life has changed completely since the laws changed." This quote, or one like it, appears in the transcripts of so many of my interviews of immigrants in the 2009 sample that it is impossible to attribute it to one person or even a subgroup of Hispanics in my study. Changes in the legal and political landscape were obvious to immigrants, from educated community leaders to the lowest wage workers. With few exceptions, participants in my immigrant sample reported new and severe barriers to employment. But how did these profound changes in the legal landscape occur? To understand this change, a brief history of the legal and political environment as it evolved over the course of my research in South Carolina is in order.

The Failure of Congress

The federal government, and Congress in particular, has the power and responsibility to enact laws regulating immigration. In 1986, the US Congress passed the Immigration Reform and Control Act (IRCA) and for the first time used the regulation of employment as part of the legal framework to control immigration. At the time, Congress understood that fortifying the border was not a solution, so it made an attempt to address the primary pull factor, employment. IRCA restrictions make it unlawful "to hire, or to recruit or to refer for a fee, for employment . . . an unauthorized alien with respect to such employment." The act provided a method of employment eligibility verification for employers to follow that indemnified them from liability. Employees had to prove eligibility by submitting either a valid US passport or permanent resident card (i.e., a "green card"). Since many workers had neither, an employee could submit a Social Security card along with a state-issued identification card bearing a photograph. After reviewing the employees' documents, the employer then attested that it had verified the documents and would keep the records on file for three years after the date of hire or for one year after employment terminates, whichever was longer. The final step in the process was for new employees to affirm on their form I-9, under penalty of perjury, that they were either a citizen or permanent resident of the United States or that they were an "alien who is authorized" (typically via an H1 or H2 visa) to work in the United States.

One of my interviewees, Gonzalo, a Colombian immigrant pioneer and labor broker, recounted a trip he took to Atlanta to become better informed about the legalities surrounding immigrant employment:

> The employment agency where I worked sent the local managers down to Atlanta to attend a conference put on by Immigration's district field office. They told us precisely what we needed to do as employment agency managers: "When an employee arrives, you clearly need to ask for their green card and their Social Security card, but . . . as employers, [you] do not have the authority to say, 'This document is good' or 'That document is bad.' Only the people who work for Immigration can make that determination." They told us very clearly that our job was to receive the documents in good faith and that if we did that, we would steer clear of any problems. When we got back to [town], we explained this to our employer clients, and, as you can imagine, it put them at ease with the legal issue of hiring our Hispanics. So that is how we began to introduce larger numbers of Hispanic workers into the local factories.

As Gonzalo correctly pointed out, IRCA put no requirements on the quality of the employer's review of documentation other than that the employer make a "good faith effort" to verify the documents. As long as employers made that effort and retained their records, they were indemnified from culpability related to hiring an unauthorized worker.

And if employers violated IRCA by willfully hiring an unauthorized worker, fines were minimal, between $250 and $2,000 for a first violation and between $2,000 and $5,000 for a second violation. Only with a "pattern of violations" did employers face potential criminal liability.

The risk-benefit calculus created by IRCA's low compliance bar and light penalties made it easy for employers to operate comfortably with less-than-perfect compliance.

Evidence of IRCA's purported failure was that 11.4 million unauthorized immigrants lived in the United States between 2015 and 2018.[1] The ease with which employers can recruit and hire undocumented workers in the post-IRCA US is probably one of the biggest factors leading to the exposure of so many undocumented workers to substandard labor conditions with extremely limited avenues for recourse. But since IRCA was passed in 1986, a series of attempts, from conservatives and liberals alike, to "fix" immigration have ensued. The battles have frequently come down to creating a path for citizenship for the millions of immigrants who reside in the United States and creating a system that would prevent the country from having to have the same discussion fifteen to twenty years hence.

In 1996, Congress passed the Illegal Immigration Reform and Immigrant Responsibility Act (IIRIRA), which provided for substantial upgrades to enforcement activities at the border, civil penalties for illegal entry, enhanced immigration enforcement in the interior of the country, and increased penalties for smuggling and document fraud. IIRIRA also provided for the "removal" (i.e., deportation) of undocumented immigrants convicted of "aggravated felonies," which range from the forgery or counterfeit of documents—of particular importance to unauthorized job seekers, who frequently pass off fake Social Security cards or other documents as real—to theft to rape and murder (8 USC, § 1101). The focus of IIRIRA was clearly on enforcement, but where IRCA made an attempt to address the pull factors related to plentiful employment in addition to enforcement, IIRIRA, in what can now be seen as an about-face, focused for all intents and purposes exclusively on the creation or enhancement of penalties related to the immigrants themselves.

But the numbers of the undocumented grew steadily from 1990 to 2007, with roughly half a million immigrants added to the total every year.[2] With this demographic backdrop, many members of Congress felt an increasing need to break from the status quo. In 2005, the House passed the Border Protection, Anti-terrorism, and Illegal Immigration Control Act (also known as the "Sensenbrenner Act" for its sponsor, F. James Sensenbrenner Jr., a Republican member of the House representing Wisconsin). The Sensenbrenner Act, like IIRIRA, focused ex-clusively on enforcement and, as such, failed to garner sufficient support in the Senate. In 2005 and again in 2006, bills were introduced in the Senate, but each time, they, too, failed to generate enough support to become law.

On July 24, 2006, President George W. Bush spoke on national tele-vision with the idea of pressuring the Senate to act. Despite substantial tension between competing factions in Congress, the overall tone of the speech was still hopeful, and it sounded as though political differences were reconcilable. That optimism was not lost on the immigrants in my study, most of whom would have heard a translation of at least part of the speech. They were left with the hope that immigration reform would come to pass and bring them an opportunity to finally emerge from the shadows. Manuela, a secondary migrant who arrived in South Carolina from New Jersey, shared,

> Things have gotten tougher with the new laws and how employers are now checking papers, but in my case, and it is the same for my siblings, we are all hopeful that immigration reform will give us an opportunity to get permanent residency. The thing is, we know that means that we'll need a record of our work, so while we could go buy better papers and work under someone else's name, we've been taking jobs that pay less, sometimes a lot less, but where they still aren't checking papers. That way, we can use our real name and develop a history of working and paying taxes. It's hard, but we've been doing this since before we left New Jersey.

In 2007, Senate Bill 1348, also known as the Comprehensive Immigra-tion Reform Act of 2007 (CIRA 2007), appeared to have a solid chance of passage. CIRA 2007 was a slightly modified version of the 2006 at-tempt and would have provided for increased enforcement and a path to citizenship for most undocumented immigrants with a history of work-ing in the United States. CIRA 2007 also incorporated the Development, Relief, and Education for Alien Minors Act (DREAM Act) as a way of promoting the integration of the undocumented into mainstream so-ciety.[3] CIRA 2007 ultimately failed to make it to the floor for a general vote, and the Senate proved unable to reform the immigration process or address the growing concerns of individual states.

The State-Level Response to Congressional Failure

Only days after the Senate announced that there would be no immigration reform at the federal level, the *New York Times* reported that a frustrated Janet Napolitano, the Democratic governor of Arizona, signed the Legal Arizona Workers Act (LAWA) into law. LAWA mandated that employers in Arizona use the federal E-Verify system to verify the work authorization of new employees or face penalties including the suspension and revocation of their business license.

E-Verify was set up by the Department of Homeland Security as an optional program that employers could use. LAWA was the first law that made E-Verify mandatory, and because it carried harsh penalties, it was at the time widely considered to contain the toughest sanctions on the employment of undocumented immigrants to pass at the state level. Even though Napolitano felt that the bill was less than perfect, she explained that something had to be done because "Congress has failed miserably."[4] LAWA announced the beginning of an era of state-level immigration policy that foreshadowed legal battles to come.

Arizona was not alone. In 2008, there were over 1,300 bills introduced in state legislatures related to immigration, and states signed at least 206 into law.[5] This incursion of state lawmakers into what had traditionally been the sole purview of the federal government attracted considerable legal attention. Suits were filed by a diverse set of litigants contesting different aspects of different laws, and unlikely coalitions formed, such as the US Chamber of Commerce and Mexican American Legal Defense and Educational Fund, the American Civil Liberties Union (ACLU), and even the Service Employees International Union (SEIU). Based on the independent histories of the two organizations, it is unlikely that SEIU agreed with the US Chamber of Commerce on why the laws were problematic, but they agreed that the laws needed to be challenged.

In *Arizona Contractors Ass'n, Inc. v. Candelaria* (2008), a coalition of local business organizations, Hispanic advocacy groups, and the US Chamber of Commerce filed suit in the federal court in the District of Arizona seeking an injunction to prevent the law from taking effect while its constitutionality was evaluated by the courts.[6] In December 2007, the district court ordered that judgment be entered in favor of the county attorneys. Even though the decision was rendered at a lower court and was almost certain to be appealed, it sent a powerful signal to the legislators of other states, including South Carolina, that asserting themselves into the immigration policy arena, at least in this specific area, was unlikely to be seen by the courts as being a priori unconstitutional. Many states were watching, and many acted.

LAWA Ruling Goes to the Court of Appeals

In June 2008, the same group of Arizona business organizations and Hispanic advocacy groups appealed the ruling in *Arizona Contractors Ass'n, Inc. v. Candelaria* at the US Court of Appeals for the Ninth Circuit. In *Chicanos Por La Causa, Inc. v. Napolitano*, the plaintiffs argued again that LAWA was preempted by IRCA, but they added that companies were going to be denied due process under LAWA and that the law's mandate to use E-Verify was preempted by Congress, making the use of E-Verify voluntary. The court ruled that "the Legal Arizona Workers Act targets employers who hire illegal aliens, and its principal sanction is the revocation of state licenses to do business in Arizona. . . . The Act was a 'licensing' law within the meaning of the federal provision and therefore was not expressly preempted." Further, since there was no alternative to E-Verify, Arizona could make the system mandatory. The Court added that the law "should be reasonably interpreted to allow employers, before any license can be adversely affected, to present evidence to rebut the presumption that an employee is unauthorized."[7]

The legal gambit may have been a long shot, but from a social perspective, immigration advocates were sending a message to immigrants: "There might be some people in the country that would like you to go away, but the businesses and immigration advocates are fighting for you." In other words, the battle may have been lost in the court of law, but it was still being waged in the court of public opinion.

Almost a year and a half later, in December 2010, the fight against the state-mandated use of E-Verify was argued in front of the US Supreme Court as *Chamber of Commerce of the United States of America v. Michael Whiting* (the name change reflected a change in the lead plaintiff and shifting personnel in Apache County). The plaintiffs shifted their focus to an argument that LAWA was not actually a licensing law. In the oral arguments before the Supreme Court, the US Chamber of Commerce argued that because LAWA essentially imposed "the death penalty [on a] business" for hiring an undocumented worker, businesses would be very reluctant to hire any worker who even remotely appeared to be an immigrant, and therefore the law discriminated against many authorized workers on the basis of race or ethnicity.[8] In a friend of the court brief, SEIU argued, among other things, that IRCA had been carefully and purposefully crafted to balance the penalties for hiring undocumented workers with the penalties for discriminating against foreign-looking workers. As it stood, five of the justices found the arguments to be insufficient to meet the rigorous burden of proof required to overturn a legislative act, affirming that states were within their rights to establish mandates that private businesses utilize the E-Verify system. The Supreme Court also set the precedent that such mandates could be "given teeth" by specifying the revocation of a business license as the penalty for noncompliance.

Legislatures across the Country Move to Close Doors on Undocumented Workers

Back in South Carolina, legislators did not wait until for LAWA's day before the Supreme Court. Bill H4400, the Illegal Immigration Reform Act (IIRA), signed into law in June 2008, was the first piece of legislation related to immigration ever passed in South Carolina. Enacted after Arizona's LAWA had passed its first hurdle at the district court but before it had been heard at the Ninth Circuit Court of Appeals, IIRA mandated the use of E-Verify or a South Carolina driver's license for all employers, public and private. It went beyond LAWA and prohibited immigrants who were in the United States illegally from attending any publicly funded institutions of higher learning in South Carolina. Although IIRA was phased in over twenty-four months, with public employers and larger businesses facing the mandates sooner than smaller businesses, my interviews revealed that with many employers confused, implementation was much less organized and uniform than the law would have suggested.

Arizona's passage of its "own" immigration law encouraged South Carolina and other states to do the same, and in the mass media, immigration-related laws were "news" regardless of where they were being passed. Immigrants in South Carolina were well aware of the laws being passed in Arizona, Alabama, Georgia, and other states. My interviewees consistently mentioned changes in South Carolina's laws but also understood and reported that immigrants arriving in South Carolina were fleeing even more restrictive laws in Alabama and Georgia. Subsequently, Utah, Minnesota, Indiana, Michigan, and other states passed restrictive laws related to employment and immigration status.

And in June 2012, in *Arizona v. United States*, the Supreme Court upheld an Arizona provision that allowed a police officer to check the immigration status of an individual while the officer was in the process of enforcing other laws, as long as the officer has reasonable suspicion that an individual is in the US illegally. The court was silent on the definition of reasonable suspicion but left the door open for future challenges to the law on the basis of issues stemming from the actual implementation of the law. The same Supreme Court ruling struck down portions of the Arizona law that it deemed preempted federal authority: namely, making it a state crime to be in the US unlawfully without registering; making it a state crime to seek work or to work without authorization; and authorizing warrantless arrests of immigrants solely on the basis of probable cause that they are deportable.

Summarizing the State's Efforts to Restrict Immigrant Access to Employment

Five years of courtroom drama related to state-based immigration laws followed. Those years of litigation brought about tangible effects related to actual policy changes and intangible but real perceptual changes related to the process itself. The case law created by the various decisions left little doubt that federal law preempted state laws in all areas of immigration policy except for the very narrow niche of license-related legislation. While this shielded undocumented immigrants from the "show me your papers" provisions of many of the statutes, it also served to intensify the states' laser-like focus on business licensing. The net result was that eight states (Alabama, Arizona, Georgia, Mississippi, North Carolina, South Carolina, Tennessee, and Utah) mandated the use of E-Verify for all employers. Fifteen more states (Colorado, Florida, Idaho, Indiana, Louisiana, Michigan, Minnesota, Missouri, Nebraska,

Oklahoma, Pennsylvania, Rhode Island, Texas, Virginia, and West Virginia) mandated the use of E-Verify for public employers.[9] Businesses operating in states with E-Verify mandates found hiring undocumented workers riskier. The effects on workers were clear and immediate. Prior to these laws, companies found to be employing undocumented workers could plead ignorance by maintaining that they did, in fact, check for documents and that the documents appeared to be authentic to their untrained eyes. The practical effect was that if an employee was willing to show an employer anything even resembling a Social Security card, the employer was able to meet the standards required by federal law. Even if the employer's plausible-deniability defense failed, it could pay a small fine for the transgression. With mandates to use E-Verify, however, not only were employers given much less room for ambiguity and a defense based on plausible deniability, but they also faced the possibility of having their entire operation suspended temporarily or in some cases having their business licenses revoked altogether.[10] The bottom line was that with the passage of these laws, and their subsequent affirmation in the courts, many jobs that once were available to immigrants with questionable documentation were rendered inaccessible. The appearance of the E-Verify logo in employment agencies and on the walls and windows of businesses sent a chill throughout the immigrant community.

Employers have two primary concerns related to hiring undocumented workers. The first is compliance with the laws governing employment, although it might be more accurate to say that they were concerned mainly with not being caught failing to comply. The second concern is the negative reputational effect of becoming embroiled in a public scandal surrounding the employment of undocumented workers. Clearly, these concerns weigh differently for different firms serving different markets. Well-known firms may be much more concerned with maintaining the integrity of their brand than they are with the small fines that could arise from an investigation. Smaller, struggling firms may be more concerned with the fines.

The bottom line is that all employers were affected. Even the most legally sophisticated employers in the region were struggling to keep up with immigration policy. The legal landscape for employers became dramatically more complicated after the states entered into the immigration regulation business.[11] After the attacks on September 11, the Homeland

Security Act of 2002 divided INS responsibilities into three agencies: US Citizenship and Immigration Services (USCIS), US Customs and Border Protection (CBP), and US Immigration and Customs Enforcement (ICE). With many states also concerning themselves with immigration, dozens, if not hundreds, of agencies were vying for control of policies and regulations in this realm. For employers that operated businesses in multiple states, this had become a serious burden; but even for businesses fully contained in one state, the situation had gotten considerably more complicated, and uncertainty ruled the day.

As impactful as the E-Verify mandates might have been, my participants' comments regarding generic and vague "changes in the laws" as well as comment in the vein of "they don't want us anymore" led me to conclude that the intangible effects could have had even more impact on the immigrants. Laws are enacted through a relatively open political process, and that process is detailed widely in the media. The result is that public debates are seen as reflections of the desires and mood of the public. So when a state passes a law that says the local police should be checking the papers of every person who looks like an immigrant, it is difficult for immigrants not to feel that the native-born do not want them in the country. When another state proposes an "English only" law, immigrants do not need an interpreter to tease out nuanced meanings. Of course, there was some relief that the courts invalidated the "show me your papers" provisions, but, for the immigrants watching from the sidelines, it does not change that the laws were not only proposed, they were also passed with wide margins of support.

Additional Forces at Play with Employers

In addition to operating within the letter of the law, employers, especially large regional employers with a long history in the area and multinational corporations with brand recognition, have reputations to protect. Part of their strategy to maintain their reputation involves avoiding public scandals.

As BMW found out, even companies that try to stay out of the news do not always succeed. In 2007, BMW's South Carolina plant made a splash in the news with a July 27 headline of "Immigration Sting Nets 7 Food Workers at BMW."[12] The article started out mentioning that the workers were cafeteria workers and followed that with details on their nationalities (Mexican and Honduran) and the charges that they would face: "charges include Social Security fraud, misuse of visas and false claims of citizenship." To be fair, the *Spartanburg Herald-Journal* then made it clear that the employees were not actually BMW employees but employees of its cafeteria subcontractor, Eurest. Toward the bottom of the article, it was even reported that a spokesman for ICE said that "neither BMW nor Eurest were responsible for the actions of the seven employees and that the companies would not face any charges." But for a company that, according to a 2011 Reuters news story, was willing to spend an estimated $140 million annually on developing and maintaining its brand in the United States alone, trusting that its customers would read past the headlines would be risky business indeed.[13]

South Carolina was home to branches, large and small, of many large, well-known companies: Avery Dennison, Black & Decker, BMW, Caterpillar, Coca-Cola, Fluor, General Electric, Goodyear, Lockheed Martin, McGraw-Hill, Michelin, Northrup Grumman, Pepsi, 3M, and Xerox lead the list. These companies made it their business to stay abreast not only of where current policies were but where they were likely to go. It should not be a surprise that most of the larger companies in the region had, by 2009, gained a reputation in the immigrant community for requiring solid proof of work eligibility.

Shift from Racialized Inclusion to Racialized Exclusion in Hiring

During the first phase of my research in South Carolina, conducted in 2005–6, many companies used temporary employment agencies to provide legal cover for the hiring of undocumented workers. Although most of the temporary employment agencies at that time already demanded to see proof of employment eligibility from all prospective employees, the scrutiny that they gave the papers was often exceedingly light. As such, many companies provided opportunities for immigrants with "good," albeit inauthentic, papers to secure employment in light industrial jobs that were both more stable and more lucrative than most of the short-term and part-time jobs that were offered directly by companies that dealt purely in underground employment. This was a form of racialized inclusion. As the political mood in the country shifted after pro- and anti-immigrant marches in 2006, so too did the willingness of companies to pretend that they were unaware of the constitution of their workforce and to use racialized inclusion in hiring. As I mentioned in the opening of this chapter, by the time I returned to my research site in 2009, even though most employers were not yet obliged to use E-Verify, one of the most consistent themes I heard from immigrant interviewees was how much things had changed "since they changed the laws." Many had heard that states had passed "show me your papers" laws, but that these laws had, by and large, been struck down by the courts was of little consolation to the immigrants. Employers were still demanding that they "show their papers." My data, in fact, are replete with references to the negative effects of "show me your papers" laws. Hiring had shifted from racialized inclusion to racialized exclusion. That it was an employer, not a police officer on patrol, that was asking for their papers was irrelevant. They were still being asked, and it definitely had an impact.

Immigrant workers were caught in a crossfire: on one side, the legal and political contexts were shifting against them, and on the other side, the quantity of qualified immigrants seeking good jobs was increasing, the latter in the form of a combination of newly arrived immigrants and experienced immigrants relocating to South Carolina to escape the even-less-hospitable legal environment in other states such as Georgia and Alabama. The legal shifts in these few short years led directly to the comment that opened this chapter: "La vida ha cambiado totalmente desde que cambiaron las leyes" (Life has changed completely since the laws changed).

6

Racialized Shocks and Out-Group Boundaries

There was a time when the image of Hispanics was very positive. People believed that Hispanics were hardworking. They believed that Hispanics had Christian values, that Hispanics had family values, and that Hispanics were the best workers you could have. All of it was positive. But all that has changed. Now we have a negative image. The negative image of all those things I mentioned gets expressed in multiple themes. People believe that we are here illegally, that we are breaking the law, that we are taking advantage of all the programs and services of the community, that we are diseased, undisciplined, and guilty of causing all the social maladies that exist. That's what dominates now. I'm not saying that it's 100 percent this way, but it's close. Our reality is totally different from the way it was just three years ago or even two years ago.
—Roger, Hispanic community leader, 2009 interview

Of all the identities that the Hispanic immigrants in the region had, one of the most salient, and seemingly most robust, was that of the *exceptional worker*. For many, the seeds for this identity were planted before leaving their home country, through conversations with friends and relatives who had spent time working in the United States and shared stories about how positively employers reacted to their willingness and ability to work hard and get things done. Others heard similar messages from recruiters at employment agencies: "the employers like us, Latinos, because we are dependable and we know how to work hard and we do really good work." For most, the identity was consolidated by the comments that they heard on the job from their managers, who often asked, "Do you have any friends or relatives that work like you do? We need a few more good people here." This identity, in an absolute sense, was strengthened by Latinos' experiences in the workplace, its salience accentuated by the fact that they spent the overwhelming majority of their waking hours involved in work activities. In a relative sense, their work identity overwhelmed their identities in other domains, in part because it was an identity of which they were proud but also because it was an identity that blurred the boundaries between themselves and mainstream society. This identity is in sharp contrast to their identities in other domains, such as race, language, education, ethnicity, and to a certain extent even religion, which all tend to brighten the boundaries between themselves and the mainstream.

Over the course of my research in South Carolina from 2005 through 2009, many events, including marches and protests in South Carolina, the US Congress's failure to produce immigration reform, anti-immigrant legislation coming out of the states, the increased enforcement of immigration laws by federal authorities, and state and local law enforcement, combined to change the legal and political landscape in the United States in general, but the changes had a particularly profound effect in states like South Carolina where legislatures were especially concerned about immigration. These changes challenged the views of both the employers of immigrants and the immigrants themselves. Specifically, the changes led to the rapid and extensive erosion of the exceptional worker identity that characterized the immigrants who had come to this area.

Roger, the community leader quoted in the chapter's epigraph, summarizes in detail the main focus of this chapter. The argument here is that race relations took a sharp turn from positive to negative, increasing the sense of alienation and marginalization of Hispanics in US society. The shift in race relations happened in sync with three important regional shocks—social movements, factory raids, and anti-immigrant policies—that brightened the boundaries between Latinos and the native-born and consequently resulted in a more crystallized sense of otherness for Latinos. Following group position theories and ecological arguments and drawing from the perspectives of many Latino immigrants and community leaders, this chapter argues that regional shocks accumulated to tarnish the positive image that many people had of the Hispanic population in the new immigrant destination of South Carolina.[1]

The events described in this chapter emphasize the influence of structural rather than exclusively symbolic aspects of otherness on the crystallization of boundaries between immigrants and the native-born. With expressions such as "We need to hold employers responsible if they hire illegals!" and "Arrest the traitors!"—in reference to employers of unauthorized immigrant workers at an anti-immigrant rally contextualized in detail later in this chapter—and in stressing the role of employers of immigrant labor, whites identified structural elements accentuating the white-Latino boundary. Protesters' demands specifically pointed to overlaps between out-group members (i.e., undocumented immigrants) and in-group members (i.e., US employers that prefer undocumented workers), suggesting that a powerful contingent of the in-group attracts rather than rejects members of the out-group (i.e., undocumented Latinos). This conceptual "attraction" does not neglect the relationship of exploitation and abuse, extensively documented in this and other studies, between employers and unauthorized immigrants.

Existing research shows that employers prefer immigrants to native-born workers.[2] Clearly, this is the preference for jobs at the bottom of the labor market and, in some cases, even for intermediary positions.[3] From the perspective of Hispanic immigrants, however, their dual frame of reference gives a different quality to the status of jobs that Americans reject.[4] Thus, if Latinos perceive their relationship with employers and advocates as favorable to achieving their economic goals and settling in US communities, they are likely to feel less alienation from US society. In contrast, when powerful US employers eliminate or reduce the value they bestow on immigrants, feelings of alienation crystallize. The series of nativist shocks that excluded immigrants from the labor market not only made their economic survival more precarious but also undermined their most valued role and sense of belonging to US society: that of the exceptional worker.

This chapter relies on interviews and conversations with immigrants, employers, supervisors, and community leaders and on my observations working as a supervisor primarily at HiCap. I focus on four specific nativist shocks: (1) the 2006 immigrant rights marches, (2) the 2006 Council of Conservative Citizens anti-immigrant rally, (3) the economic boycott identified in popular discourse as "A Day without Immigrants," (4) the 2009 ICE raid on the House of Raeford, a poultry plant. This series of events occurred in and around South Carolina over the course of this research and dramatically shifted the nature of race relations in

the region, highlighting the importance of regional shocks on race relations and immigrant integration. Specifically, community responses
evolved from praising Hispanics as "God-sent" people to deriding them
as outsiders.

Immigrants as "God Sent"

The strong relationship between race and employment documented
in much sociological research was palpable in Jessamine County with
the earliest wave of Latino immigrant arrivals. Starting in the 1970s,
companies brought Latinos from as far as Colombia to the US South.
Textile companies went to Medellín, Colombia, to recruit workers hailed
by a Cuban recruiter as "the most skilled textile workers in the world."
Some arrived first to Long Island and then made their way to Jessamine,
South Carolina. Others arrived directly in Jessamine. These workers
were offered homes and, in the words of one of the pioneer Latinos in
my research, "independence and as many hours of work as we wished."
Interviews with pioneer immigrants reveal the profound sense of pride
that many of these immigrants felt when integrating into this community as skilled workers. Miguel, one of the first Colombians hired by a
now-defunct textile mill, told me,

> I went for a job interview at the textile mill, and the manager tried to in-
> timidate me by saying, "But you don't speak English. What are you going
> to do here?" I responded that the machines and my work speak for me.
> He took me through a tour of the factory, and we stopped at one of the
> sections on the floor where there was a machine I knew well. A mechanic,
> an American, was fixing the machine. Through the interpreter, the man-
> ager asked if I knew what the problem was. I looked at the machine, and I
> responded that I could fix that machine in fifteen minutes. The American,
> the mechanic, had already spent three hours trying to fix the machine,
> and he still didn't know what was wrong with it. I was sure I could fix it in
> fifteen minutes. The manager asked how I was going to fix it. I told him
> this machine has this and that. This screw here needs to be tightened, and
> there is a missing spring, and things like that. I impressed the manager,
> and he told me that I could start the next day at 7 a.m. He knew I was
> looking for a lot of work, and he said I could work as much as I wanted to.

Miguel and others from the pioneer group recounted similar stories of how the desire of employers to hire Latino workers was fueled by immigrant productivity and the powerful force of chain migration.[5] He added that "once the managers saw that Hispanics were producing results, he sent the interpreter/recruiter to Colombia with the instruction to bring more textile workers." Corroborating Miguel's story, Carlos, a recruiter sent to Medellín in search of textile workers, shared that the managers "were enamored with the Hispanic workers": "They sent me to bring more Colombian workers. They didn't care if they were mechanics or not. They just wanted them to know about textiles, and that's how everything started. We brought one, and this person recommended another one, and this one recommended another one, and Colombians started arriving one after the next." Fabricato and other textile mills that have since closed filled the vacancies in their shops with Colombian immigrants. Ramiro recalled that "the companies started to fill with workers that weren't legal because those arriving after the first group were not coming under contract. They came illegally because the Colombian recruiter went to Bogotá and brought people that didn't have jobs. And here, and at that time, they didn't know the meaning of an illegal person, a person without papers, so those people just started to work in the factories, and the managers were happy with them."

More than two decades after the arrival of the Colombian pioneers to Jessamine, the town in Jessamine Country where I conducted this research, the preference for Hispanic workers expanded. Following the restructuring and reindustrialization of the US South and in the wake of policy changes brought about by the Immigration Reform and Control Act (IRCA) of 1986, the appetite of employers for Latino immigrant workers in the 1990s went beyond textiles and beyond South America. Other industries such as construction, manufacturing, and agriculture drew large numbers of Latino immigrants to South Carolina. Much of the demand for these workers was fueled by employers' beliefs that immigrants were more reliable and dependable than their native-born counterparts.[6] Although South Americans hailing from countries like Colombia, Chile, and Argentina continued to immigrate to the US South, most recently, the largest contingent came from Mexico to find jobs in construction, manufacturing, services, and agriculture.

Throughout the 1990s and up to the middle of the first decade of the twenty-first century, the preference for Latino immigrant workers continued, and many Latino immigrants found employment readily available. Similar to the pioneer Colombians, it took no more than a couple of days for a Latino immigrant in South Carolina to gain employment. Often, relatives and friends negotiated employment for family members and friends before a new immigrant even started the journey. When I worked as a supervisor at HiCap, it was not unusual for a worker to ask if we "had any jobs for a relative [or friend] in transit" to their new destination. With jobs being negotiated in advance, newly arrived immigrants often joined the US workforce without even taking time to rest from the treacherous migrant journey. A respondent noted that he "wanted to rest for a day after almost dying in the desert," but the cousin who helped him had promised the boss that he "was going to start as soon as he arrived because they had a lot of work." Employers were demanding workers, and immigrant workers wanted jobs. While barriers certainly existed, they could all be navigated.

Supervisors praised Latinos as a group with expressions such as "you guys work hard" and "they are dedicated and love to work." When the number of Hispanics expanded at the factory, the manager said, "I can already see a difference in this place, these are *God-sent* people." Latino immigrants generated similar sentiments from their native-born coworkers. Rusty, a white operator, said, "Determined is what they were. They needed the job, and they learned to do it." She paused for a moment and added emphatically, "Determination is what those guys have."

Perceptions of immigrants as preferred workers resulted from an assessment of the qualities of this group relative to the available pool of workers. The default assessment was that Latino immigrants worked harder and were more productive than African American and white workers. Whether this perception was accurate or not, employers hired immigrants because they believed that "they are more efficient and can do the work faster than Americans." According to an immigrant supervisor, companies hired immigrants because they were "in the red" and they thought "Hispanics are superhuman and can save the company from bankruptcy." Employers demanded more of Latino immigrants than they did of their native-born workers. This was especially the case with unauthorized immigrant workers, who were more likely to accept the excessive demands of employers than were native-born workers.

Tremendous emphasis is often placed on the premise that immigrants work harder and are more productive than their native-born counterparts, so it deserves a brief discussion. This emphasis serves different purposes for different groups: employers use it to justify their decisions, native-born workers use it to convince themselves that the precariousness of their employment is something that they themselves have control over, and academics and policy makers wonder if it should play a role in defining our policy landscape. First, I would like to reiterate that whether the premise is true is irrelevant in the labor market. If employers perceive that it is true, they will act on it. In the context of trying to understand motives and policies, it is critical that we keep in mind that working harder or being more compliant are not the same as being more productive. My research in the factories of South Carolina showed that, without a doubt, the most vulnerable workers will be the workers who can be pushed to work the hardest. This vulnerability takes many shapes, from needing medical benefits for a sick family member to being undocumented or unable to speak English to having a criminal record that precludes finding a comparable job. These vulnerabilities are real, and they subject their possessors to abuses that are equally real. In my research, I saw many cases in which the vulnerable, often undocumented immigrants, worked harder. They had to. That being said, hard work in the context of a job that requires skill and experience only goes so far, and what I saw, or more accurately, what I did not see, were productivity gains achieved by exploiting vulnerable workers and abandoning those with experience.

Awakening a "Sleeping Giant"

After the December 2005 passage of the Sensenbrenner Act (HR 4437) in the US House of Representatives, Latinos throughout the United States publicly protested the bill as it went to the US Senate. The legislation, named after F. James Sensenbrenner Jr. (R-Wisconsin), would have made the unauthorized status of immigrants a felony and would have criminalized providing aid to those living in the United States without authorization. The draconian provisions of the bill resulted in the mobilization of Latino immigrants, documented and undocumented alike, awakening this political giant and bringing its members out from the shadows and into the public view in dozens of cities across the United States. A series of immigrant marches across the country were held in April 2006 to unite Latinos of all ethnicities. They were an effort to send a message to the US public and US Senate that HR 4437 was bad legislation. The marches and demonstrations were to culminate on May 1, May Day, with a nationwide "Day without an Immigrant." Although the Sensenbrenner Act had wide support in the House of Representatives, the bill ultimately died in the Senate.

In workplaces in South Carolina, the awakening of this sleeping giant was unexpected. Employers were unprepared to cope with the marches and the possibility that their businesses would be affected if a large percentage of their workers missed work. At HiCap, information on the marches reached employers through their subcontracted temporary employment agency. The agency received an unsigned letter requesting that it allow its workers to be absent from work on April 10 if a worker wished to participate in the march that was planned for that day in Jessamine. According to Andrea, one of Ready Hands' recruiters, the agency "made a big deal because [they] thought the Hispanic workers were not going to show up to work." While individuals at the agency may have been sympathetic to the cause of the marches, their business was to supply reliable workers to the local industry, so they made a point of notifying the management at HiCap. They also called all the bilingual supervisors the day before the march to have us tell our workers that the agency was counting on them to be at work the next day. The warning had the intended effect.

Responses from immigrant workers at HiCap toward the marches were mostly favorable, and participation (or lack thereof) was based primarily on economic circumstances. Of the nearly one hundred Hispanic workers scheduled to be on that shift at the plant the day of the marches, only one Hispanic immigrant, Manuel, missed work and attended the march in Jessamine. Those who did not attend indicated that they could not afford missing work, although most expressed that they "supported the marches in spirit." A couple of the workers did disagree with the movement for reasons I discuss later. When I asked Manuel about the marches, he downplayed his participation: "I went, but there was no march, just a demonstration, and it didn't last that long. It only lasted two hours. They said it was going to start at 11 a.m. and end at 3 p.m., but it was over by 1 p.m." He concluded that "it didn't last that long because they didn't get permission for the demonstration." I interpreted the dismissive nature of his response as a form of disillusionment with a cause that was meant to be important to support the rights of Latino workers.

The request that employers made that workers work on the day of the marches is open to two interpretations, which are tied to how employers' control influences race relations. On strictly rational terms, employers were certainly concerned with productivity, and worker attendance was essential to meeting this goal. Although practically every worker in a factory can be replaced, even with advanced notice it would simply be impossible for an employer to replace even 10 percent, let alone 20 percent or more, of a trained workforce for one day. If a sizable population failed to show up for work, the production line would at best run in fits and starts, but more likely than not, it would simply cease to run. Along these same lines, workers do not want to miss work because their livelihood depends on it. From a conflict perspective, employers have incentives for maintaining control of their labor force, but the irony of production being halted by the very workers whom management brought in to leverage control in the first place may have been too painful to bear. That managers resorted to threats to maintain control over immigrant workers may have had as much to do with the irony as it did with the absolute maintenance of control. HiCap had hired Hispanic workers as replacements for "difficult" native-born workers, and they simply could not have those replacements causing problems. They chose to deliver a subtle threat, in the form of a reminder that all employees were replaceable, to the supervisors, allowing the managers to maintain control without overtly threatening anyone. But Armando, a Cuban immigrant working for Roberto, interpreted Roberto's request that everyone attend work the day of the marches as a direct threat: "I understood the warning for what it was," he said during lunch the week after the marches. "Roberto's warning meant that I was going to lose my job if I didn't show up to work." Armando talked to Richard, who, not wanting to keep information to himself, communicated with other workers. In less than a week, the message that missing work to march for immigrant rights would probably cost workers their jobs resonated loud and clear for Hispanics at HiCap. Ultimately, Richard himself asked me, "Is it true that Armando was threatened with losing his job if he didn't show up to work on the day of the marches?" Roberto and I talked to the Hispanic workers about the employer's threats, but our efforts met with only limited success.

A Day without an Immigrant

As a follow-on to the marches around the country, a grass-roots effort was made to organize a nationwide economic boycott on the part of immigrants. The newspapers ran stories about May 1 being "A Day without an Immigrant," no doubt co-opting the title of the 2004 movie *A Day without a Mexican*, which dealt with that very subject. The premise, according to fliers, was to show the powerful impact that immigrants have on the US economy by refusing to participate in it that day. Accordingly, immigrants across the country were urged not to work, spend money, sell anything, or attend school for the day.

It became clear that, at least at HiCap, managers did not need to see a day without any immigrants to know that the effect would be devastating. Upon hearing about the proposed boycott, the managers were doing their part to reproduce the sense of threat generated in response to the possibility that workers would abandon work to go to the marches just the week prior. A week and a half before the economic boycott involving Hispanic workers, Dave, the general manager at HiCap, approached me as I was running a count of units on the assembly line. He told me to carry on with my work as he talked to me. I followed his directive, moving back and forth from my count on the conveyor belt to my notes on the production schedule, pausing only briefly to interact with him:

> DAVE: What have you heard about May 1?
> LAURA: I haven't heard anything.
> DAVE: Have you heard if people are going to be coming to work?
> LAURA: I have not.
> DAVE: Tell your workers that we are supportive of the issue but the plant needs to run. The reason the company has the Hispanic enclaves and created opportunities for the Hispanic workers and su-

pervisors like Roberto, Gabe, and you to work at the plant is because you are good workers.

LAURA: I understand.

DAVE: Tell your workers that the reason we have the enclaves and all of you here . . . [he paused to choose his words carefully] is because we think you are responsible and show up to work. You need to respond in kind and show up for work, or I'm going to give these jobs to people that really want to work. The company needs people that want to be at work every day. Do I make myself clear?

LAURA: Yes.

I wanted to respond with a sarcastic remark to admonish him for being threatening. I abstained. He could have fired me on the spot and simply have the agency or Roberto issue an even more severe threat to the workers and increase the growing sense of anxiety at the plant. I clenched my jaw and left things as they were, letting Dave return to his office, seemingly frustrated.

Three days after Dave warned that Hispanic workers, including supervisors, were replaceable, the company fired Manuel, the one worker who attended the march on April 10. Manuel's coworkers connected his termination with his participation and quickly drew the conclusion that their preferred status at HiCap was far from unconditional; in fact, their preferred-worker identity was contingent on adhering to the employer's rules, contingent on their willingness and ability to show up to work and to get work done.

Marcus alleged that he fired Manuel because he was always missing work, maintaining the charade of fairness and equality that justified recruiting-, hiring-, and firing-related behaviors at the plant. However, the actions were not explained by the policies that were in place. HiCap policies called for termination after two unjustified absences in a thirty-day period, and Manuel had missed only two days of work since he started, one of which resulted from the company sending him home (along with other workers) early in a shift due to overstaffing on that particular day. Workers were surprised that Manuel had been fired because many thought he was "a good worker." This fueled their suspicion that his termination was directly related to his participation at the march. Supervisors agreed. For example, when I told Darius that Marcus had fired Manuel, he threw his production schedule to the floor angrily, exclaiming,

DARIUS: Fuck him! Fuck him! Why he'd fire him?

LAURA: He said he wanted to make a point. He didn't want the other workers to think that they could play games with him.

DARIUS: Manuel, nah, not Manuel? Playing games with him? He said that? Fuck him!

But Marcus, the African American manager in my section, wanted to send a clear message about his expectations from Hispanic workers and "make a point." Firing workers sent a clear message that efforts to mobilize have consequences. Just as workplaces are embedded in the labor market, workers are embedded in networks of social relations, and these interconnected influences can have an effect on how members of a group develop understandings of their place in society.

The warnings from employers to suppress any interest in participating in the marches and boycott were reinforced by messages that Latinos received from friends and family members in the region. At HiCap, for example, concerns about the presence of undocumented immigrants in factories increased. Juan, an employee who left my section for a job in North Carolina, returned to Jessamine warning workers that immigration authorities were going into workplaces in North Carolina. He called friends from different workplaces, and several workers in my section and Roberto's section heard from Juan that immigration authorities were starting to go into factories and workplaces in South Carolina. They even heard that ICE was starting to go into workplaces in Jessamine. Clearly, events in other immigrant destinations were affecting workplaces and neighborhoods in this study. Mostly workers felt intimidated, and some were wondering if mass protests were a good idea after all.

Large events can impact communities. Inversely, micro-level decisions can influence social relations with broader implications, for instance, in the way people draw boundaries of acceptance and rejection. Firing Manuel added to the intimidation produced by the employer's threats. These combined tactics sent a chilling message to many Hispanic workers who had perceived their growth relative to native-born workers at the plant as a source of group strength. These decisions weakened the hopes for in-group inclusion with white Americans. This was illustrated poignantly when Rosalba, a Mexican immigrant, told Richard, "The company terminated Manuel. I don't think they like us." Rosalba had succumbed to the risk of associating the actions of individuals with those of the group, in this case associating the firing of Manuel with the race of the manager.

Immigrant workers were clearly aware that their favored standing in the labor market was fragile. They knew that employers could easily dispose of and replace them. Although almost always overheard as a warning to the native-born, they nonetheless heard employers repeatedly saying, "If you don't like the work, there are hundreds out there happy to take your job." These statements gave immigrants the sense that their favorable standing with employers was predicated on working by the employer's rules. Economic survival, then, was contingent on meeting the expectations of the employer and the rules of the workplace. Immigrants knew that the ethnic economy offered an alternative work environment where loyalty and ethnic solidarity led to more stability in employment relations, but many in my research did not see it as a desirable option. As Lisa Catanzarite and Michael Bernabe Aguilera also found, many immigrants in new destinations avoid working in the informal economy or working for coethnics.[7] A Mexican immigrant once told me, "I don't like to work for Hispanics because they don't pay you the going wages, they abuse you, and there is no record that I worked anywhere. I want a job where I can clock in at 8 a.m. and I can clock out at 5 p.m. If I do overtime, I want to be paid for that too." The ethnic economy, immigrants learned, was more prone to relationships of exploitation and abuse.[8] In the United States, anti-immigrant policies further diverted immigrants from the ethnic economy and into formal. mainstream jobs. Contrary to what I found in my research in the health-care field, where immigrants reacted negatively to the paper trail created by the electronic medical records requirements of the Affordable Care Act (ACA), the prolonged promise of immigration reform, with its associated exit from marginalization, drove immigrants to seek opportunities that provided a paper trail showing their contributions to the US economy.[9] Faced with this difficult choice, most immigrants in my study chose to work by the rules of the employer, rather than embracing the flexibility that they might have found in the ethnic economy, reflecting their long-term goal of incorporating more fully into US society.

As the date for the proposed boycott approached, my observations of the shop floor showed reluctance on the part of immigrants to discuss the event. Immigrant workers talked about it only if asked. Manuel, prior to his firing, said, "They [community leaders] are asking people not to go outside at all, not to go to school, to the stores." The planning of the events surrounding the boycott reached the ears of employers, who returned to the supervisors to discuss the potential consequences of boycotting work on May 1.

The Friday before the boycott, race relations with Latinos at the plant were once again challenged. The once-robust identity of Latinos as "exceptional workers" and as "reliable and dependable" came into question as the boycott approached. HiCap's general manager approached me once more to ask, "Where are your people about Monday?" I told him that I only heard of one person who was thinking about missing work, but the rest of them were planning to be there. At this point, the company had already fired Manuel, the worker who attended the immigrant rights march two weeks prior, and the message was not lost on the workers. Later that day, I was with a group of workers from my section at the plant's cafeteria, and workers started talking about the event:

At lunchtime, I sat with Rosa, Mariela, and Brenda. I told them that Dave asked if people were thinking about showing up for work on Monday. Rosa was surprised that he knew and asked, "Do they know about Monday? How do they know?" I told her that they must read the newspapers. Rosa said she already knew that she was going to be absent the Monday following the boycott and that she didn't want to get fired for missing two days in a month, like Manuel did. She said she needed the money, but if she could somehow afford it, she would boycott. Brenda said that she wasn't planning to work on the day of the boycott. Brenda and Mariela both said that had to work because, like Rosa, they too needed the money. After hearing that everyone else was planning to be at work, Brenda changed her mind. "If you are coming to work, then I am coming," she responded, seemingly not taking the event as seriously as the other workers. Rosa smiled sarcastically before admonishing her, "You have to do it from your heart, not because other people are going to do it. At first you said you were not coming to work, and now you are.

You have to do these things from your heart." The discussion with the workers at the plant cafeteria revealed that the workers had not anticipated the company's managers finding out about the boycott, perhaps explaining the notable absence of conversations in the plant about the event. Further, some viewed the event as important but incompatible with the individual economic realities that they could not ignore. Similarly, supervisors were aware of the potential consequences of Latinos missing work but were sympathetic to the movement. In a conversation with Roberto, the supervisor from the Back End, he shared that the workers in his section had plans to be at work on the day of the boycott but wanted to do something about it. They were planning to wear white clothes to work that Monday. Roberto's workers asked if the workers in my section wanted to join them in dressing in white to show support for the people who were boycotting or demonstrating in the streets. In this way, there was an effort to mobilize in a symbolic way within the plant, even though most were prevented, for economic reasons, from supporting it in deed.

Some of the workers, however, were attuned to the implications of even a symbolic demonstration of solidarity on the shop floor. A handful of workers were concerned about tarnishing their identities, as seen in this excerpt from my field notes:

> I went around the assembly line telling the Hispanic workers in 418 (our section) about wearing white to work on Monday in support of the immigration boycott. They thought it was a good idea, and Mariela suggested wearing a white baseball cap as well. Norma said she didn't agree with the boycott. She thought there were other ways to demonstrate, but she was afraid that boycotts would only lead to more raids in factories and intimidation. When I told Belinda, a Cuban worker, about wearing white, she actually got upset. She said she didn't agree with the boycott. She lifted her index finger into the air and asked, "You know what May 1 reminds me of?" Tantalized, I responded. "International Workers' Day?" She corrected me with abundant energy: "Communism! That's what May 1 means for us Cubans. May 1 was when they forced us to march. I am sure that there are Castro people behind this boycott. You won't believe what they look like. They are clean cut, they speak English better than a native, they're highly educated. Those are Castro's people."

The Second Giant Awakens: Community Nativism and Scrutiny

Two days before the boycott and less than three weeks after the April 10, 2006, marches for immigrant rights in Jessamine and elsewhere across the United States, a crowd of an estimated seven hundred people gathered in downtown Jessamine to rally against illegal immigration. This event was one of the central catalysts that dramatically shifted how Latinos saw their standing in the racial hierarchy. The marches across the country brought the immigrants out of the shadows and into the political light and energized the debate at a national level. Locally, some combination of the march and the widely publicized marches in cities across the country clearly activated nativist spirit, as well. On the Saturday before the nationwide immigrant boycott, a crowd gathered in Jessamine carrying signs calling for the "deportation of illegal aliens" and the deportation of Lindsey Graham, the US senator from South Carolina who favored immigration reform, with a path to citizenship for undocumented immigrants already in the United States. Many others waved signs questioning, "Why have laws, if we don't enforce them?" Hispanic community leaders came to know the rally as the awakening of "the second giant."

On Saturday, April 29, 2006, the South Carolina Council of Conservative Citizens was organizing the anti-amnesty rally, calling supporters to gather outside Senator Lindsey Graham's office and counter all the momentum that the immigrant marches had generated. I put away the newspaper and headed to the meeting, not knowing what to expect.

As I approached the gathering, I spotted a crowd of white people—I saw only three Black men in the crowd, and two of them were from the media. The crowd was gathered around a pickup truck flanked by Confederate flags. Men and women waved anti-immigrant signs that read, "More INS, Less IRS," "Illegals: Go back home!" "Vote for Pedro to Go Home," and "I Didn't Fight in Iraq for Illegal Aliens." I was standing next to a skinny white man about fifty years old and wearing red plastic glasses. A large red cell phone was hanging from his neck. A Mexican flag languished in his left hand as he tightened his grip on an anti-immigrant sign. He started talking to me in heavily accented Spanish. He said he was a church leader and that he "worried that there are too many immigrants in this country and pretty soon there isn't going to be room for everyone." He "was worried about the direction the US was going." I was not sure what to say and stood there staring, saddened. He asked, "Where are you coming from?" I answered that I was from California. He asked whom I was with. I said that I was with Stanford University. I asked, in English, if I could take a picture of his signs. He responded that I could and began telling me, now in English, what he tried to say in Spanish. I thanked him for the picture and walked away.

Now at a good spot to watch the crowd, I felt a hand tapping my shoulder. Standing next to me was a Fox News reporter flanked by a cameraman. She said, "Excuse me, who are you with?" I replied that I was with Stanford University. She said, "Ah, I thought you were with . . . the media. . . . I've been trying to reach Roger [the community leader I introduced earlier] to ask about tomorrow, and all the phone numbers that I have are either canceled or nobody answers." I suggested that she call the nonprofit where Roger works to ask. She said she was going to do that and left.

As I watched more people arrive, I witnessed a conversation among three of them:

> GUY 1: They can find one cow with mad cow disease, but they can't find twelve million Mexicans.
> GUY 2: If you wanna find them, just go to Little Mexico [the pejorative name for the Hispanic neighborhood in town].
> GUY 3: You mean, El Mexico. That's what they call it, El Mexico. It ain't no coincidence that this thing is happening on May Day.

A talk-show host stood in front of the crowd: "If these people wanted to be part of this country, they'd learn the language!" He continued, "I'll tell you what to do on Monday: Go shopping! If you are going to make a big purchase, do it on Monday!" Someone from the back of the crowd yelled, "Remember the Alamo?" An even louder voice followed, "Take Mexico's oil and pay for the fence!" The crowd got quiet for a few seconds before chanting the Pledge of Allegiance.

The talk-show host returned to the loudspeaker, shouting, "We need to do four things! First, we need to stop providing health care for illegal immigrants. Second and third, we need to stop providing welfare and education for illegal immigrants—I can't barely pay for my children's education!" The crowd applauded, obviously energized. He continued, "And fourth! And this is going to be the hard one!" He shouted even louder: "We need to hold employers responsible if they hire illegals!" The crowd clapped effusively, even more energized. He asked if people knew how they are being labeled for wanting to enforce the laws. A guy wearing a cowboy hat and a Dixie T-shirt standing next to me yelled, "Red necks!" The orator ignored him and said, "They're calling us xenophobic! racists! And I don't care! I want the law enforced!" Everyone got quiet for a few seconds. A woman standing next to me shouted, "Arrest the traitors!" referring to employers hiring undocumented workers. After the talk-show host spoke, a former Republican candidate took to the podium, so to speak. He stepped onto the back of the truck, flanked by Confederate flags, and waved to the crowd. The crowd started chanting, "We don't want reform! We want enforcement!" A white female shouted in my ear, "We are going to lose this country! They are 'dumbing' down the population. They're driving wages down!"

As I walked away, I saw a Mexican flag burning on the ground. My heart sank. As a dual citizen with Mexican and US nationalities, I respond to the symbolism of these flags. I thought of my father and how, when I was growing up, he used to make me stand up from my chair to pay respect to the flag as the Mexican national anthem played after the nightly news. "Flags are symbols of respect for us and for others," he always said. I swallowed with difficulty and had to fight tears as there was nothing but hostility for people of my group around me. I closed my eyes to regain composure when I saw the Fox News anchor rushing in my direction. She must have seen me react to the flag burning. As she hurried, seeking to capture the coveted decisive moment, I could see the headline: "Mexican Cries as Her Flag Burns on the Ground." I wanted to run away from the crowd, but I did my best to simply turn and walk away. My jaw was locked, my fists tight and glued to my side. I understood why the Hispanic media had not attended the rally. No Hispanic could leave this gathering unscathed.

There are many elements in this vignette from my field notes that can be discussed. For the purposes of this chapter, however, I briefly focus on some of the central actors and their demands. To begin, the media, politicians, and church leaders played a central role in tarnishing the image of Latinos in this region. The effects of the meeting organized by South Carolina's Council of Conservative Citizens did not end that day when everyone disbursed from the square. Anyone exposed to the media, politicians, and religious leaders sharing the values of the council were exposed to durable anti-immigrant messages. Second, looking at the terms and demands found on the signs people carried and the speeches people gave at the meeting, there was a clear and generalized sense of threat of the type discussed by Leo Chavez and Douglas Massey, portraying Latinos as "invaders" and as "law breakers."[10]

Clearly, the boundaries of otherness in US society are not drawn along a simple white-Latino racial divide. In fact, a dynamic body of research focuses specifically on the nature of the color line in US society.[11] My research weighs in on this debate, too. The main perspective that this chapter brings to this line of research is one that portrays the color line as a dynamic and rapidly evolving construct susceptible to regional shocks with racial undertones. Drawing from Bobo and Hutchings, and casting aside the constructs of race as white/nonwhite or Black/non-Black, we can interpret the perceptions of group threat with regard to Latino immigrant relations in a multifaceted context situated relative to both white and Black individuals.[12]

The minimal discussion of Black responses to the immigrant rights marches reflects the absence of a change in the stance of members of this group. Local Latino community leaders discussed establishing a collaboration with an African American reporter from a major local newspaper that brought a nonconservative perspective to the overwhelming context of local, conservative radio talk shows and editorials espousing anti-immigrant rhetoric—many of these inspired by the Fox Business Network television host Lou Dobbs. The reaction of African Americans, however, in my 2006 study was minimal, if not absent, and in the workplace, it primarily took the form of increased questioning. By 2009, however, a newly formed Hispanic advocacy association included both African American and white allies. But returning to the initial stages of the crystallization of otherness in Jessamine, the town where HiCap is located, Latinos gave no indication of changes in their relationships with African Americans. As I discuss later, these relationships were not driven by racial undertones but, rather, by competition in the labor market and criminal activity in neighborhoods. This observation is relevant because the overwhelming majority of my respondents indicated that they had more in common with white people than with African Americans, in spite of describing high levels of interaction with African Americans in the labor market.

The anti-immigrant rally, I argue, shows that facets of the color line can vary independently, as the rally sharpened the boundary of otherness between Latinos and whites but had almost no effect on the nature of Black-Latino relations. For example, the day after members of the Council of Conservative Citizens gathered outside the office of Senator Lindsey Graham, I attended a birthday party at the house of Mariela, one of the HiCap workers. Mariela invited Hispanic workers from HiCap, but most guests met working at other factories. Generally, the party conversations revolved around work and family, but at one juncture in a conversation, Juan, the itinerant worker I mentioned earlier, asked people if they had heard of the anti-immigrant meeting downtown. Juan said it was all over the news. Valeria, a worker I met in one of the other plants, said that she had heard about it. Fully half of the group had not heard about the rally, but they shared a common sentiment: "Americans [whites] want us deported." Then people started sharing experiences of discrimination related primarily to not speaking English, having papers, or the exploitation associated with having an unauthorized status. The stories were usually followed with, "but we are here to work hard," "we work harder than Americans and *morenos* [Black Americans]," and "without us, American business would fall apart because no one else would do the jobs we do." There seemed to be a sense of relief after they reflected on their work identities and positive traits.

Although the rally had an effect on race relations, and particularly on the way Latinos saw their relation to whites, Latinos resisted confirming negative stereotypes and further increasing their distance from whites. This desire to keep the focus on their exceptional worker identity and keep the Hispanic/mainstream boundaries as blurry as possible was evidenced in the events that unfolded after the anti-immigrant rally.

The boycott was scheduled two days after the counter-rally, and immigrants were torn about whether skipping work and keeping their children home from school was the right strategy to employ in the fight for their rights. As was my custom, the day the boycott was scheduled, I picked up Mariela, Brenda, and Barbara for the drive to work. We had agreed to wear white clothes in support of the movement, but Mariela and I were the only ones who did. Mariela even wore a white baseball cap to show her support for the movement. Surprisingly, Brenda, the only worker who initially said she was actually going to join the boycott, did not even wear white that day. In fact, she wore a black velvet outfit. Brenda wore a purple T-shirt, but she had not seemed terribly interested in the boycott at any point. Mariela said that she felt guilty to be going to work when we were supposed to be supporting the economic boycott for immigrant reform. She had heard in the news that to show our support, we were not supposed to send the kids to school, buy in the stores, or go to work: "the opposite of what we are doing." Other workers at the plant felt the same way, but several expressed concerns about fueling the idea that they were not reliable workers. Roberto came to my section and said that all of his people were at work as well. When his boss inquired why they were all wearing white, he said it was in support of the boycott.

For the subcontracting employment agency, the concern that workers expressed in maintaining their untarnished identities as exceptional workers reinforced the perception of Latinos as hardworking. The reputation of Hispanic reliability and dependability was more firmly established when the agency learned that all the Hispanic workers showed up for work as scheduled. Whether this reliability was the result of veiled threats from management, the firing of Manuel, which workers associated with the consequences of standing up for their rights, or simply an economic reality facing the immigrants was irrelevant. What mattered was that the Latino workers were at the plant as promised, that the agency maintained its commitment to the plant management that Latinos would be there. I must have shown my frustration with the agency's pleasure that workers at the plant rejected the boycott because upon my return to the shop floor after talking to the employment agency, Mariela took the Makita gun, lifted her head, and adjusted the white baseball cap as she said with emotion, "Laura, we are here with you." After I left the plant several months later, I interviewed Mariela and other workers who said that they would have left the factory had I decided to walk out that day. These statements suggest that supervisors have powerful influence on the organized reactions of workers.

On the day of the boycott, managers expressed a heightened interest in the attendance of Hispanic workers. I interpreted this unusual interest as evidence of management's readiness to act on their threat. Marcus, my manager, had not requested our attendance sheet in weeks, yet it was the first thing he did that morning. Henry, the training manager for the Lean Manufacturing Initiative, came to my section checking for Latino workers. Later that day, Roberto, the Back End supervisor, told me that he was surprised that the managers had requested his attendance sheets. The requests, as Roberto and I saw them, injected credibility into the threat that managers had hung over bilingual supervisors and shop-floor employees. After all, without an interest in intimidating the workers and the supervisors, the managers could have requested the attendance directly from the employment agency, bypassing supervisors entirely, as was their habit.

My observations of HiCap for the months preceding the marches showed me that references to the documentation status of Hispanic workers occurred solely among supervisors, managers, and the employment agency. Typically, when these conversations occurred with managers and the agency (or in a few rare cases, on the shop floor), they involved workers who were no longer at the plant. These were usually cases when the agency found that the worker's Social Security number was associated with an anomaly, typically a criminal record (ironically, not the actual worker's criminal record but that of the person who sold them the Social Security number). Thus, the Latino workers who remained at the plant were those with reputations untarnished by documentation status. After the Council of Conservative Citizens–organized anti-immigrant rally, however, a number of discussions and accusations about working without papers emerged from native-born coworkers.

The work environment changed for Latinos. I was building an air conditioner with two of the Latino workers when Thomas, the Black assistant supervisor, approached me, asking loudly, "Laura, how would someone get a green card?" I answered vaguely that one could get a green card via marriage, family, or maybe employment. He said he was asking Norma, a Mexican worker on the assembly line, what people needed to do to get a green card. I did not engage in his questioning to avoid raising anxiety among Hispanic workers. More than one worker on the floor cautioned that, like Darius, Thomas would "stab you in the back." Rose, one of the welders, told me that "he threw Kesha under the bus," removing her from her supervisory role in the Front End. Given this reputation, the last thing I wanted to do was talk with him about the papers of Hispanic workers. After trying to talk to me about papers, Thomas walked away whistling and parked himself next to Rosa and started questioning her. After they talked for a few minutes, Rosa called me to her workstation. I stood between her and Thomas. She asked, "Laura, what's a green car?" I responded, "A green card?" and explained to her that it was a permanent residency card. Rosa turned toward me and said, "Ahh! A green card! I thought he was asking me if I had a 'green car,' and since my car is green, I told him I do have one." I smiled and told her that he should not be asking those questions. Lowering my voice, I murmured to her that she needed to be careful with him. I went back to the table to finish the board. A couple of minutes later, Norma asked Rosa, "What did he ask you, Rosa?" Thomas had already moved to the other side of the conveyor belt and was interrogating Barbara and Mariela. Rosa told Norma that he asked her if she had a green card, but she thought he was asking if she had a "green car," sharing the humorous anecdote.

All humor aside, Hispanic workers perceived the questioning as a form of scrutiny and would have refrained from talking to workers like Thomas if they had foreseen the exposure of their documentation status. Most workers do not have the benefit of knowing every worker's reputation and become disappointed when their trust is violated. I noticed that Norma had her head down. She seemed mortified, and I went to talk to her. I asked if she was okay. She said that during the break, Thomas asked her why she looked so sad. She told him that it was because she had seen in the news that Americans do not like Latino immigrants. She told him that she saw a sign that said, "God damn Mexicans! Go back home!" posted on the road. She said that it saddened her to see that Americans do not like Latino immigrants: "because we are not bad people; we are here to work." Thomas asked her if she had a green card. She told him that she did not. She felt like she could tell him because he was not going to talk to anyone about it. I told her that she may have misjudged him, that he had just asked Rosa if she has a green card and he is talking to everyone about the people who do not have a green card. She needed to be careful. She apologized. She had not wanted to lie: "What can he do? I don't think he is going to be so heartless as to report us to Immigration. What's the worst that can happen? That we lose our job?"

While it is difficult to know precisely what Thomas or anyone did with the information, his immediate effect on Hispanics was humiliation. In general, immigrants were candid about revealing their documentation status to people they trusted, but they hunkered down when they were ridiculed for not having papers. Lacking the work authorization that the native-born take for granted embarrassed and humiliated them. They would rather that the focus be on their work ethic than the absence of a work visa or green card. After the rallies and the awakening of the anti-immigrant giant, their documentation status was a status that few people ignored at the plant. Still, few thought the consequences called for desperation, at least up to this point. "What's the worst that can happen? That we lose our job?" In hindsight, these questions were prescient.

Instances in which Latino workers described that "Americans don't like us anymore" focused mainly on white Americans. In part, this was because the face of the Council of Conservative Citizens rally was uniformly white. In spite of this feeling, the immigrant workers received messages that helped them cope. The plant still preferred hiring Latino workers, and Ready Hands continued to laud Hispanics as its "best workers." Employers said that "the undocumented workers [were] the most hardworking people, the best workers you can hire." In addition, Latinos found the support of some white operators (mainly men), which attenuated the negative reactions from many whites in the city. The topic of immigration continued to attract attention for a few days after the anti-immigrant rally and boycott. I was assembling a baseboard when I overheard Mike, one of the white operators, ask T.J., "Did you hear about the meeting in [Jessamine]?" I thought he was talking to me and replied, "What?" He seemed surprised that I heard him, and signaling that it did not matter, he continued, "There was a meeting in Greenville. . . . They're a bunch of racists!" Carlos and J.T. continued working. They pretended indifference and did not get involved in the discussion at all. Mike said that the demonstrators were a bunch of Republicans with nothing better to do. I was surprised to hear someone criticizing Republicans, because it did not happen often. He told me that he was a "conservative Democrat."

Over the previous few months, Mike had shifted his behavior toward Latinos. From being indifferent and at times rude toward Latinos when they first arrived at the plant, he began to support and even care for

Hispanics as he interacted with and trained them. Black workers and white females, as discussed elsewhere, were more antagonistic toward Hispanics—with some differences along gender lines—in part because the Hispanic newcomers were replacing them in jobs on the assembly line. Although I never asked Mike why he had changed, it seemed related to his increasing exposure to Latinos. It was also clear that Mike, unlike the white females and the Black workers, was not afraid of losing his job to the immigrants. It also became clear that he had come to appreciate the positive attitude of the new arrivals.

This is not to say that, prior to these events, native-born workers were unaware of undocumented immigration. But before the marches, there was little discussion, at least openly, about the status of workers on the floor. After the anti-immigrant rally and on the day of the boycott, native-born workers at HiCap began asking about documentation status and consequently increased the salience of documentation status as an identity, sharpening the boundaries between immigrants and native-born workers.

Raids and a New Enforcement Regime: The House of Raeford

Fear of being apprehended and uprooted is a uniquely immigrant fear. This fear lives under the skin. It wakes up and goes to bed with immigrants and even haunts them in their worst dreams. This fear begins before immigrants set foot on US soil and cuts across class lines. In the immigrant imagination, *la migra*, the immigration authorities, is a powerful force that is both hard to fight and hard to ignore. Even after having a blue US passport in hand and a pristinely framed naturalization certificate, I still fear them. Many years after becoming a US citizen, I still feel uneasy every time I go through an immigration check point. The boundary of "us" versus "them" persists as long as an immigrant remains a member of an ostracized ethnic group and as long as society flexes its arm to persecute and intimidate out-group members with institutional agents.

It was not simply a matter of seeing their undocumented status grow in importance that shocked the immigrant workforce in South Carolina. Enforcement was also becoming a salient concern. On October 7, 2008, more than a hundred Immigration and Customs Enforcement

(ICE) agents descended on the House of Raeford Farms poultry plant in Greenville County. As the agents fanned through the poultry-processing plant, workers scurried through the hallways to evade capture. Ultimately, over three hundred immigrant workers were arrested that day, and from my discussions with family members of the workers, I learned that many of those detained were later deported. As with most information that is passed along through the immigrant "grapevine," the details of the *redada de la pollera* (the poultry plant raid) were vague for most immigrants. Typically, they knew that *la migra* (ICE) had raided the plant and that many were arrested and deported. Many also heard firsthand or secondhand accounts of the raid and how humiliating it was for the workers and their families.

The Associate Press coverage painted a bleak picture, as shown in this story from October 6, 2008:

> Federal agents detained more than 300 suspected illegal immigrants Tuesday in a raid at a chicken processing plant that has been under investigation for months. The raid took place during a shift change, when police and federal agents spread through the House of Raeford's Columbia Farms plant and ordered all workers to show identification, according to officials and witnesses.
>
> Maria Juan, 22, was one of about 50 relatives and friends of workers who huddled at the edge of the plant after the raid, some weeping and others talking frantically on cell phones. She was seeking information about her 68-year-old grandmother, a legal immigrant from Guatemala who went to work without identification papers but was later released. "Families are going to be broken apart," Juan said. "There will be kids and babies left behind. Why are they doing this? Why? They didn't do anything. They only wanted to work."[13]

Although undocumented workers would probably not need a reminder of the potential to have their families "broken apart," seeing it reported in mainstream outlets made that reality feel all the more immediate. But to really drive home the issue, the undocumented in my study needed only attend Sunday Mass in the weeks following the raid. Muted whispers and furtive glances from the pews betrayed the presence of the humiliated wives and mothers who had been caught in the raid. Spared immediate deportation by the fact that they had children to care for, they were under "house arrest," and they wore long skirts in an attempt to conceal their GPS-enabled ankle monitors, which they referred to euphemistically as "ankle bracelets."

What the immigrants did not know was that this raid was far from a random event. Earlier in 2008, eleven supervisors (all immigrants from Mexico) and the HR manager were arrested on charges ranging from aggravated identity theft to filing false I-9 employment identification forms. For ICE to show up with over one hundred agents took considerable effort, given that the total of ICE agents assigned to the entire state of South Carolina was twenty-two. The raid at House of Raeford happened because ICE believed that 777 out of 825 workers at the plant had submitted false documents to prove their eligibility when they were hired. An informant with ties to law enforcement told me that the word on the street was that ICE had warned management at Columbia Farms that it needed to overhaul hiring practices and that ICE was upset by the lack of attention paid to the warning. Regardless of the actual circumstances surrounding the raid, it was large and well covered in all the English and Spanish news outlets, from print to radio to television. Whether the raid was part of an enhanced enforcement regime is open to debate, but its huge impact on the psyches of undocumented immigrants living in the state was undeniable.

An immigration raid in a town of just over sixty thousand people gets noticed. The raid at the House of Raeford reframed immigrants' presence in the community from *exceptional workers* to *law breakers*. As noted, many Hispanic immigrants were arrested and exposed in a disturbingly public way. Interviewing non-Hispanics eight months after the raid, many noted that "immigrants don't follow the rules of this country" and "they take American jobs." For immigrants, however, flexing the enforcement arm of the US government pinched the already sensitive nerve of tenuous employment, leaving many in the community nearly paralyzed. Many in my study were affected either personally or through the experiences of relatives and friends. For example, Juana, a Mexican immigrant, summarized the experiences of many of the women under house arrest as a result of the raids:

LAURA: How was it for you when immigration arrived at the plant?

JUANA: It was horrible. . . . Immigration showed up on October 7. I was inside the factory working, and when they descended on the factory and people starting yelling, "La migra! La migra! La migra! La migra!" I was scared. I looked everywhere for exits, but there were none in sight. I didn't know where to go, where to run.

LAURA: Nobody alerted you that they were coming?

JUANA: No, by the time I heard, they were already inside.

LAURA: Were there people who were able to escape?

JUANA: I heard that some did, but only five or six. They caught almost all of us, and then they took us to a place like a warehouse, not too far away. They drove us in groups of about twelve people, I think, in the immigration vans. After the vans, they used buses.

LAURA: How many people did they take?

JUANA: We were 370 people. They let me go in the evening because I have a child born here. They asked if I had children born here or if my children were born in Mexico. They asked if they were minors. I told them that I have four children, all of them are minors. They had me call my husband to tell him to take care of the children and to tell him that they were going to release me but that I didn't know when. They let me go at five in the afternoon. I arrived here at six in the afternoon.

LAURA: What was going through your mind when all this was happening?

JUANA: I was . . . I was just crying and crying, crying, crying, and crying. And when I called my family, then we were all crying. It was so traumatic because I didn't know what was going to happen to me, to my children. I just cried and cried.

LAURA: And your children?

JUANA: The older one was just arriving from school, so she didn't know. It was just my husband and my sister who were at home. When I arrived home, they [her children] asked, "Mom, what happened to you? What do you have on your foot? What happened? What did they do to you?" I told them, "Immigration caught us all. They put an ankle bracelet on me." I didn't know what else to tell them. I am going to be wearing this thing [the bracelet] like I am branded. It's

embarrassing. It's like telling everyone that you got caught for working, caught for working as an illegal.

LAURA: How is your life now?

JUANA: It's difficult. I live with the ankle bracelet, and I have to charge it
two hours, one hour at night, every twenty-four hours. I don't know
when they are going to take it off.

LAURA: Are you working with the lawyers from the Hispanic Council?

JUANA: No, because apparently to have a lawyer to fight your case, you
need to have been here for ten years. The judge told me they can only
help people that have been ten years in this country.

LAURA: What are your plans?

JUANA: I don't know, depends on the judge and what they decide. I
don't know yet what is going to happen to me.

LAURA: Are you going back home . . . ?

JUANA: No, no, I am not leaving without my children, they are American. If I leave, I will be taking my children with me.

Like Juana, immigrants with less than ten years in the United States
faced a distressing future. At the time of this research, many were still
working with consulates and pro bono lawyers in search of ways to remain in the United States. Unfortunately, the negative effect of the raids
complicated immigrants' lives in multiple ways. Women's earnings as
production workers in factories had helped balance their already precarious economic situation during the Great Recession. With the economic downturn and the dying out of the construction industry, many
men barely made enough to make ends meet; others did not even make
that much.

Fidel, a Guatemalan immigrant from Huehuetenango, was in this
situation. I met Fidel and his wife in 2006. At the time, he was full of
optimism about starting a small business in his hometown with his
hard-earned savings. He was an active community leader spearheading
literacy efforts for Guatemalan women in Greenville County, a devoted
father, and committed worker. With his wife, Ramona, he worked at the
House of Raeford and any other job that came his way. Still in 2006,
fighting high turnover rates, the poultry plant was attracting a steady
immigrant stream to fill its vacancies. Many immigrants were from Fi-

del's network, a Mayan-origin Guatemalan group. I reunited with Fidel and his wife for a follow-up interview in 2009. We were meeting at the local church he started with other Guatemalan community leaders. The church had doubled its size and met the needs of many in this community.[14] When I walked in the room where we scheduled the interview, I was expecting to see the strong and optimistic community leader I met two years ago. I found a devastated man. I saw a man sitting in the chair with none of the sparkle that made so many in this community look up to him. He was hunched in a chair, leaning heavily on the armrests. The wrinkles in his face were deep and hardened. He was somber. Deep shadows framed his eyes. He was fidgeting with the tips of his fingers, anxiously.

Ramona, Fidel's wife, was sitting next to him. I could not see her face because her head was lowered, her chin tucked in her neck. She wore a long denim skirt that reached the floor. I had not seen women wearing these garments since my high school days in Mexico—many years ago. Her outfit caught my attention because the weather was almost one hundred degrees out, and we were all drinking ice water. When I met Juana at a church gathering two years prior, she seemed shy but made eye contact and carried herself comfortably when we talked. She never attended school in Guatemala, but, in the US, she was determined to learn Spanish and was in a literacy program. She told me then, "I want to learn for work. I want to talk. I want to understand what people say." I assumed she also wanted to lessen some of the teasing and abuse deriving from ethnic and linguistic differences. The poultry plant was staffed with Spanish-speaking Mexican workers who teased her and belittled her and her coethnics because they did not speak Spanish. The bilingual supervisors on the floor "yelled at [her] all the time" because she "didn't know Spanish." Like many other women from this Mayan community, she conducted her life in Chuj, her home language. Like Fidel's, Ramona's enthusiasm with her new life in the United States evaporated when her life took a dramatic turn.

Immigration authorities arrested Ramona during the immigration raid at the House of Raeford. Ramona worked the night shift at the plant for more than five years. One of her eldest sons was also arrested and deported two months after the raid. Fidel, her husband, escaped deportation because he had left the plant prior to the raid due to injuries to his hand. When I interviewed Ramona and Fidel, they were both shocked by these events. The more than two hours I spent with them were filled with long pauses between questions and tears. Fidel responded to most of my questions and served as an interpreter when Ramona responded in Chuj:

LAURA: How long did you work at the poultry plant?

RAMONA: Five years, until immigration arrived and I had to leave. . . .

LAURA: How was that for you?

FIDEL: Very difficult. She is staying here because she has an American child. They [ICE authorities] let them go, those with American children, the same day. They only detained them like six or seven hours. ICE arrived at 9 a.m. The last people left around 11 p.m. or midnight, I think. But they let her go around six in the afternoon.

LAURA: What happened when Immigration arrived at the plant?

FIDEL: They detained them. . . . After they detained them, they took them to a different place, investigating. They went through a list of questions.

RAMONA: They asked questions about how we arrived. . . .

LAURA: Did you talk to your family?

FIDEL: No, we found out that they detained her because the people with papers were able to contact family members immediately, and that's how we found out.

RAMONA: They asked if I had American-born children. They said that because I had American-born children, I could stay, and those without American children, they took them all at once, and they left.

LAURA: How is your life now?

FIDEL: She has an appointment every month or two. Every two months she has to go to North Carolina to check in. I have to find someone to give her a ride because I have to work and I can't take her. I don't have a license [to drive], and I can't take her. I have to pay for someone to take her.

RAMONA: They put an ankle bracelet on me. They have to check that I am here.

FIDEL: She has to connect the bracelet to a power outlet, and they can see through a satellite in the computer, I think.

LAURA: How are you holding up?

RAMONA: It's horrible, totally horrible to wear the ankle bracelet.

LAURA: How has this situation been for you and your family?

FIDEL: It's very difficult, because our plan was to return to Guatemala in May of next year. She was going to return to Guatemala to pick up our older children to bring them and educate them and give them a future here. Our town is very poor. There is not enough food, schools, transportation. But then Immigration arrived and started arresting people. At the same time, I was out of work for two months, two months with no work, and she just can't work. This has been very difficult for us.

LAURA: How is your son dealing with the deportation?

FIDEL: He is okay. He is in Guatemala now.

LAURA: Did they deport him directly to Guatemala?

FIDEL: He spent two months in Atlanta in a detention center before they sent him to Guatemala.

LAURA: And how is he dealing with things?

FIDEL: He told me it was really hard for him. He felt humiliated, real bad. He was in jail, and he was hungry. He didn't have food, only clothes. He'd never been in jail or arrested and spent two months in jail.

Ramona was no longer working in the 2009 follow-up interview. Before the raids, she had refused to get help from the government or charitable organizations. After her arrest, she spent hours going to churches and seeking aid to help pay for her rent and food. Her focus on learning to read and write has been replaced by a focus on learning about the immigration enforcement regime. She interacts with immigration authorities frequently and struggles to understand complicated immigration forms that she has to sign usually without clearly understanding what they say. She travels great distances to legal appointments and is constantly aware of the ankle bracelet that she tries to disguise by wearing long skirts.

The impact of the raid on those who were arrested cannot be fully gleaned from the interview excerpts or from newspapers reports of the events. When the fear of immigration authorities becomes something real and materializes in devastating events such as arrests and deportation, it takes time for people to process their feelings, feelings that defy being fully conveyed. In fact, in an interview with Mariano, a Mayan community leader I had known for more than three years, he told me that the women who were apprehended during the raid were having difficulty gaining help from community organizations because they "have a hard time expressing themselves about the event, and it's hard for lawyers and community advocates to get their story." Some in the community attribute their brevity and silence to linguistic and educational barriers. My observations of the women in safe spaces like catechism sessions, weddings, or family visits leads me to believe that the shock of their arrest and interacting with the enforcement regime has had a psychological impact that has surpassed any literacy or communication barriers.

Some sectors of the community were particularly devastated by the raids. Two years ago, I studied a Mayan group that was thriving, lauded as a model of integration and upward mobility in spite of the linguistic and educational challenges they faced. Pastors, priests, and advocates talked about how they "admired" the group's solidarity and commitment to the communities where they lived.[15] The raids at the poultry plant shifted the course of their future and initiated a downward spiral that showed no signs of relenting:

LAURA: How did the raids influence the community?

ARMANDO (COMMUNITY LEADER): Some people returned [to Guatemala] voluntarily, but there were others that Immigration sent back. From our community, there were about twenty people that went back. But there are other Mayan communities in the area, and from this one other community, about thirty-six or thirty-seven went back to Guatemala.

LAURA: Did they return as families, because I understand that some women stayed here and the men were deported?

ARMANDO: Yes, first they sent the men, but after that, one by one, the others followed. The wives returned as well. We also worked with the consulate in Atlanta. We have been working with them, and they were doing what they could to accelerate the deportation of women and children after the husband was deported and was already in Guatemala. So that the family could be reunited, the women followed their husbands, and they have returned as well.

LAURA: What was the feeling in the community? The response of the people?

ARMANDO: It was hard. It was very hard. People in the community were very scared because we thought that it was going to be like that everywhere, and then the news, all of that was in the news. For a while people didn't go out at all. They preferred to stay in their homes because we kept hearing that ICE was all over town, . . . going into Walmart, going into the stores and the gas stations. Fortunately, and thank God, we are still here. Following the raid, people from the consulate came here. They held meetings with us trying to help families that were left behind after Immigration deported several of the men. Those of us who were working were working in fear after that. It was—there was so much pressure falling on us all at once. We were so afraid. We knew that raids don't happen so easily, but we had to be careful because the laws were also changing. We were being hit from everywhere. We had to be careful at work, careful driving, careful walking in the street. We had to be careful everywhere we went. There might be another raid or not, but we had to be careful.

The immigration raids had a trickle-down effect on the lives of many immigrants in the region. As can be inferred from the descriptions of the community leaders, many people felt persecuted after the raids at the factory, even if they were not directly affected. The interdependence that exists between immigrants contributed to this expanded effect. Armando noted,

ARMANDO: Since the arrests at the poultry plant, our community has been in decline. . . . The economy in this community depended on collective donations, and without members, we are hanging by a thin thread, . . . struggling to survive, . . . trying to do what we can for those that are without work. . . . My cousins had to move in with us because of their situation, because he can't find work. So we are really worried, but we help each other, between families. My brother had to leave. In the United States, whether you work or not, you still have to pay rent, so it is a very difficult situation because we are out of work. We cannot pay the rent, and we cannot survive. The situation is so bad that many people make the decision to return to Guatemala instead of staying here without money.

LAURA: Have people actually started returning to Guatemala, or are they just thinking about it?

ARMANDO: Yes, . . . the laws have changed in all the states, so it's not like you can just move somewhere else anymore. So definitely there are people that have made the decision to go back to their country. We always communicate with each other and talk about whether there is work. And if there is work in another state, well, people go to that state, but if there isn't work and especially if we find that laws there are strict, well, we really don't have any choice but to return to our country. Many people have returned because the doors are closing on us.

Although this community, marginalized linguistically and culturally even among the Hispanic population, was especially hard hit by the backlash from the marches and fallout from the raids, Armando introduces another source of difficulty that was rapidly emerging in importance, not only for the Mayan communities but for all immigrants: changes in the laws.

State Laws and the Sharpening of Group Boundaries

At the anti-immigrant marches, many white Americans waved signs questioning, "Why have laws if we don't enforce them?" The immigrant marches struck a chord and threatened the status quo. It was no surprise, then, that many states, including South Carolina, passed anti-illegal-immigration laws, often with wide margins of approval from state legislators. The effect of anti-illegal-immigration laws compounded with previous events to create a sense of alienation far more profound than that captured in any of the events previously discussed. The severity of this effect resulted from laws that changed the relationship between immigrants and employers, weakening and often destroying the immigrants' identity as an exceptional worker. With the exceptional worker identity intact, my data show that the immigrants were able to simply shrug off or ignore the subtle but commonplace slurs or sideways glances directed at minority populations that Bobo and Hutchings describe as "laissez-faire racism."[16] My data even show that the immigrants were able to get past frequent and violent armed robberies and assaults at the hands of the African Americans with whom they so often lived in close proximity. Furthermore, my data from 2005–6 show that they not only were able to deal with these injustices but were able to deal with them and remain positive and optimistic about their place in the area and their prospects for the future. The recurrent theme seemed to be that they were valued by the "Americans" who surrounded them. Given their ability and need to compartmentalize being the victims of crime, it is probably relevant that in my interviews with immigrants, "Americans" almost always meant the mainstream of "white Americans." So strong was this connection that, when my respondents referred to all Americans, they would use some form of "Americanos y morenos" (Americans and Blacks). This association with the mainstream seems to indicate that the immigrants' own view of the color line in the US more closely resembled the Black/non-Black model posited by Jennifer Lee and Frank Bean than the white/nonwhite model traditionally and recently seen in sociological literature.[17]

In contrast to the optimism the immigrants expressed in the early interviews, the following quotes from 2009 show how painful it was for them to see the fading of their exceptional worker identity, crushed by laws that were aimed at eliminating access to employment for the undocumented immigrants of South Carolina. Carmela, a Mexican immigrant from the state of Puebla, arrived twenty-one years ago in the United States. She lived in New Jersey for about fifteen years before moving to South Carolina. Carmela liked the tranquility and the availability of jobs in South Carolina compared to the crowded housing conditions and labor markets in New Jersey. She had worked as an operator in several factories in Mexico and continued working in that type of job in the United States. When she arrived in South Carolina, she worked for several years in the textile industry. She told me, "When I first arrived at the textile factory, I was able to get all the overtime I wanted, and being one of those people—well, my husband used to get upset because I was working so much. But I couldn't see spending my money to get all dressed up and go out. I mean, where would we go? So I just worked and worked and saved and saved and eventually bought us a trailer so we could save on rent. The work was there, so that became my life." But then Carmela saw things change:

> First came the rallies, but then the laws changed, and things really got screwed up. Companies started sending people home. The companies have been telling people that they are going to call, but they don't call. Things have changed a lot. Many people lost their jobs. Before the laws changed on us, everybody was working. Many of us had jobs. We even had the opportunity to say, "If I don't like my job here, I can go apply to this other place because they are hiring people." Not anymore. They don't want us anymore. I haven't been able to find work for a year!

Surprisingly, few of my respondents in 2009 mentioned the effects of the Great Recession. Carlos, an immigrant from northern Mexico who had familiarity with both the construction and food industries, was one of those few, and he shared insights on the impact of the recession as it coincided with the changes in the legal environment. Carlos had moved to South Carolina from Atlanta after Georgia implemented stringent laws related to immigrants:

> CARLOS: We used to see people arriving from places like Atlanta, where the laws got tough. They saw South Carolina as a place where there were still opportunities. But now, the laws here changed. It got harder to make it here, and now the changes in who is here have more to do with people leaving than with people arriving. Before, when you started a job, all they wanted to see was your taxpayer ID. My guess is that it would still be that way in construction because people are pretty invisible in construction. You run your crew, and nobody ever asks you to show documents. But the economy has really slowed down, and we're getting all these construction crews from out of state, from Georgia, from Texas, even from California, and they are willing to take four or five dollars an hour less for the jobs than we were getting. So even the construction jobs are gone.
> LAURA: Are you also competing with the American construction workers?
> CARLOS: No, not really. We already got their jobs by doing the work for less than they would [he laughs, acknowledging the irony in his

commentary]. Now we're getting our jobs taken by these out-of-state immigrant crews the same way. So it has gotten really tough. In construction, there is just way too much competition for the few jobs that do exist, and everywhere else the new laws, the E-Verify laws, have made it almost impossible to land a job. The thing is, these laws haven't even gone completely into effect yet. But there are a lot of companies that are starting to use E-Verify even though they are small enough that they don't have to. The law says that they have to check new employees, but some companies have also been checking existing employees, and the ones that don't make it through the filter, well, they are out of a job, too. It used to be easy to find work, but in the last year or so, things have changed so much. Now there are really few opportunities and just too many of us fighting for them.

Theorizing "Nativist Shocks"

While the workplace provides a wealth of examples on the way nativist shocks influenced the social relationships of Latinos with the native-born, there was also an institutional response associated with the marches. Before proceeding, it is important to note that research shows that the 2006 immigrant rights marches created a sense of hope in the Hispanic community, but the reception of the marches among immigrants and native-born citizens differed according to immigration status and region.[18] As chapter 5 demonstrates, the anti-immigrant rallies and subsequent shocks sent the pendulum swinging wildly in the opposite direction, eliminating most of the gains made with this important social movement and crystallizing the boundaries between the immigrants and the native-born in the region.

In interviews with community leaders and neighbors in the period around the immigrant marches, several discussed the effects of the marches in unfavorable terms. Francisco, an immigrant from Colombia and a community leader, noted, "The marches only stirred the hornet's nest, like they say. After the marches, there was more repression against Hispanics in the companies where they work and with the authorities. The marches had a negative impact." Camila, a Mexican operator at a local factory, echoed, "Things have gotten worse since the marches. Before the marches, people didn't know about us, and they were not afraid of us. The marches showed people that we are too many, and that scared the Americans. After the marches, people started having more problems getting jobs and moving ahead. They let a lot of people go at the factory where I work."

As long as Latino newcomers in the state kept their plans and desires to themselves, the native-born appeared to be content in letting them live in anonymity. *Nativist shocks*, then, are those events or situations that promote the rapid coalescing of nativist or protectionist boundaries between mainstream society and out-groups. In this case, nativist shocks were both catalysts that provided the native-born an opportunity to react and policies that targeted the out-group. The effects of both were not lost on Luis, a Hispanic community leader who helped coordinate the immigrant rights march in Jessamine When I talked to Luis in 2009, he recounted, "We really messed things up with those marches, things were actually going really well for the Hispanics in the area before we did that. The marches were aimed at helping empower the immigrants in the area, to promote solidarity in the community. No one ever suspected that the locals would react so strongly to them. Now we have E-Verify laws and rules that prevent our children from getting an education."

When I asked another community leader, Ernesto, whether he thought race relations were getting better or worse, the topic of the marches was, again, central to his response:

ERNESTO: Up until a about a year ago, I think that race relations were getting better. Ever since, I guess, with all these Hispanic rallies across the nation and everybody trying to move to get a general amnesty in place, I think that it has gotten worse since then. But up until a year ago, I thought it was getting pretty good, really promising. Everybody was working, and there wasn't—it wasn't controversial to hire a Hispanic person for day labor, and now even that is becoming more controversial.

LAURA: Do you think that the conversations around immigration reform have had an impact?

ERNESTO: I think a significant impact, a negative impact. Definitely the rallies have only united the ones that are against it more, and the ones that are for it are mainly Hispanics, so I think, I honestly think that the marches and stuff were counterproductive, simply because it rallied the people that were against it. They felt like we were attacking them. . . . When you feel attacked, you just feel like you have to unite. And it wasn't like that at all, before. Although I did join, I did participate, and I supported it simply because I didn't want my people to think that I wasn't supporting our people, so it was a real double-edged sword for me.

Bobo and Hutchings talk about group position theory and the crystallization of intergroup boundaries as something that can take place over a period of prolonged exposure.[19] The dotted line in figure 6.1 shows graphically how that would look. It is a slow and steady crystallization process. But nativist shocks have a sudden effect on this baseline process, resulting in brief periods characterized by abnormally high degrees of crystallization. The solid line in figure 6.1 displays what happens with shocks that are event based, such as the attacks of September 11, 2001, and the marches of 2006. I contend that there is probably an overshoot in the response and that the degree of crystallization might recover somewhat as the immediacy of the event fades. In the case of developments such as law changes, the effects are institutionalized, with possible

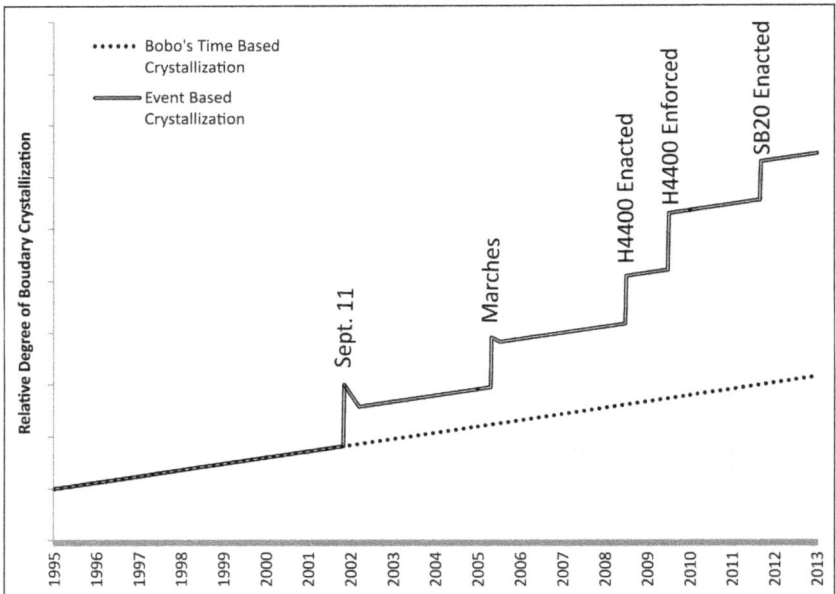

Figure 6.1. Racialized shocks and boundary crystallization over time

recovery coming from institutional adjustments—a subsequent court case invalidating a key provision or perhaps a political realignment.

Although my data in this research do not show it, I would like to make one last, and hopefully optimistic, point: the idea of the crystallization of intergroup boundaries that Bobo and Hutchings describe is not necessarily monotonic.[20] That is, I believe that it is perfectly reasonable that developments could materialize that would cause boundary crystallization to decrease as well.

Conclusion

This book addresses several unanswered questions: How and why does displacement of native-born workers with undocumented immigrants happen in the labor market? How do workers respond to racialized displacement? What are the consequences for immigrants and native-born workers involved in labor displacement? How does racial capitalism help us understand the construction of workplace segmentation and the racialization of labor markets? In answering these questions, I shed new light on questions of ethnic succession and segmentation in the labor market and reorient the ongoing debates about the economic impact of immigration. Additionally, in showing how racialized displacement works when employers use undocumented immigrants to push Black and white workers out of their organizations, the book reveals processes that are probably playing out in other contexts. The same dynamic, for example, could just as easily describe the displacement of workers unionizing, or intending to unionize, across the country.

This book provides insights into the way employers articulate race in discriminatory hiring practices. Labor market inequalities emerge from the racialization of immigrant workers and their introduction as displacements in organizations in which a Black and white color line historically dominated. In line with the theory of racialized organizations, and moving the analysis of the costs of immigration in a new direction, displacement is not a race-neutral process that results from labor market inefficiencies.[1] *Racialized labor displacement* involves employers and workers constructing social structures on intersecting categories of class, race, and gender. Furthermore, the consequences of displacement go beyond atomistic analyses of wage depreciation and economic-based competition. Racialized displacement fragments social relationships along class, race, gender, and other categories of vulnerability, such as criminal record and documentation status.

This book introduces racial capitalism to the analysis of segmentation in organizations, as it connects *the process* of capital accumulation to sorting mechanisms involving categories of distinction and vulnerability. Additionally, it shows how racial capitalism more accurately captures the labor market experiences of post-1965 immigrants of color arriving from Latin America and the Caribbean who are settling in new immigrant destinations.[2] Furthermore, the book responds to the important call for restructuring "our conceptualization of immigrants from ethnic people to racialized individuals" and the call to incorporate racism as we examine uneven structures such as those emerging through the struggle between capital and labor in racialized organizations.[3] To this end, I join other scholars who call to incorporate race perspectives into the analysis of documented and undocumented immigration in contemporary studies of the labor market.[4]

This book shows how new immigrant destinations are perfect settings to study immigrant racialization in the context of labor market competition. It teases out the role of employers in this process. In most new immigrant destinations, first-generation immigrants are new arrivals to the labor market and concentrate in "ethnic niches," enter occupations as managers, or are translating country-of-origin human capital into country-of-destination occupational advancement.[5] This variation makes it important to examine whether immigrants integrate as *replacements* or *displacements*. Additionally, in incorporating the less told story of undocumented immigrants in the US South, a place with sharp white and Black racial lines, the book shows how and why current animosity toward immigrants—especially toward undocumented immigrants—is part of a continuing pattern of ostracizing nonwhite people.

This book spotlights how workplace dynamics remain coupled with broader societal influences. In particular, it shows the importance of taking into account the embeddedness of racialized organizations in communities and government structures. Legislation banning employers from using race and gender in hiring (Title VII of the Civil Rights Act of 1964) contributes to the orchestrated but hidden encoding of racialized displacement. Community responses toward immigration respond to political forces framing immigrants as "criminals" and "job thieves." To understand changes in the color line of organizations, the book offers an analysis of the relationship between discriminatory practices and immigration backlash in communities in which racialized organizations are embedded.

I rely on racial capitalism theory to show how white managers use race, gender, and other intersecting categories of vulnerability to change the racial composition of the workforce. The resulting racialized displacement is the process by which employers orchestrate the removal of Black and white workers (mainly women) to create vacancies for more vulnerable and exploitable undocumented immigrant workers. While many people think that they have seen displacement, most have not. The evidence to date is for replacement and primarily after the fact, rather than of displacement, but see Vanesa Ribas's and my earlier work for analyses of these processes.[6] Examined after the fact, the two are frequently indistinguishable, as the results are, at least on the surface, the same. Understanding the differences between displacement and replacement is more than semantic, as the processes that drive them are quite distinct. The core of the immigration debate is whether immigrants integrate as substitutes or complements of native-born workers. Furthermore, scholars still grapple with why immigrants, who purportedly have lower human-capital skills relative to domestic workers in the secondary market, are more successful than African Americans are in employment access and retention. The book provides an answer to these questions by looking at displacement apart from replacement and in the context of racialization.

This book adds to the scant research on displacement by laying out mechanisms that can enrich our understanding of labor force turnover along class and racial lines and bringing in the perspective of employers. While displacement in new destinations has gained some attention, *the process* of introducing immigrant workers as displacements and the resulting effects on labor market segmentation have been difficult to document. Studies of displacement typically view the entrance of immigrant workers as resulting from replacement, a racially neutral process in which employers hire immigrants as complements to rather than substitutes for the domestic workforce. This study focuses on displacement, a racialized process that shows how managers integrate immigrants as substitutes for (displacements), not as complements to (replacements), native-born workers, as most academic scholarship sustains. I examine the mechanisms of displacement from the perspective of racial capitalism, a theory that allows us to examine structures of racialization and exploitation.

Displacement under Racial Capitalism

"What does it mean to assert a moral authority of those who have been marked as vulnerable, as the other, who frequently reside on the margins of authority?"[7] Racial capitalism is the process by which the dynamics of accumulation and dispossession, involving capitalists, workers, and communities, become articulated through race.[8] The analysis of racialized displacement draws inspiration from Cedric Robinson, who states that race is central to capitalism, with its roots in a history of colonization, exploitation, and systematic oppression of people of color.[9] In addition, racial capitalism allows for capturing how race and processes of racial differentiation are central components in the construction of other categories of distinction, such as class and gender, and, in this case, of the organization of economic life. Finally, as Justin Leroy and Destin Jenkins argue, the importance of racial capitalism as an analytical tool derives from helping us understand "how capitalism works rather than setting out to define precisely what capitalism is."[10]

Looking from the perspective of racial capitalism, we can see how, in workplaces like HiCap, race and racialization are central to labor relations. For example, at HiCap, lacking good papers centers undocumented Latino immigrants in a racialized position of exploitability and dispossession. Furthermore, hiring and promotion in workplaces revolve around categories of difference—"white," "Black," "Latino," "documented" or "undocumented"—in which white employers rank workers on the basis of who can be controlled most easily and who can most effectively enable the process of capital accumulation, which in manufacturing requires the constant and smooth running of the assembly line. Racial capitalism in new destinations is rooted in the vulnerability that undocumented immigrants experience (i.e., the constant threat of deportation), as well as in the growing precaritization of employment that contributes to labor market oppression. For example, fears of deportation, losing employment stability, and losing health insurance keep people locked in exploitative and oppressive working conditions while employers benefit from these vulnerabilities.

This book uses racial capitalism theory to go beyond deracialized explanations of social closure and segmented labor markets. The theory of social closure argues that changes in the composition of the workforce result from network hiring and that this hiring drives ethnic shifts and ultimately results in exclusionary closure, seen as the tendency of groups to monopolize resources by excluding outsiders.[11] Segmented labor market theory typically argues that poor working conditions at the bottom of the labor market create a situation in which vacancies are constantly produced.[12] As native-born workers churn out of jobs for any of a multitude of reasons, they create vacancies, about which the immigrant network learns. The network, in turn, supplies candidates to the labor market. In a pool overrepresented by network members, employers hire more immigrants.[13] This cycle continues, and the workplace becomes dominated by members of that particular network. This view emphasizes that it is social capital rather than human capital (in the form of skills) or reservation wages that explains the unexpected labor market success that immigrants, be they Latino or foreign-born Black individuals, have in some jobs or occupations relative to native-born Black workers.[14]

Why and how do employers turn jobs at the bottom of the labor market into undesirable jobs and directly manipulate the racial composition of the workplace? We know that employer preferences influence the pre-hire phase of the employment cycle, but a racialized displacement throws into sharp relief exactly *how* employers deploy these preferences to turn over the labor force and how workers respond to these actions.[15] Furthermore, employee demographics in an organization depend on the combination of differential inflows and outflows of workers, but existing research typically accounts for only one side of this process.[16] This book shows how employers, workers, and communities construct workplaces.

This book extends theories of labor market segmentation and labor and job queues. An additional theory I engage in this research is *split labor market theory*, which posits that segmentation occurs as a three-way conflict among employers, workers, and two different ethnic groups of workers.[17] Additionally, the theory suggests that introducing immigrants into the labor market is inconsequential for the higher-priced group that ends up in a protected segment of the labor market. The relevance of this theory for racialized displacement lies in what happens when employers introduce vulnerable workers (the "cheap labor") to threaten and displace native-born workers (the higher-priced labor). Contrary to this theory, under racialized displacement, no group is safe in the labor market. Employers segment the market not under the dichotomy of "low-cost" versus "high-cost" labor (or newcomer versus dominant worker) but in a more complicated manner, which includes vulnerable versus nonvulnerable labor. The displacement resulting at HiCap ended up segmenting the market along lines of documentation status, gender, and criminal record.

Furthermore, my focus is on the mechanisms that produce displacement and replacement and on the way race patterns the dynamics of hiring and promotion as employers try to expropriate more value from undocumented immigrant workers. Undocumented immigrants have little legal recourse in the United States and are subject to employers' oppression and abuse. Displacement can take many forms, but, in general, racialized displacement is a system in which workers, employers, and communities deploy their agency in constructing the racial and gendered structures that motivate workers' entry into or exit from jobs.

What Managers Want and Do in Racialized Displacement

Looking at how HiCap orchestrated the displacement at the company illustrates that a racialized displacement is no simple matter, and employers go to great lengths to create the illusion that they are engaging in simple replacement—as occurs in segmented labor markets, filling vacancies resulting from high turnover with workers who want to take jobs. At HiCap, the company not only used hiring agents to recruit and hire workers using race in hiring but also engaged in *preemptive asserted equality*, affirming that its hiring practices were colorblind when they were not. Managers constructed what I term *exploitative labor queues* built on racial stereotypes and the degree to which a group of workers is more exploitable. Unlike split labor markets, the price difference (in wages) between immigrants and nonimmigrants, under racial displacement, does not determine changes in the ethnic composition of the workforce. The degree of oppression and exploitability, as in racial capitalism, drives the change.

Under racial capitalism, and from the perspective of managers, displacement deploys race in hiring via an orchestrated process. This process starts with employers ranking workers in relation to the profits and extraction of labor they can get. At HiCap, the ranking involved both race and gender. With these markers of difference, Black, white, and Latino men and women were placed in a labor queue on the basis of perceived productivity and exploitability. With regard to ranking, at the top of the labor queue, HiCap placed immigrant men (under the gender-coded misnomer of "heavy lifters"), but it would take immigrant women when men were unavailable. Because of the Latinization of immigration, immigrants and Latinos are interchangeable categories in the exploitative labor queue, and Latinos in this context are a proxy for undocumented immigrants. HiCap's next choices in the labor queue were white women, followed by Black women. The latter were a majority of the female category and typically enjoyed the protection of Black female supervisors, gaining a degree of insularity from exploitation. The last groups in HiCap's queues were white and Black men. White men in operator positions were almost nonexistent (typically fewer than three out of thirty-six workers in a section) and made almost no trouble, as though they wanted to be invisible. Latinos eventually displaced two of the white men at the Front End. Once HiCap started displacing those at the bottom of its exploitative labor queue, it started creating vacancies for the workers it preferred to hire: Latino immigrants.

Colorblind discrimination under racialized displacement works precisely because it resonates with the individualistic attitudes that many white and Black workers hold toward hard work. It also works because the racial rhetoric masks discrimination and hyperexploitation in the labor market. Employers seeking low-cost and tractable labor rely on the narrative of "hard work" under capitalism to justify discriminatory hiring practices. Immigrants adopt these narratives to overcome their outsider status and the rampant xenophobia against their group. Racialized displacement drives the workforce demographics in three central ways. Employers develop labor queues ranking the most vulnerable workers ("the preferred workers") on top and the least exploitable at the bottom. In the absence of workers' resistance, they keep the workers at the top of the queue (Latino immigrants) and change the color line of the organization in the direction of this racialized group. Second, employers preemptively and strategically frame discriminatory practices by talking the talk and walking the walk of equal treatment, all the while masking the disparate impact. Finally, both employers and native-born workers themselves frame the qualities of undocumented workers in nonracial terms, allowing employers to carry on a racial displacement while masking the framework of race.

Orchestrating Displacement with Intermediaries

In addition to managers holding a labor queue that informs their preferences under racialized displacement, they are orchestrators, not implementers, of displacement. Like an orchestra conductor, managers hold the baton, but it is through the actions of the different players that their symphony is performed. In other words, we learn in this book how employers, to minimize legal and reputational risks, direct the displacement from a distance, as they delegate discrimination to agencies and other key players.

To carry out racialized displacement, employers engage labor market intermediaries who participate in an industry that thrives on mediating the participation of undocumented immigrants in oppressive and risk-loaded situations.[18] Labor market intermediaries (brokers) facilitate or hinder access to employers that seek to expropriate as much labor from their workers with the lowest level of risk to their bottom line. Getting workers to do what managers want—work more than is humanly possible—falls on these intermediaries, most often supervisors. Because the shop floor is generally decoupled from managerial supervision, intermediaries provide employers with plausible deniability when using race and gender in hiring and firing and ultimately drive the labor force in the direction of the workers whom employers want.

The labor market intermediaries at HiCap were bilingual immigrants. Immigrant labor market intermediaries are typically one short step removed in the hierarchy of vulnerability. Their competitive advantage in racialized labor markets lies in cultural traits, not in skills. Therefore, employers can easily dispose of them if the labor market shifts to a new preference category that is not under the cultural purview of current labor market intermediaries. Consequently, they are actors that cooperate with the employer to hedge opportunities and secure their place in the labor market.[19] Bilingual intermediaries like Diego, Roberto, and Carla go to great lengths to maintain the advantage that their structural position provides.

Structurally, we can conceptualize the bilingual intermediaries in displacement as brokers. Brokers are social actors or individuals that connect immigrant and nonimmigrant populations with employers and organizations. Under racialized displacement, intermediaries are ubiquitous in mediating the incorporation of newcomers and in processes of racializing workplaces. While not in organizational charts, ethnic recruiters and temporary employment agencies in the business of supplying immigrant workers are the central node that connects managers with vulnerable displacement labor. They also provide support to workers to enhance their exploitability and make their bosses happy.

The power of brokers in mediating the relationship between workers and employers lies in their ability to broker resources for workers beyond the labor market. In network theory, the sociologist Ronald Burt notes that brokers are individual intermediaries that have a degree of advantage due to the centrality of their position in the social structure.[20] Intermediaries connect employers and workers and serve both of these groups. At HiCap, brokers connected Latino immigrant newcomers with social service organizations and other services in new destination communities. Consider the example of the supervisor calling a school on behalf of a worker about a parent-teacher association (PTA) meeting or the example of a bilingual manager translating for a worker whose car broke down and needed repairs. The intermediaries, fluent in English and Spanish, are skilled in navigating societal institutions and minimizing situations of productivity risk for employers and workers. The more brokerage there is in a community, the more available workers there will be to sell their low-cost labor to capitalists and the higher the level of exploitability and oppression in the labor market.

While employers more openly deploy their preferences for immigrant workers when recruiting and selecting new hires, firing workers using race and gender categories was a covert strategy at HiCap. This made sense, as employers want to minimize the risk of conflicting with the law. HiCap moved to displace white and Black women with Latino immigrant men, but rather than firing workers directly, it degraded the jobs. In the punitive fashion that racial capitalism predicts, HiCap implemented a "lean" strategy in which it added more work to each worker, forcing them to work harder. It also made the jobs more unpleasant to "push them to quit." Managers transformed the workplace, asking workers to clean their workstation—jobs that nonimmigrant workers considered beneath them but "good for the Mexicans," according to some workers. Managers assigned contentious workers to workstations in which employees incurred the risk of repetitive injury and respiratory illnesses to "force out" these workers from the jobs and create more vacancies. This was followed by introducing more undocumented workers to fill the vacancies. When employers can get workers to leave their jobs voluntarily, they are not, at least not in terms of EEOC compliance, engaging in discriminatory practices. To an outsider, the exit of native-born workers is not a displacement but simply a replacement. Without the organizational obfuscation, however, this process is clearly an orchestrated racialized displacement.

Unlike the workers in Michael Burawoy's *Manufacturing Consent*, the workers I observed responded in categorically divergent ways to disciplining methods that forced them to work harder in order to save their jobs.[21] White and Black women initially resisted the exploitation that came in the sudden change in working conditions and tried hard to stay in the jobs. Still, under racialized displacement, for native-born women, resistance was futile because of the presence of a vulnerable group ranked higher in the exploitability labor queue. Employees felt that they could not complain that working harder was impossible when the more exploitable undocumented Latino workers were showing daily that the onerous levels of work were, in fact, achievable, at least in the short run.

In the racialized displacement at HiCap, when employers asked workers to exert more effort, rather than joining forces with Black and white women workers, immigrants cooperated with the white managers and their bilingual supervisors. Their cooperation manifested itself in working harder than native-born workers did and maintaining the "hard worker" schema that their bosses held for them. On the surface, employers' use of immigrant labor to threaten workers resonates with the dynamics described in split labor market theory, in which employers use immigrant labor as strikebreakers to threaten the workforce.[22] Under racialized displacement, however, the labor queue is not determined by price. Women, both Black and white, and documented Latino immigrants end up "forced out" of the workplace through employers' access to the more exploitable undocumented Latino immigrant workers.

Managers as actors in racialized displacement not only change the racial composition of their organizations but also use undocumented workers to change working conditions from the "good jobs" to "bad jobs" that many American workers no longer want.[23] When displacement results in permanent workers leaving the plant, and when employers fill these positions with temporary workers—which at HiCap were the only type of workers the company was hiring—displacement also results in jobs turning more precarious and becoming firmly anchored in secondary labor markets. From a race-relations perspective, the involvement of management in segmenting the labor market creates workplaces in which documented and undocumented Latino immigrants and Black and white workers see each other as competitive threats. Ethnic antagonism almost certainly emerges when employers threaten to displace native-born workers if they resist the same untenable standards imposed on the undocumented group.

Given the political nature of immigration and race relations in US society, in drawing conclusions about racial displacement, it is imperative to remark on not only what displacement is but also what it is not. Displacement is not a process in which immigrant workers "take jobs from Americans"—as conservative arguments maintain. My research shows no evidence that immigrants enter the job market to take jobs from American workers or that they are to blame for changing the working conditions that create the vacancies that agencies fill with immigrant hires. Immigrants are not doing this; their employers are. Displacement, as articulated in this study, happens because employers manipulate the labor market along the lines of race, gender, and legal status to create a segmented labor market. The existence of displacement should not surprise us but should drive us to think about how history repeats itself. Employer manipulation of labor markets has been a historical characteristic of US racial capitalism. Thus, to the extent that employers manipulate the market and profit from the vulnerability of immigrant workers and other minorities, employers, not immigrants, will remain the main source of labor displacement.

What Workers Want and Do in Racialized Displacement

Just as employers have preferences for workers and develop a labor queue based on exploitability and vulnerability, different groups of workers develop schemas about the jobs they prefer. At HiCap, workers thought of their jobs in relation to their degree of vulnerability, the opportunities they had in the wider labor market, and the history they had with the plant. While the young "floaters" had little justification for defending their jobs, other native-born workers were on a different footing when displacement started. Some workers were concerned about losing their jobs or were waiting for the company to convert them to plant employees and the attendant gain in job security. Others were already permanent employees who had worked at the plant for many years and did not want to lose that security. Some HiCap workers ranked their positions high in their job queues because they lived near the plant, had children in schools around the plant, went to church near the plant, or had social networks composed of workers at the plant. Others had already lost permanent jobs in textile mills due to reindustrialization and were afraid to return to the contingent workforce. As split labor market theory would predict, workers tried to keep immigrant workers out by engaging in exclusionary movements. Workers with papers, in this case the native-born white and Black workers who had worked in the organization for many years, engaged in acts of resistance to maintain their jobs (e.g., undermining training, refusing to pass on the tacit knowledge of the labor process, or otherwise driving Latino immigrants to make mistakes). Many expressed that they "used to like the job" but stopped liking it when employers started "the project." Contrary to what segmentation theory predicts, however, many workers fought hard to defend their jobs, even after the jobs were degraded.

Additionally, segmentation theories suggest that unlike immigrants, native-born workers are in protected segments of the market and are not at risk of losing their jobs. Research on *replacement* suggests that the jobs lost are those that nobody wants, the "bad" jobs. Under racialized displacement, however, workers in the protected segment of the market, such as native-born workers and immigrants with good papers, are increasingly vulnerable. When employers introduce a more exploitable racial group, workers on both sides of the color line (Black and white individuals) must fight to defend precarious jobs and avoid expulsion from the job market. Contrary to segmentation theory, the workers in this case found themselves more vulnerable or less vulnerable, but none were protected or secure in their employment.

Immigrant workers enter the workplace dominated by an ideology of "hard work," a schema that resonates with immigrants' own perceptions and their desperation to gain dignity and respect. The ideology of hard work justifies their placement at the top of employers' labor queues. Even when immigrants' placement at the top of employers' labor queues results, in part, from their vulnerability and exploitability, these workers continue to hold to the idea of "hard work" to defend their jobs. It seems paradoxical that a hyperexploited group will hold tight to jobs where they are mistreated and abused. Yet, for many immigrants, their "hardworking" identity is their source of strength and power. They may have little, but their labor is a source of pride and self-efficacy. Holding fast to the "hard worker" identity is also how immigrants gain a sense of belonging and integration in a society that praises hard work and dedication. In doing so, they may embrace whiteness, as the sociologist Richard Alba argues, but this strategy works only until immigrants encounter rejection and backlash in the community.[24]

Bringing attention to the dynamic nature of displacement, chapter 6 of the book shows how nativist shocks challenge immigrant workers' ideals and how in 2006, many undocumented immigrants experienced pushback in the community and, painfully, received the message that they did not belong. Given the link between community responses and labor market dynamics, displacement enhances theories of immigrant incorporation. That is, under racialized displacement, labor market incorporation is not a one-way road. It is contingent on the politics of class and race.

When managers drive displacement in contexts with rigid racial boundaries (i.e., Black and white), the introduction of a new ethnic group as a displacement vector alters the racial hierarchy in ways that create more racial divisions in the social organization of work. In the context of workplaces, for example, queuing processes involve discriminatory practices that favor hiring immigrants. They risk alienating immigrants from the native-born workers whom employers displaced in the labor queue. Consequently, discriminatory hiring practices undermine the possibility of class solidarity. When managers hire immigrants as displacements, immigrants suffer a racial/nativist backlash. Workers more effectively resist exploitation when they build solidarity bonds. Managers' preferential hiring and queuing derail this possibility. Outside of the workplace, displacement feeds the perception that immigrants rather than management displaces workers. The confusion enhances nativism and the demonizing of immigrants.

What Government and Communities Want and Do

The government as an actor in the construction of racialized labor markets shapes the field of policies and practices that determine hiring. To this end, this book ends with my return to South Carolina after the Great Recession. The region had witnessed major economic disruption, coupled with a crackdown on "illegal" immigration in the form of E-Verify mandates and other employment-based policies. Immigrants who once felt themselves welcomed in South Carolina now found themselves targets of rejection. Employers turned their backs on the very immigrant workers they had recruited, and hostility rapidly replaced tolerance.

To show how government and communities contribute to the dynamics of workplaces and labor markets, I introduce the concept of *racialized shocks*. This concept refers to events or policies, such as marches, factory raids, employment enforcement, and documentation scrutiny, that drive undocumented workers away from some new immigrant destinations and, in many cases, back to their home nations. In my research, some of these shocks led to undocumented immigrants retreating to lives in the shadows and jobs in the informal economy, increasing their employment vulnerability.

Community narratives related to changes in immigration laws and immigrant mobilization and competition along race, class, and gender lines in an organization influence the perception of Latino immigrants on the shop floor. The intertwined logics of state action and hiring matter in displacement. Employers and workers are socially and politically embedded actors. As such, their actions, attitudes, and behaviors are susceptible to changes in the political and community environment. When employers use undocumented immigrants to displace existing employees in an organization, they are constrained by policies that pro-hibit the hiring of undocumented workers and federal laws that pro-hibit hiring (and firing) based on protected categories such as race and gender.

Similarly, community attitudes related to political debates about im-migration influence local responses and the narratives that employees bring to the workplace. In the case that informs this study, xenophobic attitudes from a community responding to narratives about the "threat" of immigration and the degree to which immigrants are assimilating in society produced a change in social relations on the shop floor. It also introduced fear and instability. The concept of racialized shocks helps us understand how undocumented immigrant workers make sense of changes in their relationship with white employers under racial capitalism.

This book reveals the limits of theories of replacement, queueing, and segmented and split labor markets. Unlike these theories, racial capital-ism shows that the workplace and the labor market are built on struc-tures of class, race, gender, and documentation status. This structure, however, is also local, contingent, and shifting, and it depends on what different actors do. For example, under racial capitalism, incorporation/assimilation is a changing political process. Immigrants might be in a preferred status position when nativist attitudes in the community are dormant. Dormant nativism creates the temporary illusion that immi-grants are welcomed (or accepted) and that the boundaries of inclusion are fluid. Acceptance and fear are sentiments with opposing valence that drive or block immigrants from labor market participation. If nativism increases, risks increase. The heighten levels of risk that political move-ments activate influence the participation of immigrant workers (docu-mented and undocumented) in the labor market, and their integration is likely to suffer. Immigrants shift to more precarious working conditions in the ethnic economy and run risks in multiple domains. They are at higher risk of deportation and family separation through immigration raids, living in poverty, and raising their US-born children in fear, dis-trust, and disadvantage. The politics of nativism and exclusionary poli-cies suggest that the United States, rather than encouraging immigrant inclusion and integration, is encouraging disintegration.

Racialized Displacement and Native-Born Outcomes

One of the unanswered questions from research on the structural integration of immigrants in the labor market is whether displacement results in native-born workers moving into better positions in the labor market. The classic models of ethnic succession suggest that native-born or more established immigrants leave "bad jobs" in the secondary labor market as their skills improve or, in the case of immigrants, as they become more assimilated. Given the racialized competitive situation that employers create under displacement, and the potential of displacement to generate antagonism between people of color, I examine this question from the perspective of racial capitalism.

My study shows no evidence that the arrival of Latinos coincided with African Americans moving out of "dead-end" jobs and into better jobs. In many instances, the intersection of race and "legality"—broadly defined to include criminal status and undocumented immigrant status—locked immigrant women and Black men into the worst jobs. The HiCap case is an example of how Latino immigrant women occupied the same low-status positions as African American men and suffer hyperexploitation and abuse. African American women, on the other hand, were more likely to "exit" from exploitative and discriminatory jobs, but my research did not produce any evidence suggesting that they saw a significant improvement in their socioeconomic standing. While some of the Black women left to focus on their educational pursuits in community colleges or stay at home with their children, other Black women left to work at other companies, typically as temporary workers. This suggests that some displaced workers often end up in flexible and contingent employment, with little or no security and an employment situation that is increasingly precarious.

Consequently, the labor market dynamics described in this book should drive us to question how working-class individuals who find their livelihoods threatened might react to displacement more broadly. As I talked to white and Black working-class individuals, they expressed sentiments that resembled the racial resentment that analysts have described in current public discourse. Unfortunately, however, the resentment that the native-born felt after displacement was toward the undocumented immigrants, not toward the white employers who aggressively recruited them, hired them, and orchestrated their exploitation and discrimination.

The Question of Immigrant Integration

In Alba's most recent work, he takes analytical interest in the right-wing "Great Replacement" conspiracy theory that immigrants are coming here to remake the US into a nonwhite and non-Christian nation.[25] This concern feeds white anxieties and racial resentment against people of color. The targets of white fears are immigrants who poor and working-class whites believe will change the demographics of the nation in favor of minorities. To examine this public issue critically, Alba looks at rates of intermarriage in the US Census. He finds high rates of Latino intermarriage to whites and concludes that whites have no reason to fear that the United States will turn into a majority minority nation. Whites, according to Alba, will maintain their demographic dominance because of immigration, which will increase the number of people identifying as white, and not in spite of it.[26]

Alba's findings and the question of immigrant integration are closely associated with my research. The analysis of racialized displacement relates to how the arrival of Latino immigrants, an "in-between" group in the racial hierarchy, will bring about changes in the color line. One of my central questions relates to whether Latino integration points to a white/nonwhite or a Black/non-Black model.[27] Looking at the labor market, I find that the position that Latinos are likely to occupy in the racial hierarchy is a complicated matter involving the interaction of race, gender, class, and categories of vulnerability. Still, even under an intersectional framework, my findings support the idea that Latinos are likely to follow a path toward whiteness. This path, however, is contingent on the racialized shocks that immigrants experience in society.

Immigrant workers, as shown in other research, aspire to a middle-class status. They arrive in the United States with preformed ideas about race. Similar to the beliefs that European immigrants at the turn of the twentieth century held, the immigrants in my study believed that closeness and cooperation with white individuals, those in the dominant racial group, would help them achieve their middle-class aspirations. Their aspirations, however, are contingent on whether they are accepted by those in the dominant position. As Helen Marrow shows, immigrants' closeness to whites was evident at the start of their integration in new destinations.[28] What this book also illustrates is that this closeness can be ephemeral. After the anti-immigrant marches, immigrants experienced a sense of alienation and discontent with whites. As we have seen in this book, particularly distressing in their aspiration to whiteness (as an entry point into a middle-class status) was when white employers turned their back on them.

Class also matters. In my research, Latinos in managerial positions generally had more affinity with whites in the new immigrant destinations in which they settled. Latinos with higher human-capital levels initially arrived in Latino neighborhoods, but most moved into white neighborhoods in a matter of months. They were brokers of labor in cases of racialized displacement and complied with employers because they wanted to secure their position in the labor market. Members of this group spoke English with fluency, blurring cultural boundaries between Latinos and whites. Following the pattern of other nonwhite immigrants, many of my respondents in this class category married whites and identified as white.

This book examines how immigration, race, and gender shape the color line. While I use ethnographic data from a study conducted more than a decade ago, my argument examines the mechanisms of a current process. While some scholars deny that displacement exists, the public ostracizes immigrants and insists that they "take Americans' jobs." Furthermore, the study addresses questions that remain open in scholarship and public debate. At the time of this writing, many white working-class Americans, feeling alienated from society, blame immigrants as the nation faces one of its most severe racial divisions in recent history. Immigrants are not to blame. Their employers are. Comprehensive immigration reform and labor protection programs for immigrants and working-class Black and white people are imperative to challenge racialized displacement and inequalities in the labor market. Programs such as the Deferred Action for Childhood Arrivals (DACA) that provide educational and employment opportunities for immigrant youth are small steps to take forward.

ACKNOWLEDGMENTS

To my family—in the United States and México—thanks for your understanding and patience, thanks for keeping us close and caring for us. Thank you for the wonderful visits, the phone calls, the gifts, and the tokens of appreciation even when my academic pursuits got in the way of attending family events. My mom always had the right words of advice and encouragement. Muchas gracias, familia por todo su cariño y apoyo durante este largo proceso. My husband, Bill, has been literally side by side with me throughout this journey. He took the time to learn how sociologists think to engage in lengthy conversations about research, ethnography, immigration, labor markets, social inequality, and anything related to this research. He joined me on long walks in all kinds of weather to get through the best and the worst days of writing and publishing. He never doubted that I could write this book and succeed in my pursuits. Bill, your unconditional love surpasses adjectives and metrics. I am forever grateful.

I owe the deepest gratitude to the people who made this project possible, the individuals whose lives I studied. Over more than twenty years, I have worked with countless immigrant families in different capacities. Many of these families opened their homes and lives to me without hesitation. They trusted me and embraced me. They shared lessons as valuable as the lessons of the most brilliant academics. I especially want to thank the workers and my colleagues at HiCap for their willingness to work with me while I conducted this research. They taught me more about life and work than any book I have ever read. With unparalleled grace, they showed me how the preservation of honor and dignity are vital in surviving the instability and disadvantages of the labor market. While I cannot name those who allowed me to carry on this project studying your lives and experiences, I am indebted to you in the deepest sense. I hope you see your stories faithfully described and your experiences respectfully conveyed. I also hope that this book makes some inroads in helping Americans consider possibilities for making working conditions and labor relations fairer and more humane.

This book is the result of a long process of learning and growing. I owe my gratitude to the academic institutions, organizations, and people that have supported me throughout this long and circuitous journey. I am mindful that I am where I am because of many gifts of kindness, generosity, and support.

Colleagues in the Brown Sociology Department embraced me with warmth from the moment I arrived. The university has generously supported my academic growth and development so that I might achieve my goals. At Brown, I owe my sincerest appreciation to José Itzigsohn. José has been a caring colleague. He devoted hours of his busy schedule to read my drafts and guide me through the publication process. He provided central insights as I developed my ideas and kindly shared his expertise in Du Boisian sociology and opened my eyes to the "Black radical tradition." Gracias, José, por todo tu apoyo, sabiduría, y amistad. Sandra Barnes, the newly appointed chairperson in the Sociology Department, within weeks of her official arrival at Brown University, took me under her wing. She has been a pillar, providing encouragement and guidance to see this book to its completion. She read drafts of my work and provided invaluable input on navigating the publication process. I am forever grateful to Josh Pacewicz for introducing me to Brown University. Josh and I met at Stanford, and he has provided the familiarity and camaraderie that makes me know I have a family at Brown. He has been a good friend but also provided valuable insights on my work.

I am very grateful to Margot Jackson and Nitsan Chorev, who gave me their friendship and wise counsel. Margot spent many lunch meetings with me listening and engaging in conversation as I resolved all types of life and research matters. Margot was my mainstay when I confronted some serious health issues, and I have no way to express my gratitude. Margot's fantastic sense of humor and ease in life helped me focus on the good things ahead. Together we had so much fun exploring restaurants in Providence even while dealing with real work. My friend Nitsan Chorev also helped me in so many ways. She was my go-to person as I started wrapping up my chapters. She met with me to discuss, clarify, and provide direction. Like Margot and Nitsan, Susan Short, Janet Blume (my academic guardian angel), and Leah VanWey always made me feel affirmed and encouraged. My gratitude goes out to these incredible women who have eased my path at Brown University.

My remarkable colleagues Beth Fussell, Nicole Gonzalez-Van Cleeve, Patrick Heller, Paget Henry, Dan Hirschman, Michael Kennedy, David Lindstrom, John Logan, Emily Rauscher, Andrew Shrank, Mark Suchman, and Mike White listened to my ideas with patience and interest, read chapters, and shared insights and advice. Kelly Smith, rest in peace, project coordinator at Brown's Population Studies and Training Center (PSTC), provided editorial assistance on several chapters. Thank you all for being such wonderful colleagues. Prudence Carter was a mentor of mine when I was a graduate student at Stanford. I am grateful that since her arrival at Brown, she has continued to guide and support me. Thank you, Prudence, for helping me thrive in the academy as a woman of color. Students at Brown University have been giving, kind, and supportive. You know who you are and how grateful I am for your words of encouragement.

Brown faculty outside of sociology have also provided direction and encouragement. My admired professor Evelyn Hu-Dehart has been the closest to an intellectual mother I have ever had. I cherish our many conversations about immigration and its historical framework. Your generous reading of the entire manuscript provided detailed comments and suggestions. I am grateful to have had Margaret Weir and Lina Fruzzetti serve as my faculty mentors when I arrived at Brown. Frank Donnelly, the GIS and data librarian at Brown, generously shared his time and expertise as I searched for US Census Data. Thank you, Frank, for your valuable help. Kevin Escudero, my Brown University colleague, helped me find an editor and publisher. He eased my concerns and met with me when he was busy working on his own book and on leave. He patiently answered my questions and kindly introduced me to my wonderful editor, Ilene Kalish, at New York University Press (NYUP). Ilene took on my project with enthusiasm. Thank you, Ilene, for believing that I had a good story to tell. Yasemin Torfilli, also at NYUP, worked with me through the last pieces of the manuscript and supported me as I wrestled with writing and COVID-19.

I drafted some of the chapters starting my academic career at the University of North Carolina at Chapel Hill. The final chapters I wrote and edited while at Brown University. I am grateful to my colleagues, students, and friends at UNC–Chapel Hill who supported me at the start of my academic career. Jackie Hagan was my go-to person at Chapel Hill when I wanted to discuss immigration, labor markets, and the academy in general. Jackie is a kind friend and colleague who welcomed my husband and me to her home when we moved to North Carolina. I cannot thank Jackie enough for her inspiration and guidance.

When I was working on this manuscript in North Carolina, Sherryl Kleinman, a fellow and admired ethnographer, and I met often to discuss my ideas and her insights on this book project. Our enlightening conversations over dinner at the Weathervane taught me about ethnography and the "Howie Becker" method of writing. Ricardo Martinez-Schuldt provided invaluable research assistance while he was an undergraduate student at UNC–Chapel Hill. In addition, I am grateful to Karolyn Tyson for reading early parts of this book and providing guidance on integrating the race literature. Ted Mouw always showed interest in my research. Finally, Kathleen Mullan Harris provided opportunities for me to talk about ideas and was a source of support. I am grateful to my colleagues, students, and friends at UNC–Chapel Hill who supported me at the start of my academic career.

Robert Sauté, my trusted bilingual editor, has been a friend and a guide throughout the toughest months of writing. Robert read and reread my drafts and provided valuable editorial assistance with my chapters. His help was crucial to completing the book while I dealt with the demands of an academic job and confronted health and family responsibilities during the peak of the COVID-19 pandemic. Robert, I am very grateful for your editorial assistance, your patience during consulting sessions, and your thoughtful encouragement. Muchísimas gracias por tu amistad, comprensión, y apoyo.

Similarly, Carol Stack helped with editorial assistance and direction. I will never forget my inspirational conversations with this admired ethnographer as I was starting my academic career at UNC–Chapel Hill. Sitting next to her at her beautiful home in North Carolina, near a tree she planted at the start of her career, I had the honor of hearing about her labors in the ethnographic and academic vineyards. I always admired Carol's work, but having the opportunity to work with her and learn from her was truly an honor. Our sessions were the most prized intellectual gifts I have ever received. Among the many lessons I gained from working with Carol was approaching writing with inner peace while searching for "my voice." While I am still on that journey, I am mindful of her lessons. Carol, you have been an inspiration; working with you was a dream come true.

I started developing this book as a graduate student in sociology at Stanford. My academic advisor, Monica McDermott, graciously gave me an opportunity to conduct research in South Carolina. Before I knew anything about the racial dynamics of the South, Monica alerted me to the idea of Latino integration in new immigrant destinations and accepted my request to join her in the field. We are fellow ethnographers, and we share a love for field research and a passion for good food. My meetings with Monica and Becky Sandefur helped me look at the dynamics in the field from the balcony, not only from the dance floor. Similarly, Tomás Jiménez, also my academic advisor, has strongly supported and championed my work since the moment we met while I was in graduate school. Our shared Latinidad and interests in immigration gave me a taste of what it is like to have a community while in graduate school. Tomás has continued to support me all these years. He believed I had something important to say and encouraged and guided me throughout the most difficult times in writing this book. Gracias Profe Jiménez. David Grusky advised my dissertation and engaged with me in some of the liveliest intellectual discussions I ever had on inequality and immigration. David generously guided me while I was on the job market and has been a relentless supporter of my work ever since I started taking classes with him at Stanford. Similarly, Karen Cook has been a mentor and a role model for me who taught me to be an academic leader. Karen worked hard to help me gain visibility and exposure to great people and ideas. Karen, I am forever indebted to you for showing me the path to a successful academic career as a woman.

As I immersed myself in this project, I heard of the difficulties maintaining and cultivating friendships while writing a book. There is much truth in this statement. I am grateful for the friends who stuck with me even when I had to prioritize book writing while balancing work and family caregiving responsibilities. Maria Rendón has been a dear friend and a source of strength. She is one of the most talented academic women I know. I appreciate her taking the time from her busy schedule to provide valuable insights and comments on my work. My chats with you, estimada comadre, your words of wisdom, and your love kept me going. Thank you for not letting me fall off the face of the Earth. And, of course, how could I not mention the TikTok videos you sent on those gloomy days. You lifted my spirit and gave me ánimo. When I was in North Carolina, my friends in the "Teahouse" writing group—Hana Brown, Jessi Streib, and Michaela DeSoucey—adopted me into their family when I arrived. Our monthly tea chats remain a cherished memory. Hana has been a collaborator, a great friend, and a relentless supporter. Hana, I cannot thank you enough for your kindness and generosity in helping me see this project through to the end.

My friends at UC Berkeley read early drafts of this manuscript. When I was a postdoctoral scholar at UC Berkeley, Rashawn Ray shared coffee with me over many enriching discussions on race and the labor market. Sandra Susan-Smith read early drafts and helped me think about the influence of social networks and race in a new light. Dan Dohan supported my work while I was an RWJF postdoctoral scholar. While in my postdoc at UC Berkeley, I had the fortune to work with another "dream team" of amazing academic friends and talented women. Cristina Mora, Shannon Gleeson, and Cybelle Fox, my writing group at UC Berkeley, read early drafts of this project and helped me advance my ideas. They also provided friendship and encouragement as I embarked in the early stages of my career. Thank you all for being so giving.

Several foundations and organizations provided generous support at different stages of this research. The National Science Foundation funded my follow-up study in South Carolina through a dissertation improvement grant. The Robert Wood Johnson Foundation provided generous support to draw a comparative sample of workers in California. The Ford Foundation postdoctoral fellowship at Duke University under the supervision of Professor Eduardo Bonilla-Silva funded research time for writing one of the book chapters. The Diversifying Academia Recruiting Excellence (DARE) Doctoral Fellowship Program funded two years of my research at Stanford. The Program in Comparative Studies in Race & Ethnicity (CSRE) at Stanford and the Center for the Study of Race and Ethnicity in America (CSREA) at Brown both supported my research and writing. I have presented my work in many international and domestic workshops, and I am grateful for the feedback that I gained in these venues. In particular, I am grateful to Mary Waters for giving me confidence in the story I wanted to tell: my gratitude to all of these foundations and centers. While many people and organizations have supported my research, any errors you notice in this book are my responsibility.

TIMELINE

Italicized dates indicate a South Carolina event.

November 25, 2002   Homeland Security Act transfers authorities of the former INS to USCIS, CBP, and ICE.

April 10, 2006   One thousand to twelve hundred march in Greenville, South Carolina, for immigrant rights.

April 29, 2006   More than seven hundred demonstrators rally against "illegal immigration" in Greenville, South Carolina.

March, 2007   Alabama introduces package of anti-immigrant bills.

June 29, 2007   US Senate rejects immigration reform bill (CIRA 2007).

July 2, 2007   Arizona passes LAWA, sanctioning businesses that hire undocumented workers; governor cites US Senate's inability to tackle the issues at the state level.

March 17, 2008   Mississippi enacts SB 2988 requiring E-Verify for private businesses, phased in based on size.

March 27, 2008   Rhode Island Executive Order 08-01: Illegal Immigration Control Order.

June 4, 2008   Bill H 4400: South Carolina Illegal Immigration Reform Act is signed into law:
- "An alien unlawfully present in the United States" is not eligible to attend a South Carolina public institution of higher learning.
- Requires conspicuous signage at any place where immigration assistance might be rendered stating, "I am not an attorney licensed to practice law and may not give legal advice or accept fees for legal advice."

June 9, 2008   Executive order requires all federal contractors to use E-Verify as a condition of the contract.

October 7, 2008   ICE raids House of Raeford Farms poultry plant in Greenville County and arrests more than three hundred immigrant workers. Earlier in 2008, eleven supervisors (also immigrants from Mexico) and the HR manager were arrested on charges ranging from aggravated identity theft to filing false I-9 employment identification forms.

January 1, 2009   H 4400: All public employers in South Carolina must verify employment eligibility of all new employees through E-Verify. This requirement also applies to all public subcontractors with five hundred or more employees.

July 1, 2009   H 4400:
- All private employers in South Carolina who employ one hundred or more employees must enroll in and use E-Verify for all new employees or verify that each new employee has or is eligible for a South Carolina driver's license or ID card or possesses a state-issued ID from a state whose requirements are at least as strict as the South Carolina requirements.
- All public subcontractors in South Carolina who employ one hundred or more employees must enroll in and use E-Verify for all new employees.

January 1, 2010   H 4400: All public subcontractors must enroll in and use E-Verify for all new employees.

April 23, 2010   Arizona enacts Support Our Law Enforcement and Safe Neighborhoods Act (SB 1070).

May 6, 2010   Minnesota proposes Support Our Law Enforcement and Safe Neighborhoods Act (HF 3830), patterned on Arizona's SB 1070, but the bill fails to make it out of the Minnesota House.

July 1, 2010   H 4400: All private employers in South Carolina who employ fewer than one hundred employees must enroll in and use E-Verify for all new employees or verify that each new employee has or is eligible for a South Carolina driver's license or ID card or possesses a state-issued ID from a state whose requirements are at least as strict as the South Carolina requirements.

February 22, 2011   Seventeen representatives introduce the Michigan Support Our Law Enforcement and Safe Neighborhoods Act (HB 4305), even more strict than Arizona's SB 1070. It fails to make it out of the Michigan House.

March 15, 2011   Utah enacts the Illegal Immigration Enforcement Act (HB 497), which mandates that law enforcement officials verify legal status in some interactions and makes it a state crime "to encourage illegal immigration or transport or harbor illegal immigrants." Many of the provisions of HB 497 will be struck down in a 2014 decision of a federal district court in Utah.

May 10, 2011   Indiana enacts SB 590, directing law enforcement to work with federal counterparts. It outlaws the use of consular documents as official identifications. Provisions making English the sole official language in Indiana are stripped from the bill before its passage.

May 13, 2011   Georgia enacts the Illegal Immigration Reform and Enforcement Act of 2011 (HB 87). This law establishes requirements for public and private employers (with more than ten employees) to utilize E-Verify and provides for law enforcement actions on the part of local agencies in dealing with undocumented immigrants. The bill is vocally opposed by several business coalitions. Several of the law's provisions will be struck down in court cases.

May 26, 2011   The Supreme Court upholds Arizona's law requiring employers to use E-Verify or risk losing their business licenses.

May 27, 2011   The Utah legislature moves to copy Arizona's E-Verify law in light of the Supreme Court ruling.

June 9, 2011   Alabama enacts the Beason-Hammon Alabama Taxpayer and Citizen Protection Act (HB 56). Among the toughest anti-illegal immigration laws to be passed by any state, many of its provisions will be struck down by the Eleventh Circuit Court of Appeals in 2012.

June 27, 2011   The Immigration Reform Act (SB 20) is signed into law in South Carolina.

October 4, 2011   A federal district court in Alabama allows some of HB 56 to stand (law enforcement checks and verification of public school students) but strikes down provisions that duplicate laws that already exist in federal statutes, such as "employing, harboring and transporting illegal aliens."

January 1, 2012   SB 20:
- Requires all private employers to enroll in and use E-Verify for all new employees. The use of other forms of ID verification is disallowed.

- E-Verify must be used within three days of hiring (changed from five days).
- Requires law enforcement under certain circumstances and with reasonable suspicion to determine whether a person is lawfully present in the United States.
- Makes it an offense for a person not to carry their Certificate of Alien Registration.
- Allows a civil action to be brought under certain circumstances when a political subdivision limits or prohibits a local official from seeking to enforce a federal or state law with regard to immigration or unlawful immigration status.

June 15, 2012   Deferred action (DACA) policy is announced by the White House.

June 25, 2012   The Supreme Court upholds Arizona's law allowing police officers to check immigration status while they are in the process of enforcing other laws if they have reasonable suspicion to suspect that status. The same ruling also strikes down the portions of SB 1070 that preempt federal authority, namely, making it a state crime to be in the US unlawfully without registering, making it a state crime to seek work or work without authorization, and authorizing warrantless arrests of aliens on the basis of probable cause that they are deportable.

March 3, 2014   South Carolina agrees to a settlement with groups that filed a suit against provisions of SB 20. Police officers are no longer able to prolong a traffic or other stop to check the immigration status of an individual.

When I started thinking about my research in sociology, I wanted to study the adaptation strategies of secondary migrants who leave cities with a long history of immigration for towns with almost no recent experience with immigration. Because I knew immigrant families that wanted to leave the Bay Area—I was a student at Stanford University—for safer and less expensive areas in the South, I decided to follow my *paisanos* and other Latino immigrants in what at times felt like an exodus from California to the South. There I expected to view what happens when documented and undocumented immigrants insert themselves into a historically delineated Black and white color line. Among other questions, I was interested in how documented and undocumented immigrants achieved their version of the American dream in new destinations more readily than in traditional destinations. As a student of immigration, I expected to answer this question by observing many integration domains such as workplaces, schools, churches, hospitals, neighborhoods, and leisure places. To my surprise, except for schools, racial segregation in many of these domains prevented me from observing routine interactions between Latino immigrants and Black and white residents.

When I moved to the South, I did not expect to write a book on displacement and the racialization of work. In search of theoretical and methodological heterogeneity, I ended up in an analytical space related to my initial line of inquiry—immigration in new destinations—but my focus shifted to employment as the institutional domain where I could observe white-Black-Latino social interactions and demographic change.

GETTING THERE: ENDING AT HICAP

When I arrived in South Carolina, I was greeted with a green road sign, "Welcome to Jessamine," a city of more than three hundred thousand inhabitants, printed in bold white. Jessamine seemed like a lovely place, but I was there to do research; and my first task was to find a neighborhood to settle in for a year. Coming from California, the emptiness of the streets surprised me. I could not find a soul to ask for basic directions. My old, white sedan did not have GPS; in 2005, cell phones had no Google Maps or internet access. Equipped with a town map, I drove around wide, empty roads with narrow sidewalks on the East Side. It turned out to be the nicest part of town.

Usually, an ethnographer enters the field with a list of contacts and introductions. The list may be short, and introductions may not be much more than pro forma; but most ethnographers have some social entrée. I did not. I knew that I wanted to study new immigrants in the Jessamine area. An academic advisor who had grown up in the area sang its praises as a site for examining white-Black-Latino social interactions. What she told me and what I could learn from Census Bureau data sold me on the site's appropriateness. My advisor had no firsthand knowledge of Jessamine's Latino community, but I could not let that dissuade me. I decided to take a plunge into the community, and I knew my sink-or-swim attitude would have to get me through.

It took me about a week to get to know Latino informants. The difficulty was partly because finding immigrants in a rural destination is a circuitous process. Aside from the men working in construction sites on the outskirts of town, Latino immigrants generally worked inside large buildings, usually away from the public eye and from researchers. In addition, most apartment complexes where immigrants resided were deserted on weekdays, which limited research access in neighborhoods and residential areas. To illustrate the scarcity of Latinos at first glance, my first interaction with Jessaminers was at Baja Taco, a busy Mexican restaurant, around lunchtime on a Monday. The café was crowded with white and Black people but no Latinos. The owner was a white chef, and the cooks and prep staff were white and Black. Coming from California, where I easily walked into a Mexican restaurant, talked to people in Spanish, and felt at home, it puzzled me to find that the single Mexican restaurant on one of the main avenues in town had no Latino staff. I sat at a table near the window with a map on my lap. Given how dispersed and geographically invisible immigrants were, gaining access was starting to feel intimidating. "Where you traveling to?" a Black woman in her twenties wearing a green polo shirt, black pants, and a black cap asked as she cleaned the table next to mine. "Here," I replied. After exchanging some pleasantries, I asked if she knew anything about Pioneer Road, the area where Latinos lived. She lifted her shoulders and smirked.

"That part of town is trashy."

"Why?"

"The East Side is more upscale, and the West Side, you know, over by Pioneer Road, it's pretty trashy. We call it 'Little Mexico,'" she said, apologized, and went back to work. The area was not exclusively Mexican, but as with other stereotypes, nonimmigrants lumped the Colombian, Guatemalan, Salvadoran, Honduran, and Costa Rican families under the terms "Mexican" or "Spanish."

After driving past downtown, I headed to the West Side of town and drove through vast empty roads, large parking lots, and ranch-style homes without finding others like myself. Latino presence only became apparent when I reached Pioneer Road at the city's margins. I found Spanish-language signs posted outside a handful of buildings and strip malls sprinkled in the city's periphery. On the West Side of town, almost hurriedly, someone had placed a sign for Compare Foods, a supermarket chain catering to Latino consumers, on top of a former Piggly Wiggly grocery store. A few yards away, Ritmo Latino, a salsa club that my respondents identified as the place where young white women went to find Latino men, made an impression on anyone driving around. The club was the size of a warehouse, and immigrants felt free to go there to dance and have fun. However, immigrants are rarely free to experience steady deracialized respect and autonomy. From time to time, the police parked outside the club, and once immigrant patrons heard of their presence, they avoided the area. In the same strip mall, one could eat at El Paisa, a Colombian restaurant catering to night-shift workers and couples frequenting Ritmo Latino.

Pioneer Road had a higher concentration of Latino businesses than other areas. Many apartment complexes advertised "renta gratis" (free rent) for the first two to three months to attract Latino immigrants. A strip mall with Spanish-language signs near the apartment complexes on Pioneer Road housed several grocery stores, restaurants, and a makeshift Latino Christian church in what used to be a jewelry store. Next to these businesses, some South American entrepreneurs set the offices of a Spanish-language weekly catering to a broad spectrum of Spanish-speaking immigrants, newly arrived job seekers, and longtime residents looking for a deal or news from the community. Additionally, the strip mall housed a multiservice Latino business that cashed checks, offered bail bonds, and sold international calling cards. Used-car shops with Latino names took up big chunks of the real estate in this section of town. Laundromats with television sets loudly playing Spanish-language programming filled the air. In the same shopping center, restaurants advertised "International Food" to capture the at least eight Latino nationalities (Mexican, Salvadoran, Guatemalan, Honduran, Costa Rican, Colombian, Puerto Rican, and Cuban) that converged in the city. However, the most notable home was a ranch-style house with alternating green, white, and red lights pinned on the roof, with large capital letters that advertised, "MEXICO."

As I looked for a place to live, I kept a tally of the apartment complexes that Latinos recommended for people without papers. I went to small businesses to talk to Latinos. After receiving more than ten leads to the same complex, I approached the manager. The apartment complex had about sixty to eighty townhomes, a vermin-infested pool, a laundry facility down at the heels, and a large parking lot—with a triracial composition and high immigrant density. As a new arrival, I rented a two-bedroom apartment for $425 a month. Housing complexes with advertisements in Spanish on their lawns were likely to have a bilingual housing manager who assisted new arrivals. Rather than asking for a check—Zelle and other forms of electronic payment were not an option—for a deposit and the first few months of rent, apartment managers took cash and IDs from the country of origin without asking for a Social Security number. It took me a couple of days to figure out that white and Black residents were vacating apartment complexes and moving, not always pleasantly, to better neighborhoods. Some of the white people I talked to spoke with discontent about how they were selling their parents' residence in the West Side because "the neighborhood had changed so much." A white woman was more candid when I asked why she was moving: "Walmart is all Mexican. You cannot walk without running into Mexicans in the aisles." Ethnic succession was unfolding in front of my eyes, but I was interested in the process, not the outcome.

PARTICIPANT OBSERVATIONS

In immigration research, studying processes and mechanisms is often more critical than studying outcomes.[1] Processes and mechanisms, however, are difficult to unveil using conventional research techniques, which is why I turned to sustained participant observation, a methodological strategy in ethnography that allows the researcher to unobtrusively observe and document processes and mechanisms.[2] This approach allowed me to observe changes over time in people's behaviors and attitudes, even changes they were unaware of, and to document attitudes and behaviors in a naturalistic manner as people expressed them in specific situations over a sustained time.

Furthermore, naturalistic observations gave me a firsthand view of the labor dynamics at a new immigrant destination. This window opened even wider because I played different roles in multiple contexts throughout my research. For the first half of my field study, when I lived and interacted with residents in my housing complex, people perceived me as a recently arrived undocumented Mexican immigrant. In the second half of my field study, after I moved to a different neighborhood, Jessamine Homes, residents perceived me as an English-speaking documented Latina. During the first period, I took jobs that went with my recently arrived Mexican immigrant role, while in the second half of the study, I took a job that fit the role of a more upwardly mobile immigrant. These multiple roles and contexts enabled me to observe participants positioned at different social system levels. I consistently jotted notes of my observations and developed those notes into text at the end of every day in the field. Throughout my research, and as part of the process of checking the validity of my observations as I wrote analytic memos, I consulted with an academic advisor who was conducting research on the topic of immigration and race relations in the same city.[3] I also cultivated informants in different contexts. During the last two months of the study, I formally interviewed people I had repeatedly observed throughout the year. The field notes are one of the main sources of data for the analysis that produced this book.

In addition to participant observations, during the last two months of this research, I conducted semistructured, face-to-face interviews with a sample of 118 Latino immigrants and five non-Latino respondents (two white and three Black people). I selected the sample using two different methods. I used a snowball or chain referral strategy in half of my cases.[4] The remaining half I recruited by visiting publicly accessible establishments (e.g., laundromats, restaurants, and community centers) located in different census tracts with an identified Latino population and by selecting participants from the occupants. The interviews included closed- and open-ended questions. I asked questions about immigrant integration, inter- and intragroup race relations, their work histories, and their process for getting a job. I interviewed supervisors about their positions and managing coethnics. I conducted two pilot interviews with informants whose histories I knew well to learn how my interview questions and self-presentation affected the interviewee's responses. Following the guidelines of my institutional review board (IRB) protocol, before beginning each interview, I asked participants for consent to be interviewed and audio-recorded.

NEGOTIATING ACCESS

Gaining access was a double-sided process. First, I needed a place to live in an area of town with a high immigrant concentration. Before moving to South Carolina, I located these using US Census data. Second, I planned to find a neighborhood where I could observe interactions between Latinos and Black and white residents. Because of the project's grounded nature, I wanted to guide my site selection by people's recommendations of where Latino immigrants lived. I asked community members where Latinos lived to verify the US Census data. On the ground, I found signals of class segmentation in Latinos' residential choices. While new arrivals and poor or working-class immigrants lived on the West Side of town, the more educated and upwardly mobile were dispersed in the better-off neighborhoods of the East Side—where Baja Taco was located. Segregation, at this point, started to emerge as a theme.

After three days of driving around neighborhoods and getting leads from people, I moved into Bristol Apartments, where I lived for the first half (six months) of my fieldwork. Bristol was a predominantly Latino, low-rent apartment complex embedded in a multiethnic but segregated neighborhood. In the subdivision next to my apartment complex, almost all the residents were African American. The high population density in my complex (ninety-six units), the outdoor laundry facilities, and the need to park in a common parking area provided opportunities to observe social interactions during the first two months of data collection. However, the open parking lot, the vulnerability of undocumented immigrants, and the lack of police protection in immigrant neighborhoods resulted in a crime wave that targeted undocumented immigrants in Jessamine. Five armed robberies in my apartment complex occurred within three months. Two active drug dealers lived within fifty yards of my apartment. To everyone's surprise, one of the drug dealers was an elderly white woman who appeared to be in her mideighties. Her husband, who walked with an oxygen tank, appeared to be ninety years old. His nurse helped with drug deliveries.

After the first armed robbery, neighbors stopped socializing in the parking lot, and many refused to answer their door after dark. Even after the crime wave targeting their families, almost all continued to describe the location as *tranquila*, or peaceful. While these events decreased the number of casual encounters in the parking lot, they increased the number of more in-depth interactions. When I met with people, we met in their homes. There I could observe how they interacted with roommates and family members. Sometimes I watched TV with them or shared a meal. In these routines, I learned about domains of their lives that would not be obvious from conversations at work or in the parking lot or the laundry area of the apartment complex.

My goal was to engage in the community in ways consistent with the experiences of both low- and high-status immigrants. During the first half of my research, I spoke primarily Spanish. I also took jobs at the bottom of the labor market (e.g., cleaning toilets and working assembly-line jobs). I lived in a low-rent housing complex to observe the everyday experiences of Latino immigrants in low-wage jobs. Midway through my research, after about six months at Bristol, I took a job as a supervisor and moved into a working-class neighborhood called Jessamine Homes. The neighborhood contained a mix of Black, white, and Latino families in single-family homes. Neighbors at Jessamine tended to keep to themselves, but there were occasional opportunities for social interaction. Many Latinos in the Jessamine Homes neighborhood were home owners; some either held supervisory jobs or were starting their own businesses. Living here, in addition to my work, allowed me to interact with working-class Latinos in supervisory or intermediary positions, providing new analytical leverage for this book. My next-door neighbors were white on one side and Black on another side, which gave me exposure to their opinions. However, my white neighbors had a guarded attitude and avoided conversations with me. My Black neighbors were a couple of government employees who welcomed me and took a protective stance toward me. Joseph, my Black neighbor, mowed my lawn without me asking, and Janice, his wife, made me a peach pie because she thought I was "working too much and not eating well." This community was my home base during my first fifteen months in the field (2005 and 2006) and when I returned for a follow-up study in 2009.

GETTING A JOB

The second stage of getting access meant getting a job. I wanted to follow undocumented immigrants in their everyday lives and as they interacted with Black and white residents. But how would I make sense of what I was observing? I decided to combine the general insights I had about split labor markets and the integration of immigrants with what I saw in the day-to-day lives of immigrant workers. The focus of my research became apparent when I realized that if I wanted to study the social relations among Black, white, and Latino residents, I needed to find integrated spaces. I learned that few Latino immigrants spent much time in their homes—many worked two to three jobs—and only a fraction of their time in spaces with nonimmigrants. For example, they generally went to Spanish-language services when they went to church. When they took classes, these were English as a second language courses with other immigrants, not Black or white residents. They had little interaction with government agencies, as many were concerned with issues related to their papers. The vast majority of Latino immigrants were Spanish speaking, and native-born residents spoke only English. Consequently, while the neighborhood allowed me to observe some interactions with white and Black Americans, the language barrier and a general sense of distrust made the systematic observation of triracial group relations difficult.

The places where immigrants spent most of their time were workplaces. The spaces where they interacted with white and Black individuals were jobs. Therefore, I started looking for jobs to observe how immigrants and nonimmigrants got along. I continued to attend Spanish-language religious services (Catholic and non-Catholic) and volunteered at a day-care center for immigrant parents. Through these experiences, I gained insights into how low-wage immigrants' everyday lives unfolded when they were not working. Living in the neighborhoods where workers lived and capturing changes in their work lives would have been difficult had I lived elsewhere. For example, I understood the relevance of employment agencies in recruiting and hiring because they were core organizations in Latino neighborhoods. Similarly, living in the neighborhoods where the workers I observed lived allowed me to validate that intermediaries were cultural brokers whose field of action in immigrant employment expands beyond the firm's boundaries. My observations in the neighborhood showed that labor market intermediaries mediate for workers in organizations such as schools, the courts, the Department of Motor Vehicles, and hospitals. Yet, the bulk of data collection for this research occurred in workplaces.

Lucy, one of my neighbors and informants, eased my entry into workplaces where I observed Black-white-Latino relations. "Look, if you want to study our people, you need to get a job; you need to work in factories or warehouses." Lucy introduced me to a Puerto Rican subcontractor who brokered laborers for different companies and placed undocumented immigrants in jobs. He asked if I had "any type of papers," and when I gave him my California driver's license, he sent me to clean toilets. I worked part-time with Lucy on this janitorial crew, cleaning buildings and shopping malls. The site met my interest in finding places with a triracial composition, as Latino, white, and Black people made up the labor force. At this site, I started hearing that the companies had shifted to hiring subcontractors, and the subcontractors were hiring primarily undocumented immigrants. Eventually, the few remaining non-Latino workers were people who had few options in the labor market, typically suffering from substance abuse or mental health illnesses.

When a job opened at Carolina Mills, I applied. I wanted to see how a textile mill, an industry that traditionally segregated its workforce— the best jobs went to white workers while the worst jobs went to Black people—incorporated Latino immigrants. Here, my manager, a white woman dating a Costa Rican immigrant who worked at the plant, told me that the company "was hiring one Spanish to replace two Blacks." At Carolina Mills, I became aware that trying to disentangle displacement from replacement through secondhand reports was fraught with difficulty. I needed to be there to see the process unfold myself.

I was in the crew of the Latino new arrivals, but Carolina Mills placed me in a section where the workers were white and from families that had worked in the mills for years. Lucy mentioned after work one afternoon that they had me working with white people in an "English-only" section. You are "passing," she joked. Her area was all Latino and Spanish-speaking, where they did jobs involving physical labor. I did not bother to tell her how the temp agency that hired us challenged my papers because of my Anglo husband's name. That day Lucy disappeared from work, leaving her lunch bag and the pink jacket that she bought in the children's section at Target behind. I got worried. We had arrived together at the plant. When I returned to Bristol Apartments, where we lived, I was relieved to find Lucy in her living room circling job ads in the Spanish-language newspaper. She told me the temp agency fired her because the company ran her Social Security number and it came up bogus.

I had six jobs in one year (see table A.1). My first job for this research was at Carolina Mills. I also worked with a janitorial crew, in a plastic-manufacturing company, on an inventory crew, and in a warehouse and distribution center. The final job I had was at HiCap. Turnover was high, as people searched for *la cora extra*. Immigrants constantly looked for better jobs, testing their luck with good, semigood, and bad papers. As I followed workers from job to job and overlapped with Lucy and others in more than one job, I kept hearing different versions of what I listened to on my first day at the textile mill. White and Black workers often told me some version of "workers at this company used to be Black and white, and now they are all Mexican." The Latinos also had their own view of displacement. "The *morenos* are gone, and now it's just us Latinos." In the six jobs I had over the first year of data collection, all had some degree of rapid labor force turnover that involved the departure of Black and white people in favor of Latino immigrant workers—primarily undocumented.

TABLE A.1. Research Sites and Data Collection Procedures (2005–6)

	Sept.	Oct.	Nov.	Dec.	Jan.	Feb.	Mar.	Apr.	May	June	July	Aug.	Sept.
Workplaces													
Textile mill	X	X	X										
Janitorial crew	X	X	X	X	X	X							
Plastic manufacturing			X										
Inventory crew			X	X									
Warehouse/ distribution center				X	X	X	X	X	X	X	X	X	X
HiCap: ventilation and air				X	X	X	X	X	X	X	X	X	X
Research procedures													
Participant observations	X	X	X	X	X	X	X	X	X	X	X	X	X
Working with informants										X	X	X	X
Semistructured interviews										X	X	X	X

THE HICAP CASE

This book mainly describes my observations at HiCap, an industrial company making air conditioners for different businesses, where I worked for seven months. There I was a bystander to the drama of turnover from Black and white to Latino in a big, light industrial manufacturing company. Before working at HiCap, I had witnessed the massive displacement and ethnic succession at each place I worked, but at HiCap, I followed the process in-depth through the eyes of workers, Black and white supervisors, Latino bilingual supervisors, administrators, and recruiters from start to completion.

To gain entry into the site, I used some of the knowledge I was gaining in the community about important labor market positions I wanted to investigate. Living in the community, I found a solid drive to recruit "bilingual supervisors" and "crew leaders." For example, a multiservice van for Latino immigrants parked outside Walmart had posters advertising jobs for bilingual supervisors in its windows. The billboards of employment agencies on Pioneer Road recruited bilingual operators and supervisors. When the job at HiCap appeared in the Spanish-language newspaper and Lucy, my informant, suggested that I apply, I called and secured an interview with Ready Hands, an employment agency. For companies to maintain the stream of Latino workers into their organizations, they tended to keep undocumented supervisors who were bilingual even when they were not qualified for the job.

I wondered at this point if gender mattered in hiring supervisors. Typically, those who managed the crews where I worked were men, but women were a sizable group in the migrant population. I wondered if I could get a job for a supervisory position as a woman without manufacturing experience. I wanted to find the ways that "culturally matching" supervisors and workers influenced segregation in the workforce and the social relations on the shop floor. I also saw the supervisory position as a way to achieve social proximity to top managers.

The challenge was to gain entry into these positions with no practical experience in a manufacturing setting. As an ethnographer, I drew from the biographical resources I possessed to gain access to the site and informants, but how would I get a technical job as a supervisor in a company to observe managers from a position between workers and their employers? Years before my observations at HiCap, I worked as a human resources supervisor for Hyatt hotels and used this prior managerial experience in my application. As it turned out, however, I learned from my interview with Ms. Roberts, the human resources manager who interviewed me for the position, that employers were not strict with regard to qualifications when they hired bilingual supervisors. Despite my having almost no supervisory experience in a manufacturing setting, management asked that I build a "Mexican enclave" and run a complex production line with "my team" of Mexican workers.

HiCap hired me as a bilingual supervisor to train and supervise Latino immigrant workers. Most of these workers were undocumented and hired via Ready Hands, the temporary employment agency. In the seven months I worked at HiCap, I met only eight documented (including supervisors) Latino immigrants out of the more than sixty immigrants with whom I worked at the Front End during my first months at HiCap. For seven months, I conducted participant observations while working an eight-hour shift five days a week, plus I commuted an hour each way with Latino workers. This resulted in an observation period of more than eight thousand hours (including days when I worked overtime) of exposure to HiCap and its workers.

I achieved case heterogeneity by observing multiple work groups, sections, or departments in a single organization. For example, even when I conducted most of my observations at the Front End, where I rooted my observations, this section varied regarding the racial, gender, and linguistic composition of workgroups. Because I was a cultural broker, managers also expected me to interpret for workers and translate for the organization, opening access to other shop-floor sections and administrative offices. Finally, I had exposure to top managers (even the company director), trainers, floor managers, and supervisors, and so I observed strata often missing in studies of immigration, labor market competition, and racial turnover. In the end, however, my focus was on racialized processes and mechanisms, not on the views or perspectives of managers.

One dimension of my job entailed learning the positions on the line, interpreting for Spanish-speaking workers, and coordinating with two Black supervisors (Darius and Kesha) in the successful running of the line. The second aspect of my job involved training workers and covering for them in the assembly line during breaks, periods of exhaustion, or emergencies. Although I kept busy while performing these tasks, I made sure I had enough time to jot down field notes and observe throughout the day.

Furthermore, at the start of the research, I was fortunate to have an assignment that involved observations and enabled me to examine the three shifts that the company ran and different sections of the plant. For instance, while I was in training, management gave me a clipboard and pages with section maps and sent me to the shop floor to conduct observations. The section maps had workers' head counts. Management asked me to report if people had idle time. I told them that I did not find anything unusual and that everyone was working hard. Still, I used that opportunity to gain a sense of the organization, talk to managers and recruiters, and identify areas of focus for my observations. Here, I discovered that the Front End was the next area for displacement. Once completing displacement in this section, the company planned to change the racial composition of other areas to all Latinos, as had already happened on the first and second shifts. To learn about the way displacement came to completion on the night shift and was almost complete on the second shift, I proposed a project that involved translating "safety sheets" so that I could disengage from my job on the assembly line to talk to people.

After two weeks of observing other sections and shifts, I moved to the Front End to work on the assembly line before the company started hiring Latino immigrants. There I worked with two Black supervisors, Kesha and Darius. I told the people I worked with that I was a student in sociology doing research and that I would be working as a supervisor for this purpose. In total, I conducted seven months of participant observations in a context that was 60 percent Black, 23 percent white, and 16 percent Latino. Although I started working with Darius and Kesha, the company demoted Kesha through displacement and brought Anne to take her place. Consequently, I also worked with a white supervisor and reported to a Black middle manager and a white general manager.

JANUS: THE PARTICIPANT OBSERVER AS SUPERVISOR

The Greek god Janus has two faces, each face pointing in the opposite direction, signaling duality. Researchers in management or supervisory positions, like Janus, play the dual and contradictory role of participant observer and social actor. In the participant observer position, the ethnographer follows the rules of basic research, aimed at generating or improving theory. In my case, I entered HiCap after inductively following some displacement signals in other organizations.

Additionally, as a graduate student in sociology, I could not ignore the standards of research agreed on with my academic committee, the requirements of my IRB, and the publication standards of journals and academic presses. With this in mind, I focused on maximizing exposure to the site and participants and building empathy with people. Overall, however, I followed my research goals. I acted as a participant observer while maintaining role consistency with the demands of being a supervisor (or laborer in some cases) in an organization. Maintaining consistency in the participant observer and supervisory roles was not always smooth.

A second role that the ethnographer in a supervisory role performs is that of a social and organizational actor. As an individual member of an organization, the ethnographer is a person following a set of norms and expectations associated with the skills, competence, and loyalties required by their position. Because I limited my disclosure to HiCap with regard to the research I was doing at the company, the expectation was that I had to perform the role of supervisor. Without following the organizational rules and expectations of the job, HiCap would have fired me without a second thought, and access would have ended.

In racialized and gendered organizations, the labor market intermediary is also a cultural agent serving two masters. Companies hire intermediaries because they have expertise in accessing the cultural repertoires of a racialized and gendered workforce. For example, companies expect a Latina in a supervisory position to command respect from members with similar characteristics. Workers had their expectations of coethnics and cogender supervisors. Latinas would expect their female supervisors to be helpful, understanding, and loyal to them, not to their bosses. As I explain later, my commitment was to research and to workers, but I still performed the supervisor's duties to maintain access to the site.

I modeled my behavior on other Latina supervisors to perform the intermediary role. However, before I stepped into this role, for six months, I worked as a laborer in different jobs. Working under the management of a coethnic supervisor opened a window into how intermediaries performed their roles and what the workers they supervised expected from coethnic supervisors. I also interviewed supervisors of undocumented workers to gain a more profound knowledge of the position. As a result, I became more aware of how coethnic supervisors' role extends beyond the organization's walls; it involves intertwined institutional participation. They regularly serve as interpreters for their workers in non-work-related domains such as schools, hospitals, and courts, connecting immigrants with the gray economy for papers and providing references to community allies. I lived in neighborhoods where I could observe crew leaders and supervisors and learned how they nurtured the loyalty of their workers outside the workplace. Many of these intermediaries move from one job to another with the same crew. I had workers at HiCap offer to carry me to my next position. Unfortunately, my next job was to return to my graduate program.

DEVELOPING EMPATHY IN RACIALIZED ORGANIZATIONS

I entered the field and every job I observed for this research as a Latina immigrant (Mexican-born from a working-class background) who speaks Spanish and English fluently. At the time, I was a PhD graduate student at an elite university in the United States. While I shared a common language, ethnicity, and immigration history with many of the Latinos I observed and interviewed, I was already documented and had achieved higher levels of formal education and English proficiency. I constantly reflected on the social distance that these advantages could introduce into my relationship with the participants. How would I gain empathy with these characteristics? I discovered that Latino immigrants could relate to me in more depth after they learned that my starting point in the United States was similar to theirs. When I arrived in the United States, like many of my research participants, I entered the labor market without knowing how to speak English. Additionally, I did not have papers that authorized me to work. It took years before I acquired the papers that gave me free access to the US labor market. Additionally, I had been deported and have family members who had gone through the process of arrest, apprehension, and deportation. These experiences helped me to develop empathy and have more frank conversations about the hurdles that immigrants face to get a job that provides stability.

Even when I could overcome differences in formal education, language use, and mannerisms, I maintained the insider-outsider observer boundaries. For example, I told people I was a doctoral student working on research while at HiCap. This helped lessen some of the issues that arise from power imbalances when the participant observer also plays the supervisor role. Additionally, immigrants having higher levels of education than most native-born Americans was not uncommon in my research. For example, in the inventory crew, one of the jobs I had before HiCap, all the Latinas in my crew went to college. One had an MBA and owned a hot-dog business in a shopping center, another one had been a hospital manager, and still another had been a dean at a university. One man in the crew was a business owner displaced from his coffee business by organized crime in Colombia, and one of the men in my crew at HiCap had a political science degree and returned to Mexico to run for town mayor.

Having more cultural and human capital than the average workers was not a source of imbalance when interacting with workers with less formal education. In the end, I found that people associated my high-status markers with assumptions about my country of national origin rather than with being an outsider per se. Because the most educated Latino immigrants in the region were from Colombia, people in my research commented, "The Colombians here are either doctors or lawyers, but look at them cleaning toilets," and dismissed their claims of being more educated. To the extent that people were not fluent in English and if they were working menial, low-paid jobs, coworkers disregarded high educational credentials. Thus, when I told people I was a doctoral student doing research, I had to explain why I needed them to know. Yet the question remained about how they felt about my more formal communication and mannerisms that, whether I wanted or not, signaled higher levels of human capital and could generate distrust. In low-wage jobs, people assumed that I was Colombian ("the educated" Latinos), even though I carried myself as a Mexican in the organizations where I worked and in accordance with the roles that I played. At HiCap, my more formal use of language and mannerisms were assumed to fit the role of supervisor. One of my respondents commented, "I thought you didn't curse because you work as a supervisor." I believe these identity differences helped me maintain role consistency and still get close to the research participants.

When living in Bristol Apartments, my neighbors thought I did not speak English. Weeks after I befriended Lucy, one of my key informants, we talked outside my apartment, and a Black boy came close to us playing with a ball. He asked if we wanted to play. I answered him in English. Lucy was surprised to find that I spoke English. After Lucy and other neighbors learned that I was bilingual, I managed to help them while still reminding them that I was there to conduct research.

As an organizational actor, however, I ran the risk of distancing myself from people because of power imbalances. To minimize this situation, I disclosed to the workers that I was conducting research and that my main goal was to represent what I observed to the best of my ability.

While these words can sound vacuous to many people interacting with researchers and bilingual supervisors, I had the advantage of knowing and working with some workers, like Mariela, Lola, Roberto, Richard, Manuel, Lucy, and others outside HiCap. Some knew me from working in other crews along their side, performing precarious, nonsupervisory jobs, in some cases, while simultaneously working at HiCap. This type of network overlap was common. Because many bilingual supervisors gained power and authority in precarious positions (i.e., temporary jobs) and because of the racialized nature of their employment, these workers can as easily move down the employment hierarchy as they can move up. Roberto, for example, was a bilingual supervisor at HiCap when I first met him. Eight months later, he was no longer a supervisor. He had had several operator jobs, the last one working as a technician in a primarily white biotechnology firm. I also lived in the same neighborhoods where workers lived, and we overlapped in the same jobs. For example, during the first six months of my research, I moved from job to job with a crew of almost the same people, all people living around Pioneer Road, shopping in the same store, hanging out in the same Latino strip mall, and going to the same Sunday Mass. Additionally, I volunteered at the main Catholic church and day-care center, which helped me build trust with Latinos who came to work at HiCap but with whom I had no prior history.

Unlike most Latino immigrants, Black and white workers and supervisors were skeptical of my presence, even when I told them that I was a student doing research. During the first few weeks of my study at HiCap, non-Latino workers and supervisors teased me, harassed me, and boycotted my efforts to train the Latino recruits. However, after a few weeks of training, I had become proficient in every job on the Front End, the section I supervised—except for welding. I did not train in welding because this job involved staying seated in the same position throughout the day, which would have limited my ability to observe people in different work groups and departments. The time in training afforded me the opportunity to talk to workers about their jobs and family lives. Some of them invited me to their homes and their churches. One of them knitted me a scarf when I became sick from working near the delivery door during winter. Another gave me a gardening kit after I talked to her about the weeds growing in the backyard of my rental townhouse. Still others brought home-cooked meals for me because they thought that a V8 vegetable juice and a stick of mozzarella cheese, all I had time to eat for lunch while at work, were not enough to have the energy to run a shift.

Learning the Front End jobs also helped build rapport with Black and white workers at HiCap, particularly with the men on the assembly line. Naturally, the men in the assembly line, in general, distrusted any supervisor who displayed incompetence running the assembly line. Since I had no experience managing production schedules or manufacturing air conditioners before I took this job, the workers saw me as a joke. They teased me and quipped that I probably did not know the difference between a Makita gun and a shotgun. As a woman in a supervisory role, the bar was even higher, because most supervisors were men. Therefore, I focused on gaining their trust by learning the jobs as competently as possible from Kesha, a woman they trusted, and Darius, a charismatic supervisor they liked.

I believe I was able to build empathy with the women after an accident I had at the plant. On one occasion, while in training, I severely burned my arm (with a third-degree burn the size of a quarter) and ended up in the emergency room after the burn became infected. The burn did not hurt (third-degree burns do not hurt), and I kept working the line until Kesha saw flesh hanging from my arm. The two female welders were asking for Kesha's attention and shouting, "Nurse's office! Send her to the nurse's office!" while focusing on soldering. Showing compassion, Kesha sent me to the nurse's office. After the incident, the two female welders (one Black person and one white person), who had been at the plant for more than twelve years, smiled at me more frequently and invited me to talk to them at their fixed workstation.

In situations of racial competition for jobs, it was not easy to gain the trust of the Black and white workers, but I believe the injury was helpful in crossing racial boundaries. To cite another example, the same day of the accident, before going to the nurse's office, I went to the bathroom to wash my hands and ran into Lucinda and two other Black women. I often talked to Lucinda at the cafeteria, but she warmed up more to me after the accident. She told me, "Honey, that's white, and you have no skin left there." I looked up at her, confused. She raised her sleeve and showed me several dark spots, some the size of a nickel and some the size of a dime, on both of her arms. Another woman showed me hers and said, "My burns don't show as much because my skin is darker than yours." Although I never intended to be injured at HiCap, the incident facilitated my getting closer to the welders and workers handling base-plates and gaining Kesha's respect. The vast majority of these workers had arms dotted with scars that they acquired from handling hot copper wires on the baseplates that went from one workstation to another.

Bilingualism was essential to build rapport with some of the Black workers at HiCap, as some wanted to befriend or engage romantically with their Latino counterparts. With the arrival of the first Latino workers, some non-Latina women asked that I help them communicate with the Latino men working next to them on the assembly line. These opportunities facilitated more profound and personal social relations that workers had with one another. Some women started sharing stories with me after they asked me to interpret for them. Similarly, because the resistance from Black men motivated Latino men's exit and supported Latina women's entry, the request to interpret the communication between native-born workers and Latinos, over time, came from Black and white men, rather than from Black and white women. Black and white men were interested in the Latinas arriving at the plant. On many occasions, they asked that I translate love notes or requests in which they asked someone to go out or told them that they were interested in them. These instances produced opportunities to get to know non-Latino workers in more depth.

RESEARCH ETHICS

Readers may have concerns about the ethics of the blatantly illegal behavior that I witnessed in the research for this book. I share their concerns. Throughout this research, I struggled with the ethical issue of engaging in participant observation in organizations that were taking actions that were questionable and often illegal; hiring and firing workers on racial grounds were common. I observed these behaviors as both a worker and a supervisor at HiCap. For half of my research, I worked in employers' "preferred" queue, and as such, I was one of the exploited, tractable, and disciplined workers. For the remaining half of my research, I occupied a supervisory role. Typically, persons in this role had the authority to hire and fire workers. This was not the case for my position at HiCap, however. At HiCap, I had no administrative control over hiring or firing decisions, nor did I provide input on such decisions.

The company hired me as a cultural broker, an "interpreter" or transla-tor for Latino workers. Lastly, as a participant observer in a role with the potential to discipline workers, I pushed back in particular situations when workers were mistreated, although I was not always aware of the ultimate consequences of my actions and was certainly unsuccessful in many attempts at protecting individual workers.

Processes of inequality cut across many lines of vulnerability, and the participant observer has to manage that position and minimize risk and harm across these lines. In my case, I was in a situation in which undoc-umented immigrant workers were hyperexploited. Black working-class individuals were direct targets of discrimination and firing, and white working-class workers were collateral damage in these highly dysfunc-tional, racialized workplaces. Furthermore, sexually and emotionally harassing and abusing women was normalized, tolerated, and frequent. How should the participant observer act in an environment where ra-cial, gender, and class oppression and injustice prevail? How does the participant observer continue to research in an environment where op-pression feeds economic greed and simultaneously look herself in the mirror every morning?

Everett Hughes and Erving Goffman clearly established that a key strength of ethnography derives from the ability of the ethnographer to participate fully while in the field.[5] That being said, ethnographers are constrained by the IRB that evaluates and approves their research protocols. My IRB panel explicitly asked that I focus on observations, like a "fly on the wall." I entered the field prepared to observe, take de-tailed field notes, and process my observations to follow leads. Yet, my site demanded more. The dynamics of the racialized organization I was observing brought into tension the research task as required by the IRB and my commitment to social justice.

Employers had set up the displacement as a zero-sum game, challeng-ing my initial fieldwork ideas. How should the ethnographer behave in a research site where employment and race relations are set up as a zero-sum game? The loss of one meant the win of another. As I am a Latina immigrant woman who had been undocumented and deported and had navigated these processes of oppression painfully, the Latino workers, who knew about my background and research, expected my loyalty. The displacement turned into a situation in which intervening to support one vulnerable group would still negatively affect another. For instance, interceding on behalf of Black workers would have caused Latino immigrants to lose their jobs and possibly get deported. Intervening on behalf of Latino immigrants would have caused Black workers to lose their jobs. Similarly, protecting women or poor white individuals would have caused Black or Latino workers to lose their jobs. At every turn in this research, I was faced with decisions that could lead to direct conflict with the guiding principle of "do no harm."

A novice ethnographer is rarely prepared to deal with this situation. I guided myself in the best way I could. I ignored issues that would result in write-ups or managers firing workers. For the most part, racial segregation patterned the workplaces I studied for this project, including HiCap. This segregation meant that I spent more time with Latinos and, as such, was able to intervene on their behalf. Still, to support Black workers, I avoided the directives to write up Black workers who were not cooperating with managerial demands. While, understandably, many of the Black workers resented the presence of Latino workers, I never reported workers who threatened me, mocked my accented English, or dismissed my instructions.

Researchers must identify lines related to their specific research sites that they will not cross. I knew that I would never knowingly put workers in danger, and I had decided that I would not accept jobs that put me in the position of hiring and firing decisions. Before considering the supervisory role in this research, I decided that I would quit a job before accepting an offer to replace an existing employee. This caused me to quit a job during my fieldwork. For example, I quit Carolina Mills (a large textile mill), a decision that removed me from a research context that would have allowed me to have a sharp comparison to HiCap for a longer period. Ultimately, the researcher needs to live with their decisions, and forethought in this area will pay long-term benefits.

A key goal while I was in the field was to develop cognitive empathy with research participants. Therefore, I focused on carefully managing my relationships with supervisors and workers to build trust. If I had been perceived as aligning with upper management, gaining trust from cosupervisors and workers would have been virtually impossible. Likewise, gaining confidence from managers would have been equally challenging if I had been perceived as aligning too closely with workers. For example, managers despised union leaders and demoted or fired anyone who seemed to side with workers. To address this tension, I prioritized actions geared toward protecting the most vulnerable—in this case, the undocumented Latino immigrants, working-class Black and white individuals, and women. I listened to managers and observed their behaviors but avoided providing input on displacement or engaging in hiring and firing decisions. Additionally, I modeled my behavior after that of bilingual supervisors, who I believed interacted fairly with the workers they supervised and who had gained the respect of immigrant and non-immigrant workers.

Still, HiCap was engaging in discriminatory practices. Readers might wonder whether I expressed any opinion or opposition to the displacement plan. I grappled with this issue and even considered ending the research when I realized the details of the employer's scheme. I decided, however, against overtly challenging HiCap about the displacement for several reasons. Many immigrants at the plant asked that I "do nothing" when managers made the job expectations untenable. Others asked that I stay quiet because they wanted to avoid problems and feared losing their jobs. This concern was partly because factory raids were widespread during my research stint, and workers, not employers, were more apt to lose their jobs during these situations. In addition, vulnerable white and Black workers wanted me to "keep them out of trouble." I agreed to respect the workers' desires while trying to protect as much as possible those who resisted in tacit ways.

Protecting workers in a multiracial, competitive environment of disadvantage is an almost impossible task. Social relations, in my research, functioned as a zero-sum game in which the gain of workers of a particular racial/gender group is the loss of another. While I was at HiCap to conduct research, whenever possible, I tried to improve the employment situation of all workers. For example, I persuaded managers to improve safety on the assembly line by adding safety guards to protect workers' fingers and limbs and fought to eliminate jobs used to push workers to quit (i.e., cleaning with alcohol, floaters). Still, I worked with Darius and Kesha, the Black supervisors, to find solutions that would create a fair work situation for all HiCap workers and minimize conflict.

I often thought of ways to oppose HiCap's plans for displacement. I realized, however, that openly contesting management's schemes would not have yielded different results. First, managers were primarily white men who showed little respect for women. For example, they spoke to me using curt, disrespectful commands. Moreover, two managers harassed me sexually, while others belittled me and ridiculed my accented English and "California ideas." Managers trusted me within the constraints of my role as a bilingual researcher. Because I am a Mexican immigrant, however, they seldom took my opinions seriously. Coping with constant harassment and humiliation was painful, but I wanted to complete the research. Second, I realized that managers would have continued with the displacement process whether I worked there or not. To illustrate, during Lean Manufacturing training, I observed with difficulty and anger how managers demoted and replaced a Black supervisor who resisted their plan; this decision ultimately led him to leave the job. Managers constantly ignored Sarah, a white supervisor who protested "racial favoritism." Without much power to change anything through open opposition and given the potential to cause harm, I chose not to challenge the employer directly. Participating in this ethnographic study had its challenges. The benefits associated with disseminating my research outcomes, I hope, outweigh the drawbacks.

LEAVING THE FIELD

For some researchers, fieldwork is a mechanical set of steps: arriving, gaining access, collecting data, leaving the field, and moving on to other projects. While this was not necessarily my case, I felt that way when I returned to my graduate program at Stanford after nearly two years of fieldwork. I wrote my qualifying exam in the field—the equivalent of a master's thesis. I took multiple jobs for the research and wrote field notes every night, and for about eight months, I woke up every morning at 4:30 a.m. to pick up workers and drive them to work in factories or warehouses. This routine was exhausting, and I had to push myself to write field notes at the end of every day. On Sundays, I volunteered in a day-care center at a Catholic church, conducted interviews with community members on some weekends, and worked the night shift with a janitorial crew of immigrant workers for a while.

I returned to the field two years after my initial research, during the Great Recession, looking for opportunities to help the people from HiCap and the community. At this time, I was proactive in searching for opportunities to help the people I studied in my initial research. I worked with activists and community leaders in a multifaith coalition to create "yellow" cards (the size of a credit card) that provided information about what to do after losing a job, facing an eviction, being apprehended by ICE authorities, or being separated from family members. We also printed and distributed information on experts and community leaders willing to assist with legal advice, employment, education, or health services. Additionally, because many families lost jobs and some were under house arrest after immigration raids, the multifaith organization set up a "free pantry" for people to access food when they had no employment. One of my main activities with the coalition was to tap into my existing networks to deliver aid to the marginalized. We invested resources to recruit lawyers and social workers to start a legal and educational clinic in the community. I worked with Mayan community leaders to set up a literacy program for Chuj-speaking women from Guatemala.

As researchers, we may gain more than we offer when we work with vulnerable communities. However, I hope that this work honors my respondents' requests to represent the complexities of their stories and voices in thoughtful, culturally sensitive ways and that it helps bring meaningful and lasting change to the communities that I studied.

FOLLOWING UP

One indicator of quality research is following up with respondents to keep abreast of new developments in the field that might challenge our findings and conclusions.[6] Over the years, I maintained contact with my informants via telephone and social media to check on some of the emerging themes and theories I was developing in my analysis. Unfortunately, white and Black participants did not respond to my follow-up calls. While Darius, the Black supervisor who supported my work while I was at HiCap, offered to stay in touch and gave me his phone number and email, he did not respond to my messages. I continued to read English- and Spanish-language newspapers from Jessamine and read industrial reports about HiCap, but this was not enough to validate some of my findings and do a more thorough follow-up on the research. I was fortunate that Latinos, the immigrant community that was the focus of my study from the start, remained receptive even years after I had left the field.

Two years after conducting research at HiCap, I returned to the field to work with community advocates and verify some of my findings. I took an assembly-line job in a warehouse that packaged the organic tea widely consumed in this nation and conducted 163 additional interviews to see how the severe economic downturn shaped the racial, class, and gender dynamics I observed three years prior, when the economy was robust. The region had witnessed significant economic disruption, coupled with a crackdown on "illegal" immigration through E-Verify mandates and other employment-based policies. During this return, I gathered that I could not write about displacement without paying attention to shifts in state policy and employment relations. During this follow-up, I talked to one of the Ready Hands managers, Peggy, the woman who, two years prior, drove around town chasing a van full of Latinos to offer them a job. She shared that HiCap had gone through another cycle of racialized displacement. This time the company fired many undocumented Mexican immigrants with bad papers and replaced them with Black immigrants from Nigeria and the Caribbean. The workforce was mostly immigrant, but now more workers had good papers and were Black.

I followed up with the Latino supervisors on my findings on displacement. Roberto, the first supervisor the company hired, said during a follow-up interview, "Yeah, displacement is not good for workers and is not good for supervisors. It's good only for managers." He did not want to talk much about HiCap; he had "a bad taste about the displacement." In essence, talking about HiCap reminded him of how futile having supervisory authority and status based on bilingualism was. It also left him feeling "traumatized" (*traumado*), he told me, because managers showed no respect for workers. The consequences for supervisors were dire. Roberto, for example, tried his luck in other companies after he left HiCap. He eventually settled into a job as an operator in a biotechnology company. Moreover, while there were no mobility ladders for him at this job and he had no power or authority, he preferred this low-key role to hyperexploiting workers.

I maintained a close relationship with several of the women in my study. Those without good papers were in even more precarious conditions when I returned to the field, many working in the informal economy and even in more degraded jobs. Some were victims in a major

ICE immigration raid at a meatpacking plant where they had found employment. The men were deported. The women were under house arrest
if they had children and were waiting for their immigration hearings.
Many returned to Mexico. The Latinos, my neighbors at Bristol Apartments, either returned to Mexico (mostly the women) or were living in
multifamily, group households, to make ends meet. From a theoretical
perspective, the follow-up highlighted how unstable racialized displacement could be. Finally, it demonstrated that, in studying processes in
which a vulnerable population is the unfair target of policy, ethnographers need to bind their conclusions to the period and political and economic conditions of their research.

NOTES

INTRODUCTION

1. I use the terms "Latino," "Latina/o," and "Hispanic" interchangeably. I do this primarily for practical reasons. At the time of this writing, most studies reviewed as well as my interviews with many secondary migrants in the South use the term "Latino" or "Latina/o." I use the term "Hispanic" when I refer to US Census data, as the US Census uses this term to classify the population in national statistics. I also use the term "Hispanic" when I report on interviews and conversations with southerners. While many government workers and media leaders used the term "Hispanic" in my data, others used the terms "Spanish" or "Mexican" to identify the Latino population. In instances reflecting the latter case, I use these terms to reflect participants' own views and classification of the Latino population.
2. Logan, Zhang, and Alba 2002; Portes and Manning 2019; Wilson and Portes 1980.
3. Dobbin and Kalev 2007.
4. Ottaviano and Peri 2006; Borjas 2001, 2006; Card, 2005.
5. Borjas 2006.
6. Card 2005.
7. Catanzarite 1998.
8. Greenwood and McDowell 1986; Longhi, Nijkamp, and Poot 2006; Rosenfeld and Tienda 1999.
9. Bhagwati and Srinivasan 1983.
10. Ethier 1985.
11. Abowd and Freeman 1991; Chiswick 1988; and Hillman and Weiss 1999.
12. Martin and Luce 1988.
13. Chiswick 1988.
14. Chiswick 1988.
15. Auer et al. 2019; Orupabo and Nadim 2020.
16. Bonacich 1972.
17. Weil 2014.
18. Doeringer and Piore 2020.
19. Massey 2008.
20. Kalleberg 2011.
21. Ribas 2016; López-Sanders 2009.
22. Ribas 2016.
23. Robinson 2019; Leong 2013.

24. Catanzarite 1998, 2017; Rosenfeld and Tienda 1999; Cranford 2005.

25. Robinson 2019; Itzigsohn and Brown 2020.

26. Ray 2019.

27. Pager, Bonikowski, and Western 2009.

28. Robinson 2019.

29. Hochschild 2016.

30. Kochhar, Suro, and Tafoya 2005; Singer 2008; Waters and Jiménez 2005; Zúñiga and Hernández-León 2005.

31. Hagan, Hernández-León, and Demonsant 2015; Massey 2008; Odem and Lacy 2009; Parrado and Kandel 2008.

32. Marrow 2011; Odem and Lacy 2009; Parrado and Kandel 2008; Smith and Furuseth 2006; Winders and Smith 2010.

33. Bean et al. 2011; Donato, Stainback, and Bankston 2005; E. Griffith 2005; Massey 2008; Odem and Lacy 2009; Peacock, Watson, and Matthews 2005; Zúñiga and Hernández-León 2005.

34. López-Sanders 2009.

35. Kandel and Parrado 2005; Hernández-León and Zúñiga 2000; Johnson-Webb 2002; Kandel and Parrado 2005; Marrow 2011.

36. Crowley, Lichter, and Turner 2015.

37. Donato, Stainback, and Bankston 2005.

38. D. Griffith 2005, 2008.

39. McDaniel and Casanova 2003.

40. Waldinger and Lichter 2003; Waters 2009.

41. Broadway and Stull 2008; Gouveia and Stull 1995, 1997; Grey 1999; Hackenberg and Kukulka 1995; Kandel and Cromartie 2004; Kandel and Parrado 2005; Marrow 2011; Stuesse 2008; Ribas 2016; Stull and Broadway 2008; Stull, Broadway, and Griffith 1995.

42. Grey 1999; Grey and Woodrick 2005.

43. Manson et al. 2022.

44. Kochhar, Suro, and Tafoya 2005; Odem and Lacy 2009; Kalleberg 2001.

45. Waters, Kasinitz, and Asad 2014; Stuesse and Coleman 2014.

46. Crosby, Bromley, and Saxe 1980.

47. Emerson, Fretz, and Shaw 2011; Lofland et al. 2022.

48. Hodson 2004; McDermott 2006, 2011.

49. Small and McCrory Calarco 2022.

50. Factory descriptions that are immaterial to the sociological argument have been deliberately altered to protect the anonymity of the individuals and organizations involved in this study.

51. Fernandez and Fernandez-Mateo 2006.

52. MacKenzie and Forde 2009; McGovern 2007; Neuman and Tienda 1994.

53. Kalleberg 2011.

54. Broadway and Stull 2008; Fink 1998; Gouveia and Stull 1995, 1997; Grey 1999; Stull, Broadway, and Griffith 1995; Ribas 2016; Stull and Broadway 2008.

55. Please see the appendix for a description of the broader research site and the community.

CHAPTER 1. RACIALIZED HIRING

1. Kalleberg 2011.
2. Menjívar 2021; Garcia 2017; Herrera 2016.
3. Menjívar 2021, 92.
4. López-Sanders and Brown 2020.
5. Knight, Dobbin, and Kalev 2022.
6. Wooten and James 2004; Berrey, Nelson, and Nielsen 2017.
7. Massey and Pren 2012.
8. Shannon et al. 2017.
9. Pager 2003.
10. Hirschman 1970.
11. Bourdieu 1990.
12. Rivera 2012.
13. Waldinger and Lichter 2003.
14. Turco 2010; Rivera 2012.
15. Ciscel, Smith, and Mendoza 2003; MacKenzie and Forde 2009; Waldinger and Lichter 2003; Zamudio and Lichter 2008.
16. Johnson-Webb 2003.
17. Kalleberg 2011.

CHAPTER 2. ENLISTING SUBCONTRACTORS AND INTERMEDIARIES

1. Burt 2007; Simmel 1950.
2. Burt 1995, 2001.
3. Burt 1995.
4. Choudry and Henaway 2012.
5. American Staffing Association 2021.
6. McAllister 1998.
7. McAllister 1998, 221.
8. Bouzzine and Lueg 2021; Dobbin and Kalev 2017.
9. 84 Fed. Reg. 66 (2019).
10. Bauman, Tost, and Ong 2016.
11. Ciscel, Smith, and Mendoza 2003; MacKenzie and Forde 2009; Waldinger and Lichter 2003; Zamudio and Lichter 2008.
12. Albiston and Green 2018; Weber 1978.
13. Omi and Winant 2014.
14. Goffman 1961a.
15. Menjívar and Abrego 2012.
16. Kalleberg 2011; Reskin and Roos 1990.
17. US House of Representatives 2008.
18. Simmel 1950.

CHAPTER 3. CREATING JOB VACANCIES

1. Rivera 2012; Turco 2010.
2. Tomaskovic-Devey and Skaggs 1999; Bielby and Baron 1986.
3. Donohue 1997.
4. Smith 2007; Waldinger 1997; Fernandez and Fernandez-Mateo 2006.
5. Reskin and Roos 1990.
6. Lo and Nguyen 2018; Catanzarite and Aguilera 2002.
7. Dobbin and Kalev 2016.
8. Feagin 2020; Bonilla-Silva 2015; Wingfield and Feagin 2012.
9. Chapman 2005.
10. Doussard 2013; Graeber 2018; Kalleberg 2011; Rothstein 2016.
11. Braverman 1998.
12. Goldratt, Cox, and Whitford 2004.
13. Each gap on the line was an empty spot on the conveyor that represented a unit that would not be made according to the production plan. They were obvious signals of problems on the line and almost always drew unwanted attention from the floor managers.

CHAPTER 4. SHIFTING THE LABOR QUEUE BY RACE AND GENDER

1. Reskin and Roos 1990.
2. Feagin 1991.
3. West and Zimmerman 1987.
4. Willis 1981.
5. Simmel 1950.
6. Mayo (1933) 2016.
7. Haveman and Wetts 2019.
8. Burawoy 1982.

CHAPTER 5. SHOW ME YOUR PAPERS!

1. Baker 2021.
2. Author's analysis of data from Lopez, Passel, and Cohn 2021.
3. Krutchik 2008.
4. Archibold 2007.
5. Hegen 2009.
6. Arizona Contractors Ass'n, Inc. v. Candelaria, 534 F. Supp. 2d 1036 (D. Ariz. 2008).
7. Chicanos Por La Causa, Inc. v. Napolitano, 558 F.3d 856, 859 (9th Cir. 2008).
8. Chamber of Commerce v. Whiting, 563 U.S. 582, 606 (2011).
9. Minnesota's and Rhode Island's executive orders ceased being effective in 2011.
10. It should be noted that while most of the state laws mentioned provide for a simple fine and/or a period of probation for a first offense, most also go straight to a business stoppage, temporary or permanent, for subsequent offenses.

11. Bolden 2009.
12. Anderson 2007.
13. Reuters 2011.

CHAPTER 6. RACIALIZED SHOCKS AND OUT-GROUP BOUNDARIES

1. Bobo and Hutchings 1996.
2. Waldinger and Lichter 2003.
3. Piore 1974; Hernández-León 2005; López-Sanders 2014.
4. Massey 2001.
5. Durand, Massey, and Zenteno 2001.
6. Donato, Aguilera, and Wakabayashi 2005; Waldinger and Lichter 2003.
7. Catanzarite and Bernabe Aguilera 2002.
8. Portes and Sensenbrenner 1993.
9. López-Sanders 2017.
10. Chavez 2020; Massey, Durand, and Pren 2014.
11. Lee and Bean 2004.
12. Bobo and Hutchings 1996.
13. Weiss 2008.
14. López-Sanders 2009.
15. López-Sanders 2009.
16. Bobo and Hutchings 1996.
17. Lee and Bean 2007; see also Alba 1990; Gitlin 1995; Gans 1999; Skrentny 2002; Hollinger 2005.
18. López-Sanders and Brown 2020.
19. Bobo and Hutchings 1996; see also Hutchings and Wong 2014.
20. Bobo and Hutchings 1996.

CONCLUSION

1. Ray 2019.
2. Waters and Jiménez 2005.
3. Sáenz and Douglas 2015; Bonilla-Silva 1997.
4. Romero 2008; Sanchez and Romero 2010; Menjívar 2021.
5. Ribas 2016; Singer 2015; Marrow 2011; López-Sanders 2011.
6. Ribas 2016; López-Sanders 2009.
7. Robinson 2019, 3.
8. Leroy and Jenkins 2021.
9. Robinson 2019.
10. Leroy and Jenkins 2021, 3.
11. Lieberson 1980; Waldinger 1997; Waldinger and Lichter 2003.
12. Asimakopoulos 2009; Hudson 2007; Kalleberg and Sorensen 1979.
13. Waldinger and Lichter 2003.
14. Waldinger 1997; Waters 2009.
15. Kasinitz and Rosenberg 1996; Waldinger 1997; Waldinger and Lichter 2003.

16. Reskin and Roos 1990; Sørensen 2004.
17. Bonacich 1972.
18. Hernández-León 2005.
19. Tilly 1998; López-Sanders 2014; Pattillo-McCoy 1999.
20. Burt 2007.
21. Burawoy 1982.
22. Bonacich 1973.
23. Kalleberg 2011.
24. Alba 2020.
25. Alba 2020.
26. Alba 2020.
27. Alba and Nee 2003; Lee and Bean 2004.
28. Marrow 2011.

METHODS APPENDIX

1. Portes and Rumbaut 2001.
2. Small and McCrory Calarco 2022; Emerson, Fretz, and Shaw 2011; Lofland et al. 2022.
3. Saldaña 2014; LeCompte and Goetz 1982.
4. Biernacki and Waldorf 1981.
5. Hughes 1971; Goffman 1961b.
6. Small and McCrory Calarco 2022.

REFERENCES

Abowd, John M., and Richard B. Freeman. 1991. *Immigration, Trade, and the Labor Market*. Chicago: University of Chicago Press.

Alba, Richard D. 1990. *Ethnic Identity: The Transformation of White America*. New Haven, CT: Yale University Press.

———. 2020. *The Great Demographic Illusion: Majority, Minority, and the Expanding American Mainstream*. Princeton, NJ: Princeton University Press.

Alba, Richard D., and Victor Nee. 2003. *Remaking the American Mainstream: Assimilation and Contemporary Immigration*. Cambridge, MA: Harvard University Press.

Albiston, Catherine, and Tristin K. Green. 2018. "Social Closure Discrimination." *Berkeley Journal of Employment and Labor Law* 39 (1): 1–36.

American Staffing Association. 2021. "2021 Staffing Industry Playbook." https://americanstaffing.net.

Anderson, Trevor. 2007. "Immigration Sting Nets 7 Food Workers at BMW." *GoUpstate*, July 27, 2007. www.goupstate.com.

Archibold, Randal C. 2007. "Arizona Governor Signs Tough Bill on Hiring Illegal Immigrants." *New York Times*, July 3, 2007. www.nytimes.com.

Asimakopoulos, John. 2009. "Globally Segmented Labor Markets: The Coming of the Greatest Boom and Bust, without the Boom." *Critical Sociology* 35 (2): 175–98.

Auer, Daniel, Giuliano Bonoli, Flavia Fossati, and Fabienne Liechti. 2019. "The Matching Hierarchies Model: Evidence from a Survey Experiment on Employers' Hiring Intent Regarding Immigrant Applicants." *International Migration Review* 53 (1): 90–121.

Baker, Bryan. 2021. "Estimates of the Unauthorized Immigrant Population Residing in the United States: January 2015–January 2018." US Department of Homeland Security.

Bauman, Christopher W., Leigh Plunkett Tost, and Madeline Ong. 2016. "Blame the Shepherd Not the Sheep: Imitating Higher-Ranking Transgressors Mitigates Punishment for Unethical Behavior." *Organizational Behavior and Human Decision Processes* 137:123–41.

Bean, Frank D., James D. Bachmeier, Susan K. Brown, and Rosaura Tafoya-Estrada. 2011. "Immigration and Labor Market Dynamics." In *Just Neighbors? Research on African American and Latino Relations in the United States*, edited by Edward Telles, Mark Q. Sawyer, and Gaspar Rivera-Salgado, 37–60. New York: Russell Sage Foundation.

Berrey, Ellen, Robert L. Nelson, and Laura Beth Nielsen. 2017. *Rights on Trial: How Workplace Discrimination Law Perpetuates Inequality.* Chicago: University of Chicago Press.

Bhagwati, Jagdish N., and T. N. Srinivasan. 1983. "On the Choice between Capital and Labour Mobility." *Journal of International Economics* 14:209–21.

Bielby, William T., and James N. Baron. 1986. "Men and Women at Work: Sex Segregation and Statistical Discrimination." *American Journal of Sociology* 91 (4): 759–99.

Biernacki, Patrick, and Dan Waldorf. 1981. "Snowball Sampling: Problems and Techniques of Chain Referral Sampling." *Sociological Methods & Research* 10 (2): 141–63.

Bobo, Lawrence, and Vincent L. Hutchings. 1996. "Perceptions of Racial Group Competition: Extending Blumer's Theory of Group Position to a Multiracial Social Context." *American Sociological Review* 61 (6): 951–72.

Bolden, Tyler D. 2009. "Business Interruption and Employer Liability in the Age of ICE Raids." *South Carolina Journal of International Law and Business* 5 (2): article 2.

Bonacich, Edna. 1972. "A Theory of Ethnic Antagonism: The Split Labor Market." *American Sociological Review* 37:547–59.

———. 1973. "A Theory of Middleman Minorities." *American Sociological Review* 38:583–94.

Bonilla-Silva, Eduardo. 1997. "Rethinking Racism: Toward a Structural Interpretation." *American Sociological Review* 62:465–80.

———. 2015. "The Structure of Racism in Color-Blind, 'Post-Racial' America." *American Behavioral Scientist* 59 (11): 1358–76.

Borjas, George J. 2001. "Does Immigration Grease the Wheels of the Labor Market?" *Brookings Papers on Economic Activity* 2001 (1): 69–133.

———. 2006. "Native Internal Migration and the Labor Market Impact of Immigration." *Journal of Human Resources* 41 (2): 221–58.

Bourdieu, Pierre. 1990. *The Logic of Practice.* Redwood City, CA: Stanford University Press.

Bouzzine, Yassin Denis, and Rainer Lueg. 2021. "The Reputation Costs of Executive Misconduct Accusations." Paper presented at the Academy of Management Proceedings.

Braverman, Harry. 1998. *Labor and Monopoly Capital.* New York: Monthly Review Press.

Broadway, Michael J., and Donald D. Stull. 2008. "'I'll Do Whatever You Want, but It Hurts': Worker Safety and Community Health in Modern Meatpacking." *Labor: Studies in Working-Class History of the Americas* 5 (2): 27–37.

Burawoy, Michael. 1982. *Manufacturing Consent: Changes in the Labor Process under Monopoly Capitalism.* Chicago: University of Chicago Press.

Burt, Ronald S. 1995. *Structural Holes: The Social Structure of Competition.* Cambridge, MA: Harvard University Press.

———. 2001. "Structural Holes versus Network Closure as Social Capital." In *Social Capital: Theory and Research*, edited by Nan Lin, Karen Cook, and Ronald S. Burt, 31–56. New Brunswick, NJ: Transaction.

———. 2007. *Brokerage and Closure: An Introduction to Social Capital.* Oxford: Oxford University Press.

Card, David. 2005. "Is the New Immigration Really So Bad?" *Economic Journal* 115 (507): F300–F323.

Catanzarite, Lisa. 1998. "Immigrant Latino Representation and Earnings Penalties in Occupations." *Research in Social Stratification and Mobility* 16:147–80.

———. 2017. "Occupational Context and Wage Competition of New Immigrant Latinos with Minorities and Whites." In *The Impact of Immigration on African Americans,* edited by Steven Shulman, 59–76. New York: Routledge.

Catanzarite, Lisa, and Michael Bernabe Aguilera. 2002. "Working with Co-ethnics: Earnings Penalties for Latino Immigrants at Latino Jobsites." *Social Problems* 49 (1): 101–27.

Chapman, Christopher D. 2005. "Clean House with Lean 5S." *Quality Progress* 38:27–32.

Chavez, Leo. 2020. *The Latino Threat: Constructing Immigrants, Citizens, and the Nation.* Stanford, CA: Stanford University Press.

Chiswick, Barry R. 1988. "Illegal Immigration and Immigration Control." *Journal of Economic Perspectives* 2 (3): 101–15.

Choudry, Aziz, and Mostafa Henaway. 2012. "Agents of Misfortune: Contextualizing Migrant and Immigrant Workers' Struggles against Temporary Labour Recruitment Agencies." *Labour, Capital and Society / Travail, capital et société* 45 (1): 36–65.

Ciscel, David H., Barbara Ellen Smith, and Marcela Mendoza. 2003. "Ghosts in the Global Machine: New Immigrants and the Redefinition of Work." *Journal of Economic Issues* 37 (2): 333–41.

Cranford, Cynthia J. 2005. "Networks of Exploitation: Immigrant Labor and the Restructuring of the Los Angeles Janitorial Industry." *Social Problems* 52 (3): 379–97.

Crosby, Faye, Stephanie Bromley, and Leonard Saxe. 1980. "Recent Unobtrusive Studies of Black and White Discrimination and Prejudice: A Literature Review." *Psychological Bulletin* 87 (3): 546–63.

Crowley, Martha, Daniel T. Lichter, and Richard N. Turner. 2015. "Diverging Fortunes? Economic Well-Being of Latinos and African Americans in New Rural Destinations." *Social Science Research* 51:77–92.

Dobbin, Frank, and Alexandra Kalev. 2007. "The Architecture of Inclusion: Evidence from Corporate Diversity Programs." *Harvard Journal of Law and Gender* 30:279–301.

———. 2016. "Why Diversity Programs Fail." *Harvard Business Review* 94 (7): article 14.

———. 2017. "Are Diversity Programs Merely Ceremonial? Evidence-Free Institutionalization." In *The Sage Handbook of Organizational Institutionalism,* edited by Royston Greenwood, Christine Oliver, Thomas B. Lawrence, and Renate E. Meyer, 808–28. London: Sage.

Doeringer, Peter B., and Michael J. Piore. 2020. *Internal Labor Markets and Manpower Analysis: With a New Introduction.* New York: Routledge.

Donato, Katharine M., Michael Aguilera, and Chizuko Wakabayashi. 2005. "Immigration Policy and Employment Conditions of US Immigrants from Mexico, Nicaragua, and the Dominican Republic." *International Migration* 43 (5): 5–29.

Donato, Katharine M., Melissa Stainback, and Carl L. Bankston III. 2005. "The Economic Incorporation of Mexican Immigrants in Southern Louisiana: A Tale of Two Cities." In *New Destinations: Mexican Immigration in the United States*, edited by Víctor Zúñiga and Rubén Hernández-León, 76–99. New York: Russell Sage Foundation.

Donohue, John J., III 1997. *Foundations of Employment Discrimination Law*. New York: Oxford University Press.

Doussard, Marc. 2013. *Degraded Work: The Struggle at the Bottom of the Labor Market*. Minneapolis: University of Minnesota Press.

Durand, Jorge, Douglas S. Massey, and Rene M. Zenteno. 2001. "Mexican Immigration to the United States: Continuities and Changes." *Latin American Research Review* 36 (1):107–27.

Emerson, Robert M., Rachel I. Fretz, and Linda L. Shaw. 2011. *Writing Ethnographic Fieldnotes*. Chicago: University of Chicago Press.

Ethier, Wilfred J. 1985. "International Trade and Labor Migration." *American Economic Review* 75 (4): 691–707.

Feagin, Joe R. 1991. "The Continuing Significance of Race: Antiblack Discrimination in Public Places." *American Sociological Review* 56 (1): 101–16.

———. 2020. *The White Racial Frame: Centuries of Racial Framing and Counter-Framing*. New York: Routledge.

Fernandez, Roberto M., and Isabel Fernandez-Mateo. 2006. "Networks, Race, and Hiring." *American Sociological Review* 71 (1): 42–71.

Fink, Deborah. 1998. *Cutting into the Meatpacking Line: Workers and Change in the Rural Midwest*. Chapel Hill: University of North Carolina Press.

Gans, Herbert J. 1999. "Participant Observation in the Era of 'Ethnography.'" *Journal of Contemporary Ethnography* 28 (5): 540–48.

García, San Juanita. 2017. "Racializing 'Illegality': An Intersectional Approach to Understanding How Mexican-Origin Women Navigate an Anti-Immigrant Climate." *Sociology of Race and Ethnicity* 3 (4): 474–90.

Gitlin, Todd. 1995. *The Twilight of Common Dreams: Why America Is Wracked by Culture Wars*. New York: Metropolitan Books.

Goffman, Erving. 1961a. *Asylums: Essays on the Social Situation of Mental Patients and Other Inmates*. Chicago: Aldine Transaction.

———. 1961b. *Encounters: Two Studies in the Sociology of Interaction*. Cambridge, UK: Ravenio Books.

Goldratt, Eliyahu M., Jeff Cox, and David Whitford. 2004. *The Goal: A Process of Ongoing Improvement*. Great Barrington, MA: North River.

Gouveia, Lourdes, and Donald D. Stull. 1995. "Dances with Cows: Beefpacking's Impact on Garden City, Kansas, and Lexington, Nebraska." In *Any Way You Cut*

It: Meat Processing and Small-Town America, edited by Donald D. Stull, Michael J. Broadway, and David Griffith, 85–107. Lawrence: University Press of Kansas.

———. 1997. "Latino Immigrants, Meatpacking, and Rural Communities: A Case Study of Lexington, Nebraska." JSRI Research Report 26. Julian Samora Research Institute, Michigan State University.

Graeber, David. 2018. *Bullshit Jobs: A Theory.* New York: Simon and Schuster.

Greenwood, Michael J., and John M. McDowell. 1986. "The Factor Market Consequences of US Immigration." *Journal of Economic Literature* 24 (4): 1738–72.

———. 1988. "Changing Patterns of Migration and Regional Economic Growth in the US: A Demographic Perspective." *Growth and Change* 19 (4): 68–86.

Grey, Mark A. 1999. "Immigrants, Migration, and Worker Turnover at the Hog Pride Pork Packing Plant." *Human Organization* 58 (1): 16–27.

Grey, Mark A., and Anne C. Woodrick. 2005. "'Latinos Have Revitalized Our Community': Mexican Migration and the Anglo Responses in Marshalltown, Iowa." In *New Destinations: Mexican Immigration in the United States* edited by Víctor Zúñiga and Rubén Hernández-León, 133–54. New York: Russell Sage Foundation.

Griffith, David C. 2005. "Rural Industry and Mexican Immigration and Settlement in North Carolina." In *New Destinations: Mexican Immigration in the United States*, edited by Víctor Zúñiga and Rubén Hernández-León, 50–75. New York: Russell Sage Foundation.

———. 2008. "New Midwesterners, New Southerners: Immigration Experiences in Four Rural American Settings." In *New Faces in New Places: The Changing Geography of American Immigration*, edited by Douglass S. Massey, 179–210. New York: Russell Sage Foundation.

Griffith, Elwin. 2005. "Admission and Cancellation of Removal under the Immigration and Nationality Act." *Michigan State Law Review* 2005:979–1062.

Hackenberg, Robert A., and Gary Kukulka. 1995. "Industries, Immigrants, and Illness in the New Midwest." In *Any Way You Cut It: Meat Processing and Small-Town America*, edited by Donald D. Stull, Michael J. Broadway, and David Griffith, 187–211. Lawrence: University Press of Kansas.

Hagan, Jacqueline, Rubén Hernández-León, and Jean-Luc Demonsant. 2015. *Skills of the Unskilled: Work and Mobility among Mexican Migrants.* Berkeley: University of California Press.

Haveman, Heather A., and Rachel Wetts. 2019. "Organizational Theory: From Classical Sociology to the 1970s." *Sociology Compass* 13 (3): article e12627.

Hegen, Dirk. 2009. "State Laws Related to Immigrants and Immigration in 2008." Paper presented at the National Conference of State Legislatures, Washington, DC. www.ncsl.org.

Hernández-León, Rubén. 2005. "The Migration Industry in the Mexico-US Migratory System." California Center for Population Research On-Line Working Paper Series. https://escholarship.org.

Hernández-León, Rubén, and Víctor Zúñiga. 2000. "'Making Carpet by the Mile': The Emergence of a Mexican Immigrant Community in an Industrial Region of the US Historic South." *Social Science Quarterly* 81 (1): 49–66.

Herrera, Juan. 2016. "Racialized Illegality: The Regulation of Informal Labor and Space." *Latino Studies* 14 (3): 320–43.

Hillman, Arye L., and Avi Weiss. 1999. "A Theory of Permissible Illegal Immigration." *European Journal of Political Economy* 15 (4): 585–604.

Hirschman, Albert O. 1970. *Exit, Voice, and Loyalty: Responses to Decline in Firms, Organizations, and States.* Cambridge, MA: Harvard University Press.

Hochschild, Arlie Russell. 2016. *Invisible Labor: Hidden Work in the Contemporary World.* Berkeley: University of California Press.

Hodson, Randy. 2004. "Organizational Trustworthiness: Findings from the Population of Organizational Ethnographies." *Organization Science* 15 (4): 432–45.

Hollinger, David A. 2005. "The One Drop Rule & the One Hate Rule." *Daedalus* 134 (1): 18–28.

Hudson, Kenneth. 2007. "The New Labor Market Segmentation: Labor Market Dualism in the New Economy." *Social Science Research* 36 (1): 286–312.

Hughes, Everett C. 2017. *The Sociological Eye: Selected Papers.* New York: Routledge.

Hutchings, Vincent L., and Cara Wong. 2014. "Racism, Group Position, and Attitudes about Immigration among Blacks and Whites." *Du Bois Review: Social Science Research on Race* 11 (2): 419–42.

Itzigsohn, José, and Karida L. Brown. 2020. *The Sociology of W. E. B. Du Bois: Racialized Modernity and the Global Color Line.* New York: New York University Press.

Johnson-Webb, Karen D. 2002. "Employer Recruitment and Hispanic Labor Migration: North Carolina Urban Areas at the End of the Millennium." *Professional Geographer* 54 (3): 406–21.

———. 2003. *Recruiting Hispanic Labor: Immigrants in Non-traditional Areas.* New York: LFB, 2003.

Kalleberg, Arne L. 2001. "The Advent of the Flexible Workplace." In *Working in Restructured Workplaces: Challenges and New Directions for the Sociology of Work*, edited by Daniel B. Cornfield, Karen Campbell, and Holly McCammon, 437–53. Thousand Oaks, CA: Sage.

———. 2011. *Good Jobs, Bad Jobs: The Rise of Polarized and Precarious Employment Systems in the United States, 1970s–2000s.* New York: Russell Sage Foundation.

Kalleberg, Arne L., and Aage B. Sorensen. 1979. "The Sociology of Labor Markets." *Annual Review of Sociology* 5:351–79.

Kandel, William, and John Cromartie. 2004. *New Patterns of Hispanic Settlement in Rural America.* Washington, DC: US Department Agriculture, Economic Research Service.

Kandel, William, and Emilio A. Parrado. 2005. "Restructuring of the US Meat Processing Industry and New Hispanic Migrant Destinations." *Population and Development Review* 31 (3): 447–71.

Kasinitz, Philip, and Jan Rosenberg. 1996. "Missing the Connection: Social Isolation and Employment on the Brooklyn Waterfront." *Social Problems* 43 (2): 180–96.

Knight, Carly, Frank Dobbin, and Alexandra Kalev. 2022. "Under the Radar: Visibility and the Effects of Discrimination Lawsuits in Small and Large Firms." *American Sociological Review* 87 (2): 175–201.

Kochhar, Rakesh, Roberto Suro, and Sonya Tafoya. 2005. "The New Latino South: The Context and Consequences of Rapid Population Growth." Pew Research Center, July 26. www.pewresearch.org.

Krutchik, Laurence M. 2008. "Down but Not Out: A Comparison of Previous Attempts at Immigration Reform and the Resulting Agency Implemented Changes." *Nova Law Review* 32:455–94.

LeCompte, Margaret D., and Judith Preissle Goetz. 1982. "Problems of Reliability and Validity in Ethnographic Research." *Review of Educational Research* 52 (1): 31–60.

Lee, Jennifer, and Frank D. Bean. 2004. "America's Changing Color Lines: Immigration, Race/Ethnicity, and Multiracial Identification." *Annual Review of Sociology* 30:221–42.

———. 2007. "Reinventing the Color Line Immigration and America's New Racial/Ethnic Divide." *Social Forces* 86 (2): 561–86.

Leong, Nancy. 2013. "Reflections on Racial Capitalism." *Harvard Law Review Forum* 127:32–38.

Leroy, Justin, and Destin Jenkins. 2021. *Histories of Racial Capitalism*. New York: Columbia University Press.

Lieberson, Stanley. 1980. *A Piece of the Pie: Blacks and White Immigrants since 1880*. Berkeley: University of California Press.

Lo, Ming-Cheng M., and Emerald T. Nguyen. 2018. "Caring and Carrying the Cost: Bicultural Latina Nurses' Challenges and Strategies for Working with Coethnic Patients." *RSF: The Russell Sage Foundation Journal of the Social Sciences* 4 (1): 149–71.

Lofland, John, David Snow, Leon Anderson, and Lyn H. Lofland. 2022. *Analyzing Social Settings: A Guide to Qualitative Observation and Analysis*. Long Grove, IL: Waveland.

Logan, John R., Wenquan Zhang, and Richard D. Alba. 2002. "Immigrant Enclaves and Ethnic Communities in New York and Los Angeles." *American Sociological Review* 67 (2): 299–322.

Longhi, Simonetta, and Peter Nijkamp, and Jacques Poot. 2006. "The Impact of Immigration on the Employment of Natives in Regional Labour Markets: A Meta-Analysis." IZA Discussion Paper No. 2044. SSRN.

Lopez, Mark Hugo, Jeffrey S. Passel, and D'Vera Cohn. 2021. "Key Facts about the Changing U.S. Unauthorized Immigrant Population." Pew Research Center, April 13, 2021. www.pewresearch.org.

López-Sanders, Laura. 2009. "Trapped at the Bottom: Racialized and Gendered Labor Queues in New Latino Destinations." Paper presented at the annual meeting of the American Sociological Association.

————. 2011. *Is Brown the New Black? Mediated Latino Incorporation in New Immigrant Destinations*. Redwood City, CA: Stanford University Press.

————. 2014. "Embedded and External Brokers: The Distinct Roles of Intermediaries in Workplace Inequality." *American Behavioral Scientist* 58 (2): 331–46.

————. 2017. "Trapped at the Bottom: Racialized and Gendered Labor Queues in New Immigrant Destinations." Working Paper 176, Center for Comparative Immigration Studies, University of California, San Diego, 2009.

López-Sanders, Laura, and Hana E. Brown. 2020. "Political Mobilisation and Public Discourse in New Immigrant Destinations: News Media Characterisations of Immigrants during the 2006 Immigration Marches." *Journal of Ethnic and Migration Studies* 46 (4): 820–38.

MacKenzie, Robert, and Chris Forde. 2009. "The Rhetoric of the 'Good Worker' versus the Realities of Employers' Use and the Experiences of Migrant Workers." *Work, Employment and Society* 23 (1): 142–59.

Manson, Steven, Jonathan Schroeder, David Van Riper, Tracy Kugler, and Steven Ruggles. 2022. "Persons by Hispanic or Latino Origin [2] by Race [6] Time Series Table." IPUMS National Historical Geographic Information System: Version 17.0. http://doi.org/10.18128/D120.V1.

Marrow, Helen B. 2011. *New Destination Dreaming: Immigration, Race, and Legal Status in the Rural American South*. Redwood City, CA: Stanford University Press.

Marrow, Helen B., and Tiffany D. Joseph. 2015. "Excluded and Frozen Out: Unauthorised Immigrants'(Non) Access to Care after US Health Care Reform." *Journal of Ethnic and Migration Studies* 41 (14): 2253–73.

Martin, Philip, and Stephanie Luce. 1988. "The Immigration Reform and Control Act: IRCA's Effects on Large Farms." *California Agriculture* 42 (3): 26–28.

Massey, Douglas S. 2001. "Residential Segregation and Neighborhood Conditions in US Metropolitan Areas." In *America Becoming: Racial Trends and Their Consequences*, edited by Neil Smelser, William Julius Wilson, and Faith Mitchell, 391–434. Washington, DC: National Academy Press.

————. 2008. *New Faces in New Places: The Changing Geography of American Immigration*. New York: Russell Sage Foundation.

Massey, Douglas S., Jorge Durand, and Karen A. Pren. 2014. "Explaining Undocumented Migration to the US." *International Migration Review* 48 (4): 1028–61.

Massey, Douglas S., and Karen A. Pren. 2012. "Unintended Consequences of US Immigration Policy: Explaining the Post-1965 Surge from Latin America." *Population and Development Review* 38 (1): 1–29.

Mayo, Elton. (1933) 2016. "The Hawthorne Experiment. Western Electric Company." In *Classics of Organization Theory*, 8th ed., edited by Jay M. Shafritz, J. Steven Ott, and Yong Suk Jang, 134–41. Boston: Cengage.

McAllister, Jean. 1998. "Sisyphus at Work in the Warehouse: Temporary Employment in Greenville, South Carolina." In *Contingent Work: American Employment Relations in Transition*, edited by Kathleen Barker and Kathleen Christensen, 221–42. Ithaca, NY: Cornell University Press.

McDaniel, Josh, and Vanessa Casanova. 2003. "Pines in Lines: Tree Planting, H2B Guest Workers, and Rural Poverty in Alabama." *Journal of Rural Social Sciences* 19 (1): article 4.

McDermott, Monica. 2006. *Working-Class White: The Making and Unmaking of Race Relations*. Berkeley: University of California Press.

———. 2011. "Black Attitudes and Hispanic Immigrants in South Carolina." In *Just Neighbors? Research on African American and Latino Relations in the United States*, edited by Edward Telles, Mark Sawyer, and Gaspar Rivera-Salgado, 242–63. New York: Russell Sage Foundation.

McGovern, Patrick. 2007. "Immigration, Labour Markets and Employment Relations: Problems and Prospects." *British Journal of Industrial Relations* 45 (2): 217–35.

Menjívar, Cecilia. 2021. "The Racialization of 'Illegality.'" *Daedalus* 150 (2): 91–105.

Menjívar, Cecilia, and Leisy Abrego. 2012. "Legal Violence: Immigration Law and the Lives of Central American Immigrants." *American journal of Sociology* 117 (5): 1380–1421.

Neuman, Kristin E., and Marta Tienda. 1994. "The Settlement and Secondary Migration Patterns of Legalized Immigrants: Insights from Administrative Records." In *Immigration and Ethnicity: The Integration of America's Newest Arrivals*, edited by Barry Edmonston and Jeffrey S. Passel, 187–226. Washington, DC: Urban Institute Press.

Odem, Mary E., and Elaine Cantrell Lacy. 2009. *Latino Immigrants and the Transformation of the US South*. Athens: University of Georgia Press.

Omi, Michael, and Howard Winant. 2014. *Racial Formation in the United States*. New York: Routledge.

Orupabo, Julia, and Marjan Nadim. 2020. "Men Doing Women's Dirty Work: Desegregation, Immigrants and Employer Preferences in the Cleaning Industry in Norway." *Gender, Work & Organization* 27 (3): 347–61.

Ottaviano, Gianmarco I. P., and Giovanni Peri. 2006. "Wages, Rents and Prices: The Effects of Immigration on US Natives." Discussion Paper 13/07, Center for Research and Analysis of Migration.

Pager, Devah. 2003. "The Mark of a Criminal Record." *American Journal of Sociology* 108 (5): 937–75.

Pager, Devah, Bart Bonikowski, and Bruce Western. 2009. "Discrimination in a Low-Wage Labor Market: A Field Experiment." *American Sociological Review* 74 (5): 777–99.

Parrado, Emilio A., and William Kandel. 2008. "New Hispanic Migrant Destinations: A Tale of Two Industries." In *New Faces in New Places: The Changing Geography of American Immigration*, edited by Douglass S. Massey, 99–123. New York: Russell Sage Foundation.

Pattillo-McCoy, M. 1999. *Black Picket Fences: Privilege and Peril among the Black Middle Class*. Chicago: University of Chicago Press.

Peacock, James L., Harry L. Watson, and Carrie R. Matthews. 2005. *The American South in a Global World*. Chapel Hill: University of North Carolina Press.

Piore, Michael J. 1974. *Labor Market Stratification and Wage Determination*. Cambridge, MA: Massachusetts Institute of Technology.

Portes, Alejandro, and Robert D. Manning. 2019. "The Immigrant Enclave: Theory and Empirical Examples." In *Social Stratification: Class, Race, and Gender in Sociological Perspective*, edited by David B. Grusky, 568–79. New York: Routledge.

Portes, Alejandro, and Rubén G. Rumbaut. 2001. *Legacies: The Story of the Immigrant Second Generation*. Berkeley: University of California Press.

Portes, Alejandro, and Julia Sensenbrenner. 1993. "Embeddedness and Immigration: Notes on the Social Determinants of Economic Action." *American Journal of Sociology* 98 (6): 1320–50.

Ray, Victor. 2019. "A Theory of Racialized Organizations." *American Sociological Review* 84 (1): 26–53.

Reskin, Barbara F., and Patricia A. Roos. 1990. *Job Queues, Gender Queues: Explaining Women's Inroads into Male Occupations*. Philadelphia: Temple University Press.

Reuters. 2011. "BMW North America Invites Bids for Advertising Work." March 28, 2011. www.reuters.com.

Ribas, Vanesa. 2016. *On the Line: Slaughterhouse Lives and the Making of the New South*. Berkeley: University of California Press.

Rivera, Lauren A. 2012. "Hiring as Cultural Matching: The Case of Elite Professional Service Firms." *American Sociological Review* 77 (6): 999–1022.

Robinson, Cedric J. 2019. *Cedric J. Robinson: On Racial Capitalism, Black Internationalism, and Cultures of Resistance*. Edited by H. L. T. Quan. London: Pluto.

Romero, Mary. 2008. "Crossing the Immigration and Race Border: A Critical Race Theory Approach to Immigration Studies." *Contemporary Justice Review* 11 (1): 23–37.

Rosenfeld, Michael J., and Marta Tienda. 1999. "Mexican Immigration, Occupational Niches, and Labor-Market Competition: Evidence from Los Angeles, Chicago." In *Immigration and Opportunity: Race, Ethnicity, and Employment in the United States*, edited by Frank D. Bean and Stephanie Bell-Rose, 64–105. New York: Russell Sage Foundation.

Rothstein, Jeffrey S. 2016. *When Good Jobs Go Bad: Globalization, De-unionization, and Declining Job Quality in the North American Auto Industry*. New Brunswick, NJ: Rutgers University Press.

Sáenz, Rogelio, and Karen Manges Douglas. 2015. "A Call for the Racialization of Immigration Studies: On the Transition of Ethnic Immigrants to Racialized Immigrants." *Sociology of Race and Ethnicity* 1 (1): 166–80.

Saldaña, Johnny. 2014. "Coding and Analysis Strategies." In *The Oxford Handbook of Qualitative Research*, edited by Patricia Leavy, 581–605. New York: Oxford University Press.

Sanchez, Gabriella, and Mary Romero. 2010. "Critical Race Theory in the US Sociology of Immigration." *Sociology Compass* 4 (9): 779–88.

Shannon, Sarah K. S., Christopher Uggen, Jason Schnittker, Melissa Thompson, Sara Wakefield, and Michael Massoglia. 2017. "The Growth, Scope, and Spatial Distribution of People with Felony Records in the United States, 1948–2010." *Demography* 54 (5): 1795–818.

Simmel, Georg. 1950. *The Sociology of Georg Simmel.* Vol. 92892. New York: Simon and Schuster.

Singer, Audrey. 2008. "Twenty-First-Century Gateways." In *Twenty-First Century Gateways: Immigrant Incorporation in Suburban America,* edited by Audrey Singer, Susan W. Hardwick, and Caroline B. Brettell, 3–30. Washington, DC: Brookings Institution Press.

———. 2015. "Metropolitan Immigrant Gateways Revisited, 2014." Brookings, December 1, 2015.

Skrentny, John D. 2002. "Inventing Race." *Public Interest* 146:97–113.

Small, Mario Luis, and Jessica McCrory Calarco. 2022. *Qualitative Literacy: A Guide to Evaluating Ethnographic and Interview Research.* Berkeley: University of California Press.

Smith, Heather A., and Owen J. Furuseth. 2006. *Latinos in the New South: Transformations of Place.* Aldershot, UK: Ashgate.

Smith, Sandra Susan. 2007. *Lone Pursuit: Distrust and Defensive Individualism among the Black Poor.* New York: Russell Sage Foundation.

Sørensen, Jesper B. 2004. "The Organizational Demography of Racial Employment Segregation." *American Journal of Sociology* 110 (3): 626–71.

Spartanburg Herald-Journal. 2007. "Immigration Sting Nets 7 Food Workers at BMW." July 27, 2007.

Stuesse, Angela Christine. 2008. "Globalization 'Southern Style': Transnational Migration, the Poultry Industry, and Implications for Organizing Workers across Difference." PhD diss., University of Texas at Austin.

Stuesse, Angela Christine, and Mathew Coleman. 2014. "Automobility, Immobility, Altermobility: Surviving and Resisting the Intensification of Immigrant Policing." *City & Society* 26 (1): 51–72.

Stull, Donald D., and Michael Broadway. 2008. "Meatpacking and Mexicans on the High Plains: From Minority to Majority In." *Immigrants Outside Megalopolis: Ethnic Transformation in the Heartland,* edited by Richard C. Jones, 115–33. Lanham, MD: Lexington Books.

Stull, Donald D., Michael J. Broadway, and David Griffith. 1995. *Any Way You Cut It: Meat Processing and Small-Town America.* Lawrence: University Press of Kansas.

Tienda, Marta. 1998. "Immigration and Native Minority Workers: Is There Bad News after All?" In *Help or Hindrance? The Economic Implications of Immigration for African Americans,* edited by Daniel S. Hammermesh and Frank D. Bean, 345–52. New York: Russell Sage Foundation.

Tilly, Charles. 1998. *Durable Inequality.* Berkeley: University of California Press.

Tomaskovic-Devey, Donald, and Sheryl Skaggs. 1999. "An Establishment-Level Test of the Statistical Discrimination Hypothesis." *Work and Occupations* 26 (4): 422–45.

Turco, Catherine J. 2010. "Cultural Foundations of Tokenism: Evidence from the Leveraged Buyout Industry." *American Sociological Review* 75 (6): 894–913.

US House of Representatives. 2008. *ICE Workplace Raids: Their Impact on U.S. Children, Families and Communities: Hearing Before the Subcommittee on Workforce Protections, Committee on Education and Labor.* 110th Cong., 2nd sess. Serial No. 110-92. Washington, DC: US Government Printing Office. www.govinfo.gov.

Waldinger, Roger D. 1997. "Social Capital or Social Closure? Immigrant Networks in the Labor Market." Working Paper No. 6. Lewis Center for Regional Policy Studies, University of California, Los Angeles.

Waldinger, Roger, and Michael I. Lichter. 2003. *How the Other Half Works: Immigration and the Social Organization of Labor.* Berkeley: University of California Press.

Waters, Mary C. 2009. "Social Science and Ethnic Options." *Ethnicities* 9 (1): 130–35.

Waters, Mary C., and Tomás R. Jiménez. 2005. "Assessing Immigrant Assimilation: New Empirical and Theoretical Challenges." *Annual Review of Sociology* 31:105–25.

Waters, Mary C., Philip Kasinitz, and Asad L. Asad. 2014. "Immigrants and African Americans." *Annual Review of Sociology* 40:369–90.

Weber, Max. 1978. *Economy and Society: An Outline of Interpretive Sociology.* Vol. 2. Berkeley: University of California Press.

Weil, David. 2014. *The Fissured Workplace.* Cambridge, MA: Harvard University Press.

Weiss, Mitch. 2008. "300 Suspected Illegal Immigrants Caught in SC Raid." Associated Press. *Post and Courier*, October 6, 2008. www.postandcourier.com.

West, Candace, and Don H. Zimmerman. 1987. "Doing Gender." *Gender & Society* 1 (2): 125–51.

Willis, Paul. 1981. *Learning to Labor: How Working Class Kids Get Working Class Jobs.* New York: Columbia University Press.

Wilson, Kenneth L., and Alejandro Portes. 1980. "Immigrant Enclaves: An Analysis of the Labor Market Experiences of Cubans in Miami." *American Journal of Sociology* 86 (2): 295–319.

Winders, Jamie, and Barbara Ellen Smith. 2010. "New Pasts: Historicizing Immigration, Race, and Place in the South." *Southern Spaces*, November 4, 2010. http://southernspaces.org.

Wingfield, Adia Harvey, and Joe Feagin. 2012. "The Racial Dialectic: President Barack Obama and the White Racial Frame." *Qualitative Sociology* 35 (2): 143–62.

Wooten, Lynn Perry, and Erika Hayes James. 2004. "When Firms Fail to Learn: The Perpetuation of Discrimination in the Workplace." *Journal of Management Inquiry* 13 (1): 23–33.

Zamudio, Margaret M., and Michael I. Lichter. 2008. "Bad Attitudes and Good Soldiers: Soft Skills as a Code for Tractability in the Hiring of Immigrant Latina/os over Native Blacks in the Hotel Industry." *Social Problems* 55 (4): 573–89.

Zúñiga, Víctor, and Rubén Hernández-León, eds. 2005. *New Destinations: Mexican Immigration in the United States.* New York: Russell Sage Foundation.

INDEX

ABOUT THE AUTHOR

LAURA LÓPEZ-SANDERS is the Stephen Robert Assistant Professor of Sociology at Brown University. She holds advanced degrees from Stanford and Harvard Universities. Her work has received awards from the National Science Foundation, the American Sociological Association, the Robert Wood Johnson Foundation, and the Ford Foundation.

www.ingramcontent.com/pod-product-compliance
Lightning Source LLC
Chambersburg PA
CBHW020533030426
42337CB00013B/833